Pictures of Atonement

Pictures of
ATONEMENT

A NEW TESTAMENT STUDY

Ben Pugh

CASCADE Books • Eugene, Oregon

PICTURES OF ATONEMENT
A New Testament Study

Copyright © 2020 Ben Pugh. All rights reserved. Except for brief quotations in critical publications or reviews, no part of this book may be reproduced in any manner without prior written permission from the publisher. Write: Permissions, Wipf and Stock Publishers, 199 W. 8th Ave., Suite 3, Eugene, OR 97401.

Cascade Books
An Imprint of Wipf and Stock Publishers
199 W. 8th Ave., Suite 3
Eugene, OR 97401

www.wipfandstock.com

PAPERBACK ISBN: 978-1-5326-5362-9
HARDCOVER ISBN: 978-1-5326-5363-6
EBOOK ISBN: 978-1-5326-5364-3

Cataloguing-in-Publication data:

Names: Pugh, Ben, author. |
Title: Pictures of atonement : a New Testament study / Ben Pugh.
Description: Eugene, OR: Cascade Books, 2020 | Includes bibliographical references and index.
Identifiers: ISBN 978-1-5326-5362-9 (paperback) | ISBN 978-1-5326-5363-6 (hardcover) | ISBN 978-1-5326-5364-3 (ebook)
Subjects: LCSH: Atonement—Biblical teaching | Jesus Christ—Crucifixion | Atonement | Redemption | Sacrifice
Classification: BT265.2 P84 2020 (print) | BT265.2 (ebook)

Manufactured in the U.S.A.   AUGUST 19, 2020

Unless otherwise stated, Scripture taken from the New Revised Standard Version (NRSV). Copyright © 1989, National Council of the Churches of Christ. Used by permission. All rights reserved.

To: The staff of the Hallward Library in the University of Nottingham. I continue to find this library the very best place in which to get books written.

Contents

Acknowledgements ix

Introduction xi
1 The Possibilities of a Pentecost Standpoint 1
2 Victory 13
3 Redemption 32
4 Dying and Rising with Christ 45
5 Sacrifice 68
6 Justification 105
7 Reconciliation 124
Conclusion 133

Bibliography 137
Ancient Literature Index 149
Scripture Index 150
Subject Index 157

Acknowledgements

As I NOW COME to the end of the Atonement Project, I want to acknowledge again, like I did at the start, the influence of Barrie Taylor who, in 1992, sparked in me the desire to study the atonement in as much depth as possible.

There are two other people whose chats were particularly helpful. Dr Sandra Brower introduced me to Douglas Farrow's *Ascension and Ecclesia*. He didn't get much of a mention in this book as things turned out but it was his work that first stimulated me to think of the cross from the viewpoint of the ascension, a viewpoint which later became the Pentecost Standpoint, the backbone to the thought-experiment that is this book. Then there is Dr Ed McKenzie whose constant interest in my books was very flattering and whose awareness of all the scholarship I was engaging with in this volume was really helpful. He helped confirm what I was thinking and helped to navigate me to the most important sources.

With this volume I did something I have not done before and that is let someone read it before it's completely polished. I wanted my friend Peter Hayter to read it and tell me what he thought. He represents what seems to be the main, or at least the most appreciative, audience my books have attracted so far: informed, interested non-academics. I am completely delighted with this and delighted that he was able to read it for me and give comment.

I would also like to thank, once again, my amazing editor with Cascade: Dr Robin Parry who has edited all three atonement books and whose encyclopedic knowledge and watchful eye has saved me from embarrassing myself.

Last but not least, my wife, Pearl, was completing her PhD in dietetics at the same time I was completing this book. Having her as a fellow traveler along a similar road (though hers far more demanding and stressful) has been a great comfort in what can be a lonely endeavor.

Introduction

THIS BIBLICAL STUDY OF atonement is the third phase in my Atonement Project. So far, I have been using the "Wesleyan" quadrilateral, but have ended up using it in this order: reason and tradition first, then experience, then Scripture. The first volume came out in 2014, which was my *Atonement Theories: A Way Through the Maze*. I concluded this book with what I termed the Incarnation Criterion. By this I meant that the Christ of the cross is the prime criterion for judging all theories of the cross: his person defines his work. I named Irenaeus, Anselm, John McLeod Campbell, and P. T. Forsyth as especially noteworthy examples of this incarnation-eye-view of atonement. To let the Father define the work, I pointed out, results in difficult moral problems that too easily impugn the Father as demanding and inflexible. To let our humanity define the work, results in theories, such as the Moral Influence theory, that are inadequate for explaining the extremity of the solution offered. To place the person of Christ himself at the center compels us to attend to him who is the God-Man of Chalcedon, the bridge and mediator between the divine and the human.

My second volume came out in 2016 and was called: *The Old Rugged Cross: A History of the Atonement in Popular Christian Devotion*. In it, my aim was to analyze what has been happening on the ground. How, if at all, have these atonement theories helped ordinary Christians to live more devoted lives? The key concept I came up with was the Participation Imperative. By this I meant that the one assumption that underlies the church's most formative engagements with the cross has been the assumption that Christ is the representative human. He suffers with our sufferings and dies our death yet raises us up to newness of life with him. The church's use of Eucharist, metaphor, and art has been all about the attempt to re-present, and hence to participate all over again in, the events of Gethsemane, Calvary and the tomb. Even within the evangelicalism of the nineteenth

Introduction

century I discerned a shift *away* from the strictly forensic theories of atonement to which it remained ostensibly committed and in the direction of the ever-increasing use of the word "blood" instead of "cross" or "Calvary." The atonement thus became liquefied and applicable. The hymnody and preaching of the nineteenth century was famously filled with the invitation to wash and bathe in this blood—a subjective participation to counterbalance the objective penal substitution.

In the first volume I was a historical theologian, then, in the second volume, I became a church historian, and now I change hats again, but in a way that gets me back to my true first love: I am wearing the hat of a biblical scholar. I like to live dangerously, always feeling like I am a guest at other people's debates, a visitor wondering around other people's countries of well-honed expertise, a foreign piece of mail sitting in a clearly-labelled pigeon hole. Even while writing *Atonement Theories*—which, of all the books I have written, most falls within my areas of proven academic expertise—I quickly became an intruder in other people's cherished specialisms such as Anselm studies, Luther studies, and Calvinism. Similarly, in the second volume I knew that my only well-practiced area of specialism was in the Pentecostal part of the story. Again I was an intruder tiptoeing through the quest for the historical Eucharist, Anglo-Saxon literature, and medievalism, trying not to disturb the natives. Strangely, though, with this biblical volume I feel like I am coming home. And that is for two reasons. One is that my personal meditations on the Word have centered on the themes explored here since as far back as April 1992. I am writing about a biblical place I have personally inhabited for twenty-eight years. The second reason is that the Bible is every believer's pigeon-hole. It is every Christian's specialism. The Word of God belongs to the church, which is also why I am pleased to be trying out here the new discipline of the theological interpretation of Scripture, to which I now turn.

The Theological Interpretation of Scripture

This piece of work aims to make a contribution to the new hermeneutic that has been gaining increasing traction since Stephen Fowl's seminal work of 1997.[1] The theological interpretation of Scripture (TIS) is being

---

1. Stephen Fowl (ed.). *The Theological Interpretation of Scripture: Classic and Contemporary Readings* (Oxford: Blackwell, 1997). The use of "theological interpretation of Scripture" as a technical term seems to not go any further back than 2005: Robert

Introduction

appropriated both by biblical scholars who are disillusioned with "atomistic and naturalistic"[2] historical-critical methods and systematic theologians who, like me, want to try their hand at some serious biblical work without having to engage with the kind of atomizing exegesis that empties the Word of all useful meaning, and leaves you wanting to slash your wrists.

As I introduce this concept I want to first register two oddities about the TIS movement. The first is that, despite the fact that Fowl's founding document was a reader and therefore entirely immersive, outlining only in the briefest of terms what the approach consists of, there has been a never-failing stream of prolegomena ever since. There seem to be at least as many books *about* TIS as there are books that seek to *exemplify* it as a practice. The other oddity that the newcomer will notice is that many publications that are coming out under the auspices of TIS are written by scholars who are not in any very obvious way practicing TIS and do not seem to have even fully understood it. The main reason many such publications are not really TIS gives me a reason now to introduce what, in my view, is the greatest strength and most distinguishing feature of the movement and the thing that marks it out as a clear development on the older discipline of biblical theology: it is theology done in and for the church. One avowedly TIS book I read mentioned the church right at the very end, as an after-thought, like most theology books do. By contrast, what you will find in *Pictures of Atonement* is academic research with some of the features of a devotional. It will have reflections at the end of each chapter borne out of my own daily meditations on these atonement themes.

A second strength of TIS is that, unlike biblical theology, which was always at odds with systematic theology and wary of its confessional biases, TIS tries to be a genuine rapprochement between theology and biblical studies. Laudably, Brazos are in the middle of producing a series of commentaries that are written *not* by biblical scholars but by people who, in various ways, would normally be classed as theologians: Stanley Hauerwas and Robert Jenson, for instance. This is where TIS is truly groundbreaking. However, TIS is clearly not new. All of its leading proponents are unanimous on this point. The church has always instinctively read the Bible theologically, seeking to receive it as God's Word spoken to faith for the formation of Christian character and action.

Plummer, *40 Questions about Interpreting the Bible* (Grand Rapids: Kregel, 2010), 314.

2. Goheen, "A History and Introduction to a Missional Reading of the Bible," 9.

Introduction

There is, according to one article, a form of TIS called "interested" TIS (I-TIS).[3] It is this kind of TIS that I will mainly be practicing as I will be bringing to the biblical texts the interests generated by my first two volumes on the atonement. As mentioned, these gave me two motifs: the Incarnation Criterion (in *Atonement Theories*) and the Participation Imperative (in *Old Rugged Cross*). I will be bringing both of these to the light of Scripture.

The Role of Metaphor

I will be especially interested in the role of metaphor, which I identified in *The Old Rugged Cross* as being crucial in re-presenting the cross in ever fresh ways to the faithful, rescuing it from sliding into a mere sign or logo for Christianity. This was a major plank in my Participation Imperative thesis. The re-metaphorization of the cross via the arts allowed a renewed sacramental participation in the cross. McGilchrist, in his study of the importance of right hemisphere thinking in the appreciation of metaphor, is correct in saying that "the gap across which metaphor carries us is one that *language itself creates*. Metaphor is language's cure for the ills entailed on us by language."[4] Metaphor, it is claimed, "was the first word in spoken language, and only after losing its original colour could it become a literal sign."[5] If this is the case then our never-ending words about the cross might actually be placing it further and further away from us. In this study, I will be examining the New Testament metaphors with a view to recovering their spiritual immediacy, their embodied logic, their sacramental power.

Metaphor is of interest to any biblical study of atonement since the way the earliest church understood the death and resurrection of Christ was expressed almost entirely in pictorial language. Indeed, one is hard pressed to find any New Testament interpretations of the work of Christ that are not in metaphorical language. Even the renderings of Christ dying or suffering "for us" and "for our sins": ostensibly non-metaphorical language, almost certainly make some filtered reference to the Levitical sacrifices or qualify some commonly known trope from the Greek stage about heroic deaths for others.

3. Greg Allison, "Theological Interpretation of Scripture: An Introduction and Evaluation," *The Southern Baptist Journal of Theology* 14.2 (2010), 30 [28–36].

4. Iain McGilchrist, *The Master and His Emissary: The Divided Brain and the Making of the Western World* (New Haven, CT: Yale University Press, 2009), 116.

5. Richter, cited in McGilchrist, *The Master and His Emissary*, 117.

Introduction

Metaphor is variously defined as: "the application of an alien name by transference";[6] "An affair between a predicate with a past and an object that yields while protesting";[7] "a calculated error," which, "discloses a relationship of meaning hitherto unnoticed";[8] and "*understanding and experiencing one kind of thing in terms of another.*"[9] Metaphors always involve two things: one familiar and the other unfamiliar and they are always characterized as much by *dis*similarity as they are by similarity between the familiar and unfamiliar components. They exist in an "is" and "is not" tension, with the "is" highlighted by the new relationship and the "is not" aspects left behind. The power of the new relationship that is forged between the "predicate with a past" and the object is positively revelatory. It brings out the "hitherto unnoticed" element that Ricoeur highlights as the fruit of the new and often startling relationship. It is this too that gives metaphors their explanatory power. Because of these things metaphors are absolutely ubiquitous to language and totally central to the way we learn about new and unfamiliar or abstract things. Negatively, in just the same way as a metaphor will only use some aspects of the familiar thing: called the *source*, or *vehicle*, so a metaphor will only highlight certain aspects of the unfamiliar thing: called the *target* or *tenor*. Everything else disappears from view. It must be acknowledged, for instance, that the horrible realities of the trial and crucifixion of Jesus somewhat disappear from view in Paul's atonement theology, which could explain perhaps the post-Pauline Synoptic Gospel tradition, which sought to be more attentive to the passion narrative itself. Then, by the time we arrive at the Johannine corpus, we see a marvelous synthesis between

---

6. Aristotle *Poetics* 1457b 7-8.

7. Nelson Goodman, *Languages of Art: An Approach to a Theory of Symbols* (Oxford: Oxford University Press, 1969), 69.

8. Paul Ricoeur, "The Metaphorical Process," *Semeia* 4 (1975) 78-79.

9. George Lakoff and Mark Johnson, *Metaphors We Live By* (Chicago: Chicago University Press, 1980), 5; italics original. In addition to Lakoff and Johnson, the key literature would look something like this: Max Black, *Models and Metaphors: Studies in Language and Philosophy* (Ithaca, NY: Cornell University Press, 1962); Paul Ricoeur and Harry Prosch, *Meaning* (Chicago: University of Chicago Press, 1975); Paul Ricoeur, *The Rule of Metaphor: Multi-Disciplinary Studies in the Creation of Meaning in Language*, (trans. Robert Czerny with Kathleen McLaughlin and John Costello, S.J.; London: Routledge and Kegan Paul, 1978); Hans Georg Gadamer, *Truth and Method* (rev. trans. by Joel Weinsheimer and Donald G. Marshall; New York: Seabury, 1989). In relation to theology: Janet Martin Soskice, *Metaphor and Religious Language* (Oxford: Clarendon, 1985); Colin Gunton, *The Actuality of Atonement: A Study of Metaphor, Rationality and the Christian Tradition* (Edinburgh: T. & T. Clark, 1988).

INTRODUCTION

the narrative and the theology, which became definitive of the later patristic traditions.[10] But the point is that the reason for the omissions in Paul's theology is that he is only giving us a series of pictures, none of which claim completeness.

In one very important sense the considerable use of metaphor in New Testament atonement theology was because there was no other way of expressing the otherwise inexpressible. Metaphor, far from being a frilly, aesthetic superfluity, is in fact the way we always grasp new truths, even scientific ones. Metaphor is therefore reality-depicting, perhaps even supremely so, and not a lesser category. Metaphor speaks a language that conveys deep meanings and emotions not accessible through "naked abstract formulations."[11] The first Christians had stumbled upon an unforeseen yet long foretold *new* thing: the tragic execution of the wholly innocent Jesus of Nazareth turned out to be a death-defeating, life-transforming event. It turned out to be a promised divine intervention, the power of which could be appropriated simply by receiving the Spirit. The result would be an in-rush of overwhelming experiences of God's presence, grace, and power. There was no other way to communicate this new thing than to use familiar concepts as vehicles for the unfamiliar. The main difficulty for us, of course, is that, in many cases, the familiar component is no longer familiar to us. This, needless to say, will be one of the problems I will try to rectify in this book.

Metaphors are structured in different ways by different linguists. Perhaps the most helpful way of viewing the structure for our purposes is to see a metaphor as occupying the liminal and affective space between the source or vehicle being commandeered for a new usage, and the target or tenor: the new idea needing new language. With each atonement metaphor I will be clarifying the source of a metaphor so as to re-describe, with the newly clarified metaphor, the target. Though I agree with Gunton,[12] who, like Ricoeur, elevated the role of metaphor to take its rightful place alongside other expressions of realist epistemologies, I am also an artist. This being the case, I also agree with David Brown in his enthusiasm for

10. Petros Vassiliadis, "Beyond *Theologia Crucis*: Jesus of Nazareth from Q to John *via* Paul (or John as a Radical Reinterpretation of Jesus of Nazareth)," *Greek Orthodox Theological Review* 47.1–4 (2002), 139–63.

11. Craig Ott, "The Power of Biblical Metaphors for the Contextualized Communication of the Gospel," *Missiology* 42.4 (2014), 362 [357–74].

12. Colin Gunton, *The Actuality of Atonement: A Study of Metaphor, Rationality and the Christian Tradition* (Edinburgh: T. & T. Clark, 1988).

Introduction

the non-cognitive, sacramental power of a metaphor. He points out that God is a real presence within God-ordained metaphors. In other words, God is able to inhabit well-chosen words in just the same way that he is understood in some traditions to inhabit bread and wine, and we see this in concentrated form in poetry (especially theistic poetry) where metaphors occupy such a central place. Brown then applies the same appreciation for the metaphors found in poetry to the metaphors of the Bible. He uses John 1:1 as a case study, pointing out that efforts to paraphrase John's use of "Word" to describe the incarnation, using terms such as "expression" end up introducing a whole new set of associations not native to John's original "Word" metaphor.[13] Brown thus adds a second layer of irreducibility to that established by Ricoeur: biblical metaphors are irreducible because God-inhabited.[14]

And it is this sacramental power of metaphors that joins up with the aim of TIS, namely, that of faith-formation. I will be approaching the metaphors of atonement as an appreciator of poetry and image and seeking to recapture the immediacy that was their original faith-nourishing power.

So, I bring three interests to this study. The first is the motifs of incarnation and participation which I identified during phases one and two of the Atonement Project. The second is an interest in adopting the theological interpretation of Scripture as the overall ethos of this study: it is biblical study for theological results, and the research user is understood to be the church. Thirdly, I bring an interest in metaphor. Indeed, following the lead of Colin Gunton and John McIntyre, the entire study is structured around the metaphors of atonement.[15] Appreciating the value and possible origins of these metaphors I am hoping will be the most illuminating way of studying New Testament atonement themes.

New Year 2020

---

13. David Brown, *God and Mystery in Words: Experience through Metaphor and Drama* (Oxford: Oxford University Press, 2008), 52–55.

14. However, he makes it clear that this should not be taken to mean that we must never go beyond the biblical metaphors. We should create new ones for new situations: Brown, *God and Mystery in Words*, 72.

15 Gunton, *Actuality of Atonement*; McIntyre, *Shape of Soteriology*.

CHAPTER 1

The Possibilities of a Pentecost Standpoint

At the Origins of the Metaphors

Dialectical Tensions

METAPHOR IS A WAY of dealing with the shock of the new by juxtaposing the new with the familiar. The new thing was that the Spirit, dispensed by the glorified Christ, was revealing to people that the shamefully executed Jesus of Nazareth was the glorified King of All. This belief that Jesus was the only true Savior and Lord, and his triumphant inversion of crucifixion, Rome's most powerful means of keeping the peace, put the first Christians very much on the wrong side of the political ideologies of the surrounding culture.

Philip Esler has made illuminating use of an axiom of sociologist Peter Berger, namely that the relation between religion and society is always "dialectical," always fraught with conflicting aims and values. According to Esler, Luke, in the context of a parent religion and a wider political system that were both sometimes hostile, creates ways for the new beleaguered community to find a sense of its own legitimacy.[1] Seen in this light, the metaphors of atonement would have been developed not only as a way of explaining the unfamiliar but also as a way of robustly defending a marginal and muted position that existed in irreconcilable tension with the dominant culture and its Caesar.[2] The dominant culture had strong views

---

1. Especially Esler, *Community and Gospel in Luke-Acts*. See also Esler, *The First Christians in Their Social Worlds*, 1–18.
2. Studies of the political Paul and possible traces of a critique of empire in his writings

PICTURES OF ATONEMENT

about death by crucifixion. There was nothing to defend or eulogize about somebody who had been subjected to this ultimate sanction.[3] Yet the first Christians had powerfully experienced the ascended Lord Jesus through the Spirit. The one who was crucified was now King. "The central focus of the proclamation after Easter," wrote Gunton, "was that the events of Jesus' history, and particularly of the Easter period, had changed the status of believers, indeed of the whole world. The metaphors of atonement are ways of expressing the significance of what had happened."[4]

Inspired by experiences of Christ through the Spirit the metaphors of atonement were generated, in part at least, as items of resistance to the Roman hegemony together with its lord and savior, Caesar. The metaphors were both potent and polemic. It was assumed and accepted that the dominant culture would be outraged by the claims being made:

> For the message about the cross is foolishness to those who are perishing, but to us who are being saved it is the power of God. . . . For Jews demand signs and Greeks desire wisdom, but we proclaim Christ crucified, a stumbling block to Jews and foolishness to Gentiles, but to those who are the called, both Jews and Greeks, Christ the power of God and the wisdom of God (1 Cor 1:18, 22-24. Also Gal 5:11; Heb 12:2).

Feminist Standpoint Theory

Transformative experiences of the Spirit gave the earliest Christians a certain vantage point or standpoint. Nancy Hartsock's Feminist Standpoint is a Marxist-inspired theory that has now been applied usefully to many marginalized or "muted" groups as a way of helping us to notice that marginal groups hold a perspective on many aspects of life that is wholly other to that of the dominant culture,[5] indeed, in Hartsock's original version of the theory, the viewpoint of the marginalized is the inverse opposite of the dominant view.[6] Further, this marginal viewpoint actually has a more ac-

---

are of related interest. For a recent summary of the scholarly positions see Mackenzie, "The Quest for the Political Paul."

3. Hengel, *Crucifixion*, 22-38.

4. Gunton, *Actuality of Atonement*, 46.

5. Harding, "Comment on Hekman's 'Truth and Method: Feminist Standpoint Theory Revisited,'" 382-91.

6. Hartsock, *The Feminist Standpoint Revisited and Other Essays*, 107 and elsewhere.

curate view of things, in contrast to which, the standpoint of the powerful is likely to be "partial and perverse," or, "strange and harmful."[7] This seems to be mainly because the powerful have, in true Marxist style,[8] a vested interest in maintaining the status quo and so choose not to see the things that might undermine their own legitimacy. In order to gain a more full-orbed understanding of the way things really are, therefore, the standpoint of the marginalized must be recognized. Nancy Hartsock is adamant that standpoint theory is not primarily about truth but power, not primarily about epistemology but resistance to hegemonies, so she goes no further than Marx originally did in explaining the exact nature of the epistemic advantage that the marginalized have, describing it only as "engaged" and exposing "real relations."[9] This epistemic advantage appears to be more to do with what those on the underside of society are unencumbered by rather than what they are endowed with. They are merely free from the standpoint of the oppressor. But might not the viewpoint of the marginalized have something more robustly positive to offer?

The Coming of the Spirit and the Birth of the Metaphors

The epistemic advantage of the post-Pentecost Christians over against Rome is easy to name. It is not merely an absence of skewed values but *the presence of the Spirit*. To a significant degree, the Holy Spirit *is* the epistemology—the way of knowing—of the earliest church. Pentecost revealed an ascended Lord to those who had not been eye-witnesses of the life, death, resurrection, or ascension of Christ. Their experience of the Spirit was all that was needed. It was an entirely convincing experience of the ascended Jesus, who was now Lord and dispenser of the Spirit (Acts 2:33). They knew he was raised and glorified for one simple reason: the same Spirit that raised Jesus from the dead now dwelt within them (Rom 8:11). For them, a new life had begun, which was understood to be a foretaste of the age to come. Hence, the Spirit provided epistemic access to the two least verifiable and yet the two most crucially important axes of the Christian faith: the

---

7. Cockburn, "Standpoint Theory," 335.

8. Standpoint theory apparently originates with Hegel's parable of the master and the slave (*Phenomenology of Spirit* IV, 26, B), which is thought to have been influential in the development of Marx's concept of class struggle. Marxism in turn clearly provides standpoint theory with much of its essential coloring.

9. Hartsock, *The Feminist Standpoint Revisited*, 108.

reported past of the resurrection of Christ and the uncertain future of the return of Christ.

So, it was into this Spirit-inspired epistemic breakthrough that the metaphors were birthed, as language was sought for expressing the new-found faith. Accounting for how the metaphors were generated in this way naturally leads us into the temptation to speculate about the order in which they were born.

How we arrange the metaphors seems important to any attempt to make sense of them by reference to their origins. An attempt at chronology would share with all other efforts at nailing things down chronologically in the New Testament a certain sense of inevitable doom. For a start, there is, of course, no unanimity about the dating of any of the New Testament documents. Secondly, even though striking differences are thrown up by even so blunt an instrument as "earlier" and "later," we do not know that changes over time account for this. It could have been changes over space, changes in context. All chronological development, if there was any, might well already have happened and been solidified well before Paul wrote Galatians. Moreover, the earlier portions of the New Testament are almost all Pauline, so that, in asserting a metaphor as "early" all we really might be saying is that it is "Pauline."[10]

There was one change that happened in the surrounding context that *might* be significant. As I briefly explored in *Old Rugged Cross*, the cult of the martyrs during the early patristic period played a crucial role in the ever deepening attachment to the cross as the central symbol of Christian faith. The cross, in fact, always has been the way Christians have made sense of persecution, and it continues to function in that way. It may well be that there is a similar dynamic going on in the first century as we enter the persecutions first of Nero (r. 54–68 AD) and then of Domitian (r. 81–96 AD). This might explain the dominance of sacrifice and cost language around the cross during the later period. The metaphors that dominate earlier on, it could be argued, still reflect that first flush of Pentecost, which brought vivid experiences of a kingdom breaking in now, and of participating in the victory and vindication of Christ. We might even go as far as to say that the earlier metaphors are kingdom-now metaphors: the King has triumphed and is reigning, pouring out his power.[11] He has led his people in a new

---

10. Thanks to the delegates of the Erhardt Seminar at the University of Manchester for pointing out this, in retrospect, rather obvious fact.

11. Some older studies of the relationship of Paul's conversion to his theology also

THE POSSIBILITIES OF A PENTECOST STANDPOINT

exodus. There is liberation from former demonic and carnal powers and a participation in his heavenly reign. The later metaphors might be termed suffering-now metaphors, most notably the sacrifice metaphor. These, perhaps, are designed to instill resilience to growing hostility through an appreciation for the price paid and the life laid down to reconcile God's former enemies to himself. It could be that such metaphors helped to prepare Christians to be willing to pay a price for faith, even the ultimate price, in the midst of a world full of people who are still God's enemies.

The possibility of arrangement in two phases—kingdom-now followed by suffering-now—played a part in my early deliberations. However, as I penetrated deeper into the meaning of each metaphor, I became more interested in arranging them in terms of logical and semantic relationships, which might gently imply chronological begetting of one picture by another, but which don't require a commitment to an early or late framework. Chronology is still implied but is not central to the structure. Instead I speak fancifully of one picture giving rise to another in putative chains of development, favoring the picture of mountain peaks with lower hills receiving something that somehow flows from the peak. Victory flows into redemption, which flows into participation, and sacrifice flows into justification, which flows into reconciliation. It is a thought experiment, if you will.

Cross or Kingdom: Which Gospel Is the Gospel?

> ... discourse about who will (or will not) enter the kingdom, and what the kingdom is like fills the pages of the Gospels. When we leave the Gospels and turn to Paul, however, what happens to the kingdom? We might get the impression that outside the Gospels the kingdom, except for a few mentions here and there, fades away into the background of the New Testament.[12]

Something we ought to attempt to resolve before we move onto the metaphors of atonement is the fact that there appears to be a pre-Easter message

---

speak of this triumphalistic element in the origins of Paul's gospel, especially Beker, *Paul the Apostle*, but also (though presenting a very different argument to Beker's) Bruce's, *Paul: Apostle of the Heart Set Free*, and the work of Bruce's student Seyoon Kim, *The Origin of Paul's Gospel*. See also the discussion of these in Gaventa, *From Darkness to Light*, 17–21.

12. Vickers, "The Kingdom of God in Paul's Gospel," 52.

that was all about the kingdom, and a post-Easter message that was all about the work of Christ. Some scholars and popular Christian writers don't really seem to know what to do with the cross and resurrection once they have finished waxing lyrical about the grand narrative of the God who, from Genesis to Revelation, is on a mission to establish his reign, his kingdom. An entire chapter of an edited work, entitled, "The Kingdom of God and His Mission,"[13] says only this about the work of Christ: "Through his death and resurrection, Jesus has demonstrated decisively the victory of God's reign over history."[14] Others prefer only to mention the kingdom in relation to the teaching and ministry of Christ, and proclaim the *work* of Christ, his once-and-for-all atonement for sin, as the most important thing. For them, the gospel is a gospel of the cross. On the part of some wise thinkers there has been some effort to find a synthesis between cross and kingdom. In fact, there have emerged four explanations for the apparent transition from a kingdom gospel to a cross gospel, all of which nonetheless affirm that both remain valid and interrelated. Let us consider each in turn.

Delayed Parousia

This is the oldest solution, dating back to the 1930s and the work of C. H. Dodd. He claimed that, although there is still to be found in Paul the kingdom theme of "transition from 'this evil Age' to 'the Age to Come,'"[15] there is a marked shift of emphasis away from a futuristic hope to a here-and-now gospel. In this here-and-now message, "believers are already delivered out of this present evil age."[16] In both Paul and John, there is still present the familiar "eschatological valuation"[17] of the historical facts surrounding Jesus. In short, there is an already-but-not-yet tension in Paul similar to that found in the teachings of Jesus, the speaker of parables about tiny seeds and massive harvests and slowly spreading leaven which then completely

---

13. Luc, "The Kingdom of God and His Mission," 94. William Abraham is similarly remiss in his classic work: *The Logic of Evangelism*. The gospel is defined as the proclamation of the reign of God and defined entirely in these eschatological terms. The death and resurrection is subsumed into that framework without any effort to really explain the salvific value of events so momentous as these.

14. Luc, "The Kingdom of God and His Mission," 94.

15. Dodd, *Apostolic Preaching*, 13.

16. Dodd, *Apostolic Preaching*, 13.

17. Dodd, *Apostolic Preaching*, 47.

The Possibilities of a Pentecost Standpoint

permeates. But where Jesus is trying to wean his audiences *off* the idea of a right-now and complete in-breaking of the victory of God, Paul seems precisely to offer the possibility of right now walking in newness of life: for him the emphasis is on the "already." Paul's is more of a realized eschatology than an inaugurated one.

In both Paul and John, mystical incorporation into Christ is what brings this realized eschatology about. By participating in Christ, believers are *already* risen with him and the church has *already* become the eschatological people of God. Notably in John's Gospel, in place of the Olivet Discourse predicting the second coming of Christ, there is the Upper Room Discourse in which, instead of a second coming of Christ, the coming of the Spirit after Christ's departure is predicted.

Dodd believed he had an explanation for this: "This [realized eschatology] was the true solution of the problem presented to the Church by the disappointment of its naïve expectation that the Lord would immediately appear."[18] However, I would argue that this entering of the life of the age to come into people's here-and-now experience is a phenomenon very much brought about by *Pentecost*. This, rather than some hasty revision demanded by the embarrassment and disappointment of a delayed parousia, is where I would prefer to place the emphasis:

> Salvation meant incorporation into the kingdom of God, which occurred as the Holy Spirit swallowed them. . . . Until Pentecost, Jesus and the resurrection were wondrous events outside them. At Pentecost, however, the followers of Jesus became a part of the body of Christ.[19]

Dodd's solution, then, offers a biblical hinge between the kingdom emphasis and the arguably more this-worldly emphasis of the cross and resurrection. Dodd reckoned that this hinge was basically an enormous *non*-event: the delayed parousia. I argue that it was an *event*: Pentecost. There is, of course, a case for saying that both are related. An arguably more cynical take on it would say that teaching about the present time wonders of life in the Spirit was deliberately pushed as a sort of consolation prize for the big non-event of the century. If we suppose, however, that people's experiences of the Spirit were very real and that the teachings about life in

---

18. Dodd, *Apostolic Preaching*, 63.

19. Poe, *The Gospel and its Meaning*, 20. Poe provides a helpful overview of the "quest for the historical kerygma" that was initiated by C. H. Dodd and was at its height during the '50s and '60s: Poe, *The Gospel and Its Meaning*, 15–55.

the Spirit were an outcome of these experiences, then the Pentecost explanation becomes a convincing one, regardless of whether or not there was any real anxiety about a delayed second coming.

Lost in Translation

This is my term for the explanation that, in the transition from a Jewish sect to a predominantly gentile religion, Paul translated what had been a Jewish apocalyptic idea into terms that were their gentile equivalents. Jesus had already transformed it from a "narrow-minded nationalistic hope to a universal, spiritual order,"[20] now Paul, without altering its fundamental meaning, replaced the kingdom language with dynamic equivalents.[21] In Paul's case, "the righteousness of God" was a favorite, but "salvation" and being "in Christ" also translate Christ's original message about himself as the inauguration of the reign of God. Similarly, John, also writing for a gentile audience, liked the term "eternal life," and generally avoided "kingdom of God," though he did use the term (John 3:3, 5; 18:36). Poe again:

> When the evangelists moved outside the context of a Jewish community, they no longer bound themselves to the language of the people of the covenant, wrapped up as it was with a redemptive time, place, and tradition. Instead, they employed language that communicated the same message, but to a people who never knew the Law or the Prophets.[22]

The *kerygma*, or preached message, on this reckoning, certainly retains a fixed inner core but superficially shapes itself to new contexts.

However, the transition from a gospel of the kingdom to a gospel of the cross and resurrection does seem like a change to the inner core, not just to its mode of expression. This cultural explanation alone, though illuminating, does not seem sufficient to fully explain the post-Easter transition, though it is certainly of some help.

---

20. Caragounis, "Kingdom of God/Heaven," 430.
21. Caragounis, "Kingdom of God/Heaven," 430.
22. Poe, *The Gospel and Its Meaning*, 38. See also Martin, *Carmen Christi*.

Cause and Effect

Richard Bauckham opens the way for a promising synthesis in his use of the particular and the universal as two poles between which the whole mission of God may be articulated:

> Mission takes place on the way from the particularity of God's action in the story of Jesus to the universal coming of God's kingdom. It happens as particular people called by God go from here to there and live for God here and there for the sake of all people.[23]

And the Bible, he says, is full of these journeys from the particular to the universal. God is the God of the heavens and the earth yet chooses Abraham, showing that he is both and equally the God of the particular and of the universal. The Bible is full of this "universal direction that takes the particular with the utmost seriousness."[24]

Don Carson's solution may be grouped together with this one as he resolves the disconnect using cause and effect. He is very clear that the gospel is a proclamation. It is not to be equated with any of the things that result from that proclamation, whether these are personal salvation or social action. Good news is simply to be announced because, "that's what one does with news."[25] Carson describes the popular saying, wrongly attributed to St. Francis, "preach the gospel, sometimes use words," as "smug nonsense."[26] That the Bible addresses both individual salvation and social justice he does not dispute, but "what is more doubtful is that the Bible treats *either* as the gospel."[27] The events of the incarnation, death, and resurrection *result in* the spreading of the kingdom that Jesus was predicting. Yet, this means that the message we actually preach is about the coming of Christ and what he achieved for us in death and resurrection. The kingdom is not the message but the result of the message.

---

23. Bauckham, *Bible and Mission*, 10.
24. Bauckham, *Bible and Mission*, 11.
25. Carson, "What Is the Gospel?" 158.
26. Carson, "What Is the Gospel?" 158.
27. Carson, "What Is the Gospel?" 159.

Ironic Victory

For the earliest formative remnant of them the paradoxical notion that God's anointed vice-regent was ignominiously killed became the generative center of their beliefs.[28]

The central irony in the passion narratives of the Gospels is that Jesus' crucifixion turns out to be his elevation to kingship.[29]

The very most recent scholarship tries to make cross and kingdom as indistinguishable as possible. Taking their bearings from an entire sweep of biblical theology, advocates of this view point out that, at least as far back as Isaiah, the promised Messiah-King always was destined to ascend his throne by way of suffering, just like David himself. Isaiah becomes especially illuminating once we can move beyond the sharp divisions of the text into First, Second, and Third Isaiah. Irrespective of who wrote the various parts of Isaiah and when, the final work was edited to be a literary whole. Once we see Isaiah whole again we see that there is a connection between the royal Davidic figure of Isaiah 1–39 and the Servant of the Servant Songs of 40–55. In the case of the Suffering Servant passage, if we take the unifying step of placing it back into its literary context we can see that this suffering figure might also be a royal figure. Isaiah 51 and 52 are full of references to David's Zion to which the Lord was now about to return bringing a reign of peace (52:1, 7–8), and 55:3 promises faithfulness to the covenant with David.

Fast forward to the Gospels, especially Mark, and it becomes clear that the entire journey to Jerusalem and the arrest, trial, and crucifixion is being quite deliberately portrayed, albeit with much irony, as the king marching on Jerusalem, asserting the ultimate triumph of the kingdom, and ascending the throne of the cross. The cross itself always did have ironic enthronement connotations with its built-in seat—a small wooden protuberance—upon which the dying victim would pathetically rest. As Wright points out, this accession via humiliation is really only part and parcel of the radical kingdom redefinition that had been so central a part of all of Christ's teaching throughout his ministry: "the cross *is* the sharp edge

---

28. Meeks, "Inventing the Christ," 89–90.
29. Marcus, "Crucifixion as Parodic Exaltation," 73.

of kingdom redefinition, just as the kingdom, in its redefined form, *is* the ultimate, meaning of the cross."[30]

Plenty have noted the strong notes of glory *through* suffering, glory *the other side of* suffering, but, in this view, the suffering of the Messiah, as portrayed in all four Gospels, is actually *the very means itself* of Christ asserting his sovereignty.[31] It is itself the messianic victory.[32] This crucified Messiah is hence given the titles that belong to Caesar: Savior, Lord, King (Phil 3:20), and the cross itself—not even Christ's triumph over the cross in resurrection and glory, but the suffering and humiliation of the cross—*is* the power of God (1 Cor 1:18). The crown of thorns is more than incidental, the robes and mockery are not there by accident, and the *titulum* announcing that this *is* Jesus the King of the Jews is central to the picture being painted by the Gospel writers. The crucifixion is the moment the rightful king ascends his throne. The kingdom of God, which forms the heart of Christ's teaching, begins to actualize at the cross.

This view requires a fundamentally ironic way of looking at the cross, which seems to have its beginnings in Paul but reaches a climax in Mark's Gospel. *The cross is the opposite of a cross*: an image that Paul deploys sparingly and in response to contexts where hubris of some kind is the main problem (as with the Corinthians!). At other times Paul finds himself addressing people who would have lived all their lives in fear of curses, spells, magic, and evil spirits (arguably the audience of Ephesians) and to them this message of an ironic victory is not routinely deployed. To reassure them, Paul does not tend to go via the rather convoluted and subtle route of the cross as ironic victory but cuts straight to the chase: Christ is Lord, has the name above all names, is head over all principality and power. It is certain situations that especially inspire him take his eye down from the heavenly throne of Christ to the seat of the cross, there to glory in the honor found only in shame.

Atonement, Kingdom, and Gospel

In the mid-twentieth century the trend in New Testament studies was to say "the answer is the delayed parousia; what was the question?" The assertion consequently was that New Testament pneumatology and the Pauline

30. Wright, *How God Became King*, 228.
31. E.g., Wright, *How God Became King*, 237.
32. Wright, *How God Became King*, 243.

in-Christ doctrine emerged as remedies to the delay, as consolation prizes. Emphases that are integral to New Testament theology from its very beginnings were taken to be hasty re-writings of the original teachings of Christianity's founder. There seems here to be a failure to recognize the fundamentally experiential nature of earliest Christianity. James Dunn has been exceptional in truly recapturing this emphasis, that the risen Christ was experienced as the Spirit.[33]

A way of looking at Christian origins that is less dismissive of the experiences that informed it is to say that, until Pentecost, the "already" aspect of the kingdom had only been implicit. Even seeing the cross as the inauguration of a reign required a certain way of looking at things that was not, by itself, obvious. Now, the already in-breaking reign of God came in the outpouring of "this that you both see and hear" (Acts 2:33). The Spirit came and gave the people such a foretaste of the age to come that they could now already taste it and became indomitably assured of its ultimate consummation in a new creation.

Reflection

1. Recall any experiences of the Holy Spirit, whether your own or experiences others have reported. What "epistemic advantage" took place? What were the main insights? A clearer vision of the saving work of Christ, or something else?

2. Esler believes that religion always exists in a dialectical tension with the surrounding culture. In other words, the culture is pulling in one direction and our faith is pulling in another. Where are the pressure points for you as you seek to live out your faith in your culture? Where do you find yourself rubbing up against a completely different dominant narrative?

3. What do you think of the way I have tried to harmonize kingdom and cross by using Pentecost?

---

33. Dunn, *Jesus and the Spirit*.

CHAPTER 2

Victory

> The most fundamental unifying theme throughout Jesus' ministry is that he was setting up the kingdom of God over against the kingdom of Satan. Jesus' exorcistic and healing ministry constitutes preliminary victories over this enemy, while his death and resurrection spell Satan's ultimate demise.[1]

IF WHAT WE HAVE said is true—that the metaphors of atonement came about as a result of the inrush of Pentecostal witness to the crucified Christ, who had now defeated death and was ascended to the right hand of God— then it makes sense for us to try the victory metaphor for size first of all. It makes sense to see whether this fits as the first and prime metaphor out of which some of the others might flow. We are immediately confronted, however, with the fact that in only three places in the New Testament is the *death* of Christ explicitly and unmistakably linked to the idea of a victory over hostile powers (Col 2:14–15; Heb 2:14–15; Rev 12:11), and then there are a further three or so places where such a link is very strongly implied (Heb 10:12–13; 1 John 3:8; John 12:31–33).[2]

---

1. Boyd, *God at War*, 238.

2. Richard Bell finds that, although Paul is shy of using the terms "Satan" or "devil" he seems to strongly believe that Christ's death and resurrection were the means by which humans are delivered from the clutches of Satan: *Deliver us from Evil*, 232–41. For example, being delivered from the power of darkness is equated with having redemption and the forgiveness of sins: Col 1:13–14. Further, redemption from "under the law" in Gal 4:4 is equated with having once been "enslaved to the elemental spirits" of 4:3. This is part of Paul's wider apparent equation of slavery to the law with slavery to the demonic, and serving the law with serving idols: Caird, *Principalities and Powers*, 41, and Bell, *Deliver us from Evil*, 235–41.

It may be, however, that the concept is more like a kind of background music to the New Testament understanding of Calvary, an assumed position based on an almost universally held worldview. That worldview seems to be that we share this world with various other beings that we cannot see but whose collective activity leads to concentrations of power that have a major effect upon everyone's life. These powers are sometimes good but very often overstep the mark and become a source of systemic evil. Christ's work in some way puts them all back in their place. Sometimes they are even pictured as having been reconciled to Christ (Col 1:16, 20). More often they are understood to have been defeated, disarmed, and placed beneath his feet.

Setting the Scene: Life under the Powers

Paul Hiebert famously opened the eyes of Western missiologists to the reality that, for many if not most non-Western people, this world is a world that we share with various kinds of spiritual beings.[3] In the West, it has been centuries since we believed in things like trolls and fairies, or localized deities, and only very recently have angels made a bit of a come-back. If we believe in a non-physical realm at all, it tends to be "up there" somewhere. Humans, matter, and earthly things are all safely "down here" where we can observe them, measure them, and put them to use. But the arrangement is incomplete, claimed Hiebert, until we include the "excluded middle," the zone that is neither completely up there nor totally down here. He noted, too, how the Hebrew Bible portrays God as triumphing over the gods of the middle zone, such as the Ashtoreths and the Baals.[4] Indeed, the big difference, for Hiebert, between the animistic worldview and the biblical vision is that the biblical writers present us with a "divinely ordained and maintained created order" of which the spirits of the middle zone are a part. They are mere creatures and are entirely subject to their creator. It is for certain that, for many of the earliest Christians, one of their greatest joys would have been precisely this realization. The powers that they once tried in vain to control using amulets and spells could now all be seen to lie beneath Christ's feet.

Judging from the rise of apocalyptic literature during the intertestamental and New Testament periods, the view of the cosmos as a "war

3. Hiebert, "The Flaw of the Excluded Middle," 35–47.
4. Hiebert, "The Flaw of the Excluded Middle," 41.

VICTORY

zone"⁵ between good and evil forces became increasingly widespread. All of the sources of apocalyptic literature go much further than the canonical Scriptures of Israel in the place given to gods, angels, and demons.⁶ However, even Jesus himself seems to have believed that Satan was the "ruler of this world" whom he would soon cast out by his accomplishment at the cross (John 12:31). It seems that belief in an invisible realm of powers that exist on a seamless continuum with visible powers was "almost universal."⁷

The New Testament terminology used to describe the powers is of uncertain origin. The pseudepigraphical sources normally cited as background do not necessarily predate the New Testament and may include Christian interpolations.⁸ The most common New Testament terms, together with customary, non-biblical usage, are as follows:⁹ *archai* is the plural form of the term for the highest authority, the top official in a region.¹⁰ In the New Testament, this normally occurs as a pair with the following term: *exousiai*. This term refers to legitimation, authorization, and those possessing such authorization. The term would include, according Wink, "ideological justifications, political or religious legitimations, and delegated permissions."¹¹ The pair is often translated as "principalities and powers." *Thronoi* means thrones. Just as today, throne refers symbolically to the seat of power. *Kyriotētes* means dominion, authority. The further we go on, the more it becomes clear that we are dealing with terms that are nearly synonymous and were almost certainly never meant to carry any specific technical meaning. These are not designations for the components of some elaborate hierarchy of spirits, fun though it has doubtless been for some spiritual warfare advocates to let loose their imaginations in this way! In fact, Wink observes that, though the pair *archai* "principalities" and *exousiai* "powers" is a common pairing (1 Cor 15:24; Col 1:16; 2:10,

---

5. Boyd, "Christus Victor View," 26.
6. Boyd, "Christus Victor View," 27.
7. Wink, *Naming the Powers*, 7.
8. Benoit, "Pauline Angelology and Demonology," 6.
9. It is to be noted that not until the New Testament writings is there any use of these terms to apply to anything other than human, earthly concentrations of power, unless we include the Pseudepigrapha.
10. Arnold, *Powers of Darkness*, 81.
11. Wink, *Naming the Powers*, 16. He is saying this in the context of having to process harrowing experiences of Latin American political dictatorships, which seems to be what adds a certain twist, perhaps a bitter twist, to his terminology. He describes his experiences on pp. ix–xi.

15; Eph 1:21; 3:10; 6:12; Titus 3:1), the various terms often occur in whole strings of assorted terms, "as though power were so diffuse and impalpable a phenomenon that words must be heaped up in clusters in order to catch a sense of its complexity."[12]

In addition to these spiritual powers, Paul also seems to view such entities as the flesh, the law, and sin as personified and monstrous powers, a phenomenon that Emma Wasserman attributes to Middle Platonic influences on Paul. Plato first developed the idea of the uncontrolled force of appetite in a person's life, comparing it to a tyrannical ruler who takes over a city.[13] The Middle Platonists wrote of the tug-of-war within us between rationality on one side and the irrational passions and appetites on the other, which easily take over from our rationality and become monstrously demanding.[14] This two-part inner struggle seems quite similar to Paul's uniquely insightful view of the Christian life; we are caught between flesh and Spirit. And he, like the Middle Platonists, describes sin as a power that dominates us, enslaves us, captures us as with the edge of a spear, imprisons us, and even kills us (Rom 6:12–13, 18, 20; 7:10–11, 13–14, 23).[15]

Gustav Aulén, following William Wrede[16] (who also believed that Paul was indebted to Hellenistic concepts of flesh and spirit), was sure that Paul regarded the human plight as a state of being in bondage to the "realities," the "active forces" of flesh, sin, law, and death,[17] in addition to the more familiar demons, principalities, and powers. Christ's work delivers people from *all* of these powers. The powers are defeated through their mistaken act of crucifying the Lord of glory.[18] Interestingly, Aulén addresses himself to the question that immediately confronts anyone who has studied the history of the doctrine of the atonement and noted the dominance of the *Christus Victor* viewpoint throughout the patristic era and then studied the New Testament teaching on atonement and found that the victory motif does not immediately strike us as dominant. Compared to the church

12. Wink, *Naming the Powers*, 8.

13. *The Republic* Books IV–IX.

14. E.g., Plutarch, *Moralia*, especially *De Virtue et Vitio* (On Virtue and Vice) in *Moralia* II; Philo, *Legatio ad Gaium* 3:116–17.

15. Wasserman, "Paul among the Philosophers," 388.

16. Wrede, *Paul*. Wrede's contemporary and critic Albert Schweitzer also believed that the New Testament doctrine of redemption was essentially about deliverance from demonic powers: Schweitzer, *Mysticism of Paul the Apostle*, 64–74.

17. Aulén, *Christus Victor*, 81.

18. Aulén, *Christus Victor*, 81.

VICTORY

fathers, Aulén notes that there is far less mention of the devil in the New Testament.[19] Instead, there is a much greater place given to this great collection of entities that we call the powers, expressed using the various terms such as "principality and power," we have briefly explored.[20] And it is at this point that Aulén is able to press into service Wrede's powers—"flesh," "sin," "law," and "death"—as a kind of rent-a-crowd, if you like. The mighty host of principalities and powers are further thronged by flesh, sin, law, and death. The death of Christ dethrones these powers too. This helps Aulén to make the claim that, if we include *all* the powers, the work of Christ *is* presented as a victory in the New Testament just like it is in the church fathers. He musters Romans 7:4, 9, 10:4, 1 Corinthians 15:26, 56, Romans 5:18, Galatians 3:10, 13 and Colossians 2:14 in support, which all describe the flesh, sin, the law, and death as our enemies and declare that the cross has now vanquished them.

Like Wrede and Aulén, Beker also included flesh, sin, law, and death as powers and saw them as interlocking, with death as the main power. So that, with the defeat of death in the death and resurrection of Christ, the chief power, together with all its allies, is vanquished.[21]

Walter Wink does not focus on these four as powers but confines himself to the principality and power lists. Wink views the powers as the "inner and outer" aspects of the various structures of a society: governments, corporations, and so on. There is a visible pole (the way we see powers exercise their power) and an invisible pole (the driving force, ideology, and legitimation behind an organization). Both poles come into being together and only exist together, and neither is a problem until the particular power in question idolatrously raises itself up above God.[22] But the concept includes "every concentration of power in any authorized agent or sector."[23]

Similar to Wink is Grayston who, in his delightful little study of Colossians 1:15–20, describes the thrones, dominions, principalities, and powers

19. Aulén, *Christus Victor*, 83.

20. ". . . from the latter half of the second century onwards the demonic powers drop into the background, and their place is taken by the devil." Aulén, *Christus Victor*, 86.

21. Beker, *Paul the Apostle*, 189–91.

22. Wink, *Naming the Powers*, 5. His main basis for claiming both an inner and an outer, a heavenly and an earthly, a spiritual and a political connotation is Col 1:16: "For in him all things were created, in heaven and on earth, visible and invisible, whether thrones or dominions or principalities or authorities—all things were created through him and for him." Ibid., 11. His use of RSV is preserved.

23. Wink, *Naming the Powers*, 12.

of verse 15 as "semiautonomous accumulations of power, in society and the environment."[24] A trap is set for them by the death of Christ and they are then restored to their proper service.[25]

Boyd differs from Wink and Grayston in attributing greater personal agency to them. He insists they are personal spiritual beings.[26] Reichenbach, in turn, thinks that Boyd ends up giving the powers far too much power, making them into the apparent "centerpiece" of the whole plan of redemption."[27]

There is, then, a spectrum of views about the powers. Some view these powers as not fully personal and operating mainly within organizations (Wink, Grayston); others view them as highly personal invisible spirits, beings that would have instilled such fear in the people of the first century as to make them resort to spells and magic (Arnold, Boyd). In addition, some have viewed these powers as not wholly bad and certainly redeemable. Wesley Carr even claimed that the powers are angelic beings and wholly good.[28]

It seems that every angle that has been taken has shed *some* light on this, including those angles that include the more seemingly natural enemies of flesh and sin. Indeed, Paul and others do personify entities that we would not normally think of personifying. By means of these we, literally, become our own worst enemy. The hopelessness that death brings is perhaps the chief power without which flesh, sin, and law would have no hold over our behavior. The principalities and powers are not necessarily any more or any less personal than flesh, sin, law, and death in the minds of the New Testament writers. It is just that they operate in a different way. They are described as more diffuse, ethereal, more uncanny and numinous. Where flesh, sin, law, and death create an experience of slavery, the principalities create fear. Following Wink, this can indeed be seen in certain

---

24. Grayston, *Dying, We Live*, 136.

25. Grayston, *Dying, We Live*, 136. "It is as if God were a king surrounded by enemies in his own royal court, who wished to draw his people from their support of his enemies, allowing them to kill his Son and thus, by displaying their vicious nature, destroy their own power. When the Son is raised from the dead, he triumphantly mocks the discredited enemies, and their formerly deluded victims are reconciled to God." He references Martin, *Reconciliation*, 41.

26. Boyd, "Christus Victor View," 29.

27. Reichenbach, "Healing Response," 54.

28. Carr, *Angels and Principalities*.

monolithic human organizations, which become unaccountable and immune. They wield uncanny, unearthly power over people.

To bring us more completely up to date, contributing to the continued embracing of the victory motif by scholarship has been the "apocalyptic" turn taken in recent Pauline scholarship. The apocalyptic take on Paul was inspired originally by Albert Schweitzer,[29] then Ernst Käsemann,[30] and restarted in earnest by J. Louis Martyn and continued by Douglas Campbell and others.[31] This view takes its inspiration, not from rabbinic Judaism (as in W. D. Davies) or Palestinian Judaism per se (E. P. Sanders), but from the Judaism of the weird and wonderful apocalyptic literature. It was characterized by intense despair at present circumstances, which usually included political oppression and persecution, the use of symbolic language: often in the form of dreams or visions, a strong celestial dimension: the apocalyptic world is a world of angels and demons, and predictions of catastrophic judgement upon the earth that would issue in the vindication of the righteous. Apocalyptic writings sought to draw back the veil on political events to reveal the powers that were pulling the strings. Martyn puts it vividly: "Anti-God powers have managed to commence their own rule over the world, leading human beings into idolatry and thus into slavery," but "God will inaugurate a victorious and liberating apocalyptic war against these evil powers.... This kind of apocalyptic eschatology," he claims, "is fundamental to Paul's letters."[32]

The new apocalyptic Paul has brought a helpful and supplementary angle on Paul in addition to what was helpful about the (no longer new) New Perspective. Like the New Perspective it nestles within a certain body of Second Temple Jewish literature to see how Paul's writings start to catch the light from there. A difficulty with the apocalyptic take on Paul has been not what it claims but the force with which it denies all alternatives.[33] The stridency with which this is done seems hard to justify.[34] David Shaw

29. Schweitzer, *Mysticism of Paul the Apostle.*
30. Käsemann, *Perspectives on Paul.*
31. Gathercole supplies a helpful introduction: Gathercole, *Defending Substitution,* 42–47.
32. Martyn, *Theological Issues in the Letters of Paul.*
33. Traceable perhaps to Schweitzer's understanding of the apocalypticism of New Testament times as being itself completely at odds with the legalistic Torah-piety of the Pharisees: Macaskill, *Union with Christ,* 23.
34. It drives a wedge between rabbinic Judaism and apocalyptic Judaism: Bell, *Deliver us from Evil,* 234.

deplores the way in which we are forced to choose a Paul who is *either apocalyptic or covenantal*: "Is Paul's gospel," he says, "fundamentally about a decisive divine incursion to defeat enslaving cosmic powers or is it about promises fulfilled: the forgiveness of sins and the justification by faith of Jew and Gentile alike?"[35] To this, an answer of "both" does not seem entirely unreasonable.

Despite its name, the movement has moved away from an emphasis on the parousia in deference to a firmly this-worldly view of Paul's understanding of the coming of Christ and the Spirit.[36] The apocalyptic movement seems to derive its energy from distancing itself from any forensic view of Paul and his doctrine of justification. However, within Jewish apocalyptic literature itself there are seemingly two discernible types: the cosmological and the forensic. The cosmological type is found in 1 Enoch 1–36. This type includes God being portrayed as a warrior and liberator, focuses on Genesis 6 and the fall of the angels (rather than Genesis 3), perceives humans as enslaved to these fallen angelic beings, and proclaims the answer in a decisive liberation by God. The forensic type is exemplified by 2 Baruch and 4 Ezra. This type sees God as a judge and justifier, sees in Genesis 3 the definitive description of the origins of evil, and views the human plight as our liability to judgment under God's law; the way out is obedience to the law resulting in justification before God.[37] It does not seem that either is a perfect fit for Paul, and neither ought that to be expected. Paul is scrambling for the words to describe a completely new thing that, though foreshadowed, prophesied, and anticipated, was not quite as anyone had expected.

So, a more detailed treatment of some relevant passages still awaits but it seems there is a growing scholarly consensus that has been building for some time now. This consensus means that, if we are to be able to understand the New Testament on its own terms, the disenchanted universe that many of us in Western cultures take for granted needs to be set aside. The capacity to personify even such entities as "sin" and "the flesh" and to attribute to events a spiritual rather than a purely natural cause was clearly a significant aspect of patterns of thought in the classical period and late antiquity. Both Jews and gentiles alike viewed the world as much more comprehensively animated by personal powers than many of us do today. With this background in view, we will now look at some passages.

35. Shaw, "Apocalyptic and Covenant," 155.
36. Shaw, "Apocalyptic and Covenant," 156.
37. See Shaw's helpful table: Shaw, "Apocalyptic and Covenant," 163.

Christ's Victory: Sources of the Concept

Psalm 110:1

"The LORD said to my Lord, 'Sit at my right hand until I place your enemies as a footstool beneath your feet.'" This passage, the single most quoted Old Testament passage in the New Testament, sounded ready-made for the early interpreters of the shameful crucifixion of Jesus. The apparent defeat of the Messiah is only temporary; in the realty revealed to believers, God has exalted him to share God's rule in heaven until all his enemies are defeated.[38] With these words from Psalm 110:1 we are at the heart of the origins of the victory motif in New Testament atonement theology. It is behind every reference to Jesus being seated at the right hand of God. Jesus applies this verse to himself: Matthew 12:44; Mark 12:36; Luke 20:43, and the early church applies it to him in numerous places (Acts 2:32–36; 5:31; 1 Cor 15:22–25; Heb 1:3; 10:12–13; 1 Pet 3:21–22). Boyd draws the conclusion from these passages that, "the work of the cross was about dethroning a cruel, illegitimate ruler and reinstating a loving, legitimate one: Jesus Christ."[39] His death and resurrection were somehow "the means by which he gained the upper hand over the enemies of God."[40]

It is significant that the passage is quoted at the climactic moment of the trail of Jesus itself where Jesus applies it to himself. What seems to make Christ's designation of himself as the "my Lord" of Psalm 110:1 into something contentious enough to get him condemned by Caiaphas is the heady mixture created by combining Psalm 110:1 with Daniel 7:13–14 (especially v. 14: "I saw one like a son of man coming with the clouds of heaven"). The result is this: "'I am; and you will see the Son of Man seated at the right hand of the Power, and coming with the clouds of heaven'" (Mark 14:62). Bauckham believes it was this combination that provoked the charge of blasphemy. It made Daniel's "one like a son of man" into "an unambiguously divine figure."[41] It means that the heavenly son of man of Daniel shares the divine throne of Psalm 110.

Ultimately it is the fulfilment of this promise of heavenly exaltation that provides us with the Father's answer to the Godforsakenness of the Son on the cross. Christ quotes Psalm 22:1 in the famous cry of dereliction

38. Meeks, "Inventing the Christ," 91.
39. Boyd, *God at War*, 246.
40. Boyd, *God at War*, 244, reflecting on Heb 10:12–13.
41. Bauckham, "Markan Christology," 32.

yet probably was invoking the whole psalm, including verses 21–23, where God answers the one who has been apparently deserted. Baukham insightfully concludes:

> Perhaps this is why Mark's narrative ends surprisingly soon. He could not *narrate* Jesus's exaltation to the heavenly throne and so he leaves Jesus, beyond his death and burial, unseen by his readers[;] . . . it is clear that the story continues beyond what he narrates, even into his readers' future.[42]

This passage, then, plays perfectly into the Pentecost Standpoint narrative that I have set up. The picture it provides of a vindicated king reigning with God over all his enemies is by far the most important lens through which the earliest church saw Christ. And it was arguably Pentecost that first made this seem real: Peter's Pentecost sermon is replete with references to this heavenly reign. But not only that, this passage seems to offer the earliest church a key to the dark events of the crucifixion when Jesus' citation of it (Mark 14:62) and dauntless belief in it helps to bring about the death sentence.

Genesis 3:15

Another important source for the victory concept is the place held in the popular imagination by the *protoevangelium* of Genesis 3:15: "I will put enmity between you and the woman, and between your offspring and hers; he will strike your head, and you will strike his heel." One of the most notable things about the passage is the fact that, as far back as the date of the Septuagint (second and third centuries BCE), there has been a tendency to translate the pronoun "he" of "he will strike your head" (as in the NRSV above) as masculine when the Hebrew suggests a translation of "she"[43] or "they," that is, "the (female) descendants of Eve."[44] This indicates, according to Martin, that the association of this text with the growing messianic hopes of the intertestamental period can even be traced as far back as the Septuagint itself.[45] The masculine turn comes because the translators are

42. Bauckham, "Markan Christology," 33–34.
43. The Latin Vulgate renders it as *ipsa*, "she."
44. Martin, "The Earliest Messianic Interpretation of Genesis 3:15," 425. The passage has a forbidding list of other translation difficulties besides the pronouns: Wenham, *Genesis 1–15*, 79–81.
45. Martin, "The Earliest Messianic Interpretation of Genesis 3:15," 427.

referring back to "seed" (*sperma*), which, though neuter, is assumed to refer to the Messiah, whom the translators assumed to be male. Martin does not consider the other possibility, namely, that the translators are harmonizing with "*his* heel,"[46] which only makes sense if the owner of the heel, who does the striking of the serpent's head, is also a "he."

Julie Walsh extends a feminine interpretation of the seed of Eve by reference to Jael who literally drives a tent peg through the head of Sisera, the commander of Jabin's forces in Judges 4–5.[47] There is even a poetic justice discernible in the fact that the serpent deceived the woman in Genesis 3, thus bringing about her downfall, but in the story of Jael, the woman does the deceiving and this brings about the downfall of the evil Sisera.[48] Walsh is able to cite support as far back as Augustine for the reading that the offspring of the woman that God has in mind are specifically the female followers of Yahweh.[49] New Testament echoes of the Jael story, and back through Jael to Genesis 3:15, are traced to the unusual term that Jesus uses in the Gospel of John for his mother: "woman," this particular woman being, of course, the descendant of Eve who brought into the world the one who would strike the serpent's head. Echoes of Jael are also detected in the way Mary is described as "blessed among women" (Luke 1:42). Jael is described in the same way ("most blessed among women") by Deborah (Judg 5:24).

The promise to the Seventy in Luke 10:19 that they would trample on serpents and scorpions has obvious echoes with Genesis 3:15 as does the promise to the Roman Christians that the God of peace would soon crush Satan under their feet (Rom 16:20).

Some of these exegetical twists seem to produce tenuous results but the point seems a valid one that the *protoevangelium* was a very widely held part of the messianic expectations of the time. What is perhaps notable is that the most obvious New Testament echoes of Genesis 3:15, namely,

---

46. The Hebrew would literally read: "bruise of him [*tishuphenu*] the heal [*aqav*]." Ambrose, doubtless to harmonize with the Latin *ipsa*, has "She shall watch for your head and you for her heel." *Flight from the World* 7.43, in Louth (ed.), *Ancient Christian Commentary on Scripture, Old Testament I*, 90.

47. Walsh, "Jael's Story as Initial Fulfillment of Genesis 3:15," 22–37.

48. Walsh, "Jael's Story as Initial Fulfillment of Genesis 3:15" 25.

49. Walsh, "Jael's Story as Initial Fulfillment of Genesis 3:15" 22. Also ibid., 24: "the Serpent dealt with the woman as the representative of both humans, and God took the same approach when he cursed the Serpent: his people had 'the woman' as their representative."

in the trampling of snakes and scorpions of Luke 10 and the crushing of Satan of Romans 16, refer to followers and believers doing the trampling and crushing, a fact that assumes a participation in Christ's victory.

Christ's Victory: The Language

Colossians 2:14–15

> ... erasing the record that stood against us with its legal demands. He set this aside, nailing it to the cross. 15 He disarmed the rulers and authorities and made a public example of them, triumphing over them in it. (Col 2:15)

> Nowhere else in the New Testament is Christ's victory over the powers of darkness given fuller expression than in Colossians 2:15.[50]

So much for the cultural context and the Old Testament origins of the concept—all of which *ought* to point to a vast wealth of New Testament passages that actually picture Christ as a mighty warrior and present his death and resurrection as a great victory, but when it comes to passages that unmistakably do this we are met with meagre pickings. Boyd has already used up all his best biblical references by the time he is on the fourth page of his "Christus Victor" chapter and is already relying on passages that can be construed as referring to the cross but which do not actually do so, such as 1 John 3:8.[51]

Colossians 2:14–15 is undoubtedly our most important instance of the victory metaphor. It shares with the rest of the early part of Colossians a profusion of terms normally used to refer to the Roman Empire. Maier includes "reconciliation" (1:20), "making peace" (1:20), "rule" (3:15), and "kingdom"(1:13), as instances of imperial terminology, quite apart from the obvious reference to the Roman *Triumphus* or triumphal procession of Colossians 1:15.[52] These political references are the more remarkable for the fact that Christ's triumph is not through the military exploits so celebrated by the empire but through *a cross*, the empire's dreaded symbol of abject defeat.

50. Arnold, *Powers of Darkness*, 104.
51. Boyd, *God at War*, 238–41.
52. Maier, "A Sly Civility," 326.

VICTORY

It should be noted also that the victory celebrated in this passage is a cosmic victory first and foremost, and only secondarily a victory that applies to us individually.[53] However, what seems clear in Colossians 2:14–15 is that the main weapon that has been removed, the thing that the powers have been disarmed of, is the "certificate of debt" (Arnold) or "handwriting of requirements" (NKJV) or "charge of our legal indebtedness"(NIV), which has been taken out of the way and nailed to the cross.[54] The Greek term is *cheirographon*, etymologically meaning something that has been handwritten. The most plausible explanation for its use is probably still that of Adolf Deissmann, who described certain Papyri that list various infringements but with an enormous "X" written all across the papyrus. There is a further record of a trial in which the governor of Egypt concludes by declaring "Let the handwriting be crossed out."[55]

The element of exposure, of public humiliation, dominates the passage. It is the meaning conveyed by every key word in verse 15: *apekdysamenos* "he disarmed," *edeigmatisen en parrēsia* "he made a public spectacle of them," and *thriambeusas autous* "he triumphed over them." The first word, *apekdyō*, normally refers to undressing. Though a translation that would have Christ stripping something off *himself* is possible (the Greek is in the middle voice as in 3:9),[56] it seems more in keeping with the context to say that Christ stripped the principalities and powers. In a Roman *triumphus*, the stripping would normally be of the enemy's weaponry.[57] The next word, *deigmatizō*, can simply mean "I show," but in the right context can mean "I expose." Such is the meaning in Matthew 1:19, where Joseph wants to avoid exposing Mary to public disgrace. The addition of *en parrēsia* "with confidence" serves to emphasize that this particular exposure was done with a sense of great triumph and celebration.

---

53. Boyd, *God at War*, 241.

54. Benoit, "Pauline Angelology and Demonology," 15. Similarly Arnold, who uses Anselmian language: "How precisely did Christ's death and resurrection accomplish this disarming? Precisely because the powers could not deter Christ from making a satisfaction for sin . . . the powers thus lost their chief mechanism for holding people in bondage." Arnold, *Powers of Darkness*, 104–5.

55. Deissmann, *Light from the Ancient Near East*, 332–38.

56. So Maier, "A Sly Civility," 344, who also refers to a disrobing and re-robing ritual prior to the victory procession and claims that Christ is here pictured as disrobing in preparation for his parade.

57. Wink cites Plutarch's *Triumph of Aemilius Paulus* 32–34, Wink, *Naming the Powers*, 58 n54. Despite citing this description, Wink seems to prefer to translate "unmask" rather than "disarm": ibid., 58–9. There is no explanation for this.

Lastly, *thriambeusas autous,* "he triumphed over them": on the basis of the use of the same Greek word for "triumphal procession" in 2 Corinthians 2:14 ("But thanks be to God, who in Christ always leads us in triumphal procession, and through us spreads in every place the fragrance that comes from knowing him"), Hock proposes the following translation: "Christ, by disarming the angels [normally rendered 'principalities and powers'] of their unchecked independence and authority, leads them proudly along, parading them in himself."[58] Both passages are making metaphorical reference to a Roman *Triumphus* or victory procession. The person at the heart of the *Triumphus* would be the victorious general, but besides him there were many other groups of people included in the procession. In fact, there were six groups in all: magistrates and members of the senate in front, then the trumpeters with some of the spoils of war, then the flute-players and white oxen soon to be sacrificed, then the captives in chains, then the general on his chariot, and finally the victorious army bringing up the rear.[59] Hock's point is to exactly correlate three of the groups with the three groups that might have been in Paul's mind as he wrote. So, the magistrates and senate are the apostles, the general is Christ, and the victorious army is the angels (principalities and powers, not mentioned in 2 Cor 2:14). Hock then makes the point that this threefold identification applies to both passages: 2 Corinthians 2:14 and Colossians 2:15. Because the principalities and powers must be the equivalent to the victorious army in Paul's picture, they must therefore be seen as at least potentially good and certainly redeemable, as is also implied in Colossians 1:16, 20, where the invisible powers are made by and for Christ and God reconciles *all* things to himself. "Thus," says Hock, "the ministers and angels triumph with God in Christ. They are sharers in His victory."[60] Similarly Benoit: "there is no punishment here but a re-ordering. The Powers are not formally guilty."[61] Similarly Boyd insists that the reconciliation of the "all things" of Colossians 1:20 has to include the thrones, dominions, rulers, and powers mentioned in 1:16. Elsewhere, as Benoit admits, these same powers lie beneath Christ's feet

---

58. Hock, "Christ the Parade," 114.

59. This is described in many sources: Hock, "Christ the Parade," 117; Arnold, *Powers of Darkness*, 106; Wink, *Naming the Powers*, 56 n46, though the original source for them all might be: Versnel, *Triumphus: An Inquiry into the Origin, Development, and Meaning of the Roman Triumph.*

60. Hock, "Christ the Parade," 119

61. Benoit, "Pauline Angelology and Demonology," 15.

and are rendered powerless: 1 Corinthians 2:6; 15:4; Ephesians 1:21–22.[62] However we construe it, the result is peace (1:20), and this peace will mean that nothing opposes Christ's lordship and everything will be in its proper place. It seems impossible to avoid the conclusion that, for at least some of the powers, this proper place will be beneath Christ's feet.[63] Paul's ambiguity about the powers, their shades of grey between the malevolent and the benevolent, is something we probably will need to be content with.

One more difficulty to revisit, while we are on the subject of ambiguity, is the small matter of God deceiving the devil. Though this patristic idea is not to be found explicitly in the New Testament, there seems to be a hint of it in the passage most often cited by the patristic authors in support: 1 Corinthians 2:8: "None of the rulers of this age understood this; for if they had, they would not have crucified the Lord of glory."[64] It is highly likely that "rulers" here denotes the same group of powers that we have been describing and exegetes have long continued to draw the conclusion that when the powers thought they had the Lord of Glory in their grasp their apparent victory was turned into a resounding defeat: "unwittingly they had been mere instruments in God's hands."[65] Much as the concepts that were later elaborated by the fathers of God entering into a deal with the devil seem very crude, yet, Paul and the fathers may not be all that far apart where this passage is concerned. One thing that Aulén noted which Paul and the fathers have in common is a certain "double-sidedness."[66] In the fathers, the devil is the enemy and yet is used as God's instrument to accomplish salvation. In Paul, there is something similar going on, perhaps hinted at in 1 Corinthians 2:8, but certainly coming to the fore in his musings about the law in Romans 7. There, the law is the enemy making sin worse yet is used as God's instrument to bring us to Christ's deliverance.

Revelation 12:11

Revelation 12:11: "But they have conquered him by the blood of the Lamb . . ." is undoubtedly to be understood in the context of Satan's role as the "accuser of our comrades" (Rev 12:10). The function of the blood of the

62. Benoit, "Pauline Angelology and Demonology," 15.
63. Boyd, *God at War*, 248–49.
64. The patristic developments are explored in my *Atonement Theories*, 3–25.
65. Scott, *Colossians, Philemon, and Ephesians*, 189.
66. Aulén, *Christus Victor*, 83–84.

lamb is that it gives the accused an answer for the accuser (hence Rom 8:33–34). However, it is interesting also to note the intertextuality that exists between Revelation 12 and Revelation 20. Both include multiple terms for Satan that include the word "dragon" (12:9; 20:2); both include a reference to the dragon being overthrown (12:9; 20:2); in both passages an angel is involved in this overthrow (12:9; 20:1); both make a connection with martyred believers (12:11; 20:4); and both make the victory over Satan bafflingly temporary: he is released again to carry on going on the rampage (12:12–17; 20:7–10).[67] A clue to this apparent two-stage victory over Satan, the first of which seems somehow provisional, may be in the exodus typology that can be seen in both Revelation 12 and 20. Exodus may be a "template" for the story, with Revelation 12 concluding "between the two exodus deliverances."[68] The first deliverance was the deliverance from Egypt, effected by the blood of the lamb (12:11), via Moses (whose miraculous escape as a baby might be referred to at 12:4), on the night of Passover. The second deliverance came after the dragon, here perhaps, a symbol of Pharaoh (also: Ps 74:13–15; Isa 27:1; 51:9), went out in pursuit of the Israelites into the wilderness (12:6, 14) necessitating a second deliverance via the parting of the Red Sea (perhaps referred to at 13:1). Laure Guy concludes: "John's audience has the benefit of knowing that God came through with a second deliverance in the exodus story—despite their being hemmed in earlier on the seashore."[69] The message in both Revelation 12 and 20 is "Don't give up."[70]

Hebrews 2:14–15[71]

> Since, therefore, the children share flesh and blood, he himself likewise shared the same things, so that through death he might destroy the one who has the power of death, that is, the devil, and free those who all their lives were held in slavery by the fear of death.

---

67. Guy, "Back to the Future," 231: a helpful table is provided.
68. Guy, "Back to the Future," 232.
69. Guy, "Back to the Future," 232.
70. Guy, "Back to the Future," 236.
71. Two helpful commentaries here are: Bruce, *The Epistle to the Hebrews*, 84–87, and Ellingworth, *The Epistle to the Hebrews*, 170–75.

VICTORY

We are told here that it is "through death" that Jesus won his victory over him who held the power of death. This seems to tap into the tradition of ironic victory, chiming well with passages such as 1 Corinthians 1:18–25, 2:1–8 and Galatians 6:14. If we accept that the powers are not only the supernatural beings that inhabit the "excluded middle" but also the powers that we might class as natural, then this passage affords us a tantalizing glimpse into how these powers work in league with each other. Central to the passage is death, *Thanatos*, who in Greek mythology was personified to the point of being understood as a god and brother to *Hypnos*, sleep. *Thanatos* is personified in Revelation 20:14 to the point of being cast into the lake of fire along with Hades (see also the quote from Hos 13:14 in 1 Cor 15:55). Death is given its power by the devil, the only place in the New Testament where this is stated. Yet the devil has been "destroyed." The Greek is *katargeō*, which is a word that does not imply complete annihilation but a rendering powerless, useless, or unemployed. It is a favorite term of Paul's, who uses it in Romans 6:6 to describe how the "body of sin" has been "destroyed." Next we are given a window into exactly how death, as the devil's lieutenant, affects human beings. It is through the "fear of death" that people are held, not just in the hour of their death but all their lifetimes, subject to slavery. The only other place in the New Testament where we seem to be in similar territory is 1 Corinthians 15:56: "The sting of death is sin, and the power of sin is the law." Many involved in ministry today describe the way in which "strongholds" form in people's lives. They are formed, according to Ed Silvoso for instance, by ingrained patterns of thought that are driven by hopelessness.[72] Death seems to remove hope by continually asserting its ultimate triumph over all that lives, over life itself. This, it seems, causes people's attachment to sin to become stronger; they become enslaved to that by which they had hoped to escape or be comforted. To extrapolate beyond this seems to be to go beyond what the passage itself says, indeed I have probably already transgressed in that way.

Conclusion

If the victory metaphor can be given the prominence that an increasing number of people seem to want it to have then it offers a fresh

72. "A mind-set impregnated with hopelessness that causes us to accept as unchangeable situations that we know are contrary to the will of God." Silvoso, *That None Should Perish*, 155.

understanding of salvation itself. Unlike John McIntyre, I did not include salvation (*sōteria*) as one of my metaphors as it seems to be too much of an umbrella concept—not only in common Christian parlance today but in the New Testament as well. And the word is not normally associated with the cross and resurrection directly. However, perhaps, like "redemption," it has a limited technical meaning as well as a broad all-embracing one. And that technical meaning could simply be that it describes the "rescue" with which Christ's death on the cross has delivered us from "this present evil age" (Gal 1:4). It describes the state into which we are brought following Christ's cosmic victory over the powers.[73] It may be a concept indebted to the "salvation of God" that the Israelites would see when they were trapped by the Red Sea (Exod 14:13; also 14:30; 15:2) as well as the second exodus promised in Isaiah (43:3; 45:22; 49:8; 52:7), in which case it is specifically about deliverance from an oppressive enemy.

Indeed, the very concept of a Messiah is that of a savior, which is an expectation based on the founding story of Genesis. The seed of the woman would crush the head of the serpent. And now all the followers of the Messiah are given power to trample on serpents and scorpions and over all the power of the enemy. A central messianic promise was that he would sit at the right hand of God with all Israel's enemies being placed beneath his feet, and this promise in Psalm 110 of a seated Lord awaiting the consummation of a victory already assured becomes the founding Scripture for the Christology of earliest Christianity. Hence, the nexus of that Christology is the ascension, yet, from that position of vindication, the death of Christ becomes viewable as the true moment of the devil's defeat. The resurrection barely comes into the equation here. When it comes to vanquishing the powers that are opposed to the reign of God, the death of Christ is the secret weapon, and carries the day.

How is this victory secured exactly? In two of the three passages we looked at, the heart of the matter appears to be the wiping out of the handwriting that accused us, the overcoming of the accuser. Justification in Christ seems to be the thing that gives believers an answer, so that, even though the handwriting may be a perfectly truthful itemization of debts that are owed, yet what Christ has done can be appealed to, and the claims confidently dismissed. In the third passage, the devil has been incapacitated

---

73. Boyd, *God at War*, 250. Also 252: "Our salvation is a function of Christ's exalted lordship, and his lordship is a function of his victory over, and now enthronement above, all 'rule and authority and power and dominion, and every name that is named (Eph 1:21)." Boyd musters the following in support: Acts 26:17–18; Gal 1:4; Col 1:13–14.

by the loss of his most important general: Thanatos. Without the fear of death the power that keeps people in chains to self-destructive behaviors is broken. Accusation and the threat of death seem to be the specific weapons of the enemy that have been shattered by the cross.

However, that the victory metaphor does not give us a complete picture of the atonement without remainder ought to be clear. For a start, as Green has pointed out, there is the obvious fact that, in places such as Romans 5:8–10, it is the fact that God did *not* declare war on his enemies that is crucial to what we are to understand atonement to be.[74] It is, however, founding. It is a founding picture that gives rise to further pictures.

Reflection

1. So Christ has triumphed over the principalities and powers and disarmed them. Seemingly, he has also defeated the powers of death, the flesh, sin, and the law. An obvious comment someone might make is: "In a world still rampant with evil, exactly what kind of victory was this?" How would you answer?

2. It seems we now have an answer to the accuser. We can overcome him by the blood of the Lamb. What might this look like in practice? Should we, as some recommend, talk back to the devil?[75]

3. Think of what it means that death has been defeated. Paul says he is sure that nothing, not even death itself, shall separate us from the love of God that is in Christ Jesus (Rom 8:38–39). It is a union that cannot be dissolved by the death of our bodies and, according to Paul, becomes even more glorious once we are absent from the body and present with the Lord (2 Cor 5:8; Phil 1:23). Now think of your most stubborn bad habit, whether past or present: the writer to the Hebrews says that, with the fear of death removed, we are freed from such slavery. Do you agree? Does having eternal hope make it easier live a morally good life?

---

74. Green, "Kaleidoscopic Response," 65.
75. Tozer, *I Talk Back to the Devil*.

CHAPTER 3

Redemption

Setting the Scene: Israel, Exodus, and Oppressors

It is hard to overestimate the importance of the exodus story within the historical, political and theological worldview of Second-Temple Judaism; and, again and again, that story resonated in a world where most Jews were hoping and praying that it would come true once more, this time for good.[1]

ISRAEL WAS DISTINCT FROM other nations in that it was a nation of freed slaves with only God as their Master. Exodus was the defining event.[2] Israel would be ruled over only by God. Even after delivering Israel from the Midianites, Gideon insisted: "I will not rule over you, nor will my son rule over you. The LORD will rule over you." (Judg 8:23).[3] Even when Saul is chosen by Samuel, the word "king" is studiously avoided (1 Sam 10:9–11). In both Deuteronomy 17 and 1 Samuel 8 there is a realistic assessment of how exploitative kings can be and how vulnerable Israel was, for all its anti-master theology, to be seduced not just by Canaanite religion but by Canaanite political systems as well.[4] However, once the monarchy was

---

1. Wight, *Jesus and the Victory of God*, 577.

2. A wide consensus, and applied to atonement theory by, e.g., Green, "Kaleidoscopic Response," 62, citing Larsson, *Bound for Freedom*; Watts, "Exodus," 478–87; Watts, *Isaiah's New Exodus and Mark*; Pao, *Acts and the Isaianic New Exodus*.

3. Klein, "Liberated Leadership," 284: "Because of Israel's doctrine of God, she was opposed to anyone who would claim to be king or master over her." But see Robin Routledge, *Old Testament Theology*, 30 for a summary of discussion around the apparent inconsistencies between texts that seem monarchist and others that are anti-monarchist.

4. Block, "Burden of Leadership," 263. Note in 1 Sam 8:11–17 the repeated use of the

established and Israel and Judah were repeatedly led astray, the catastrophe of exile humbled Israel. They tried again to move away from, to quote Walter Brueggemann, the "public ambitions that imitated the great powers" and tried to return to "covenant and Torah."[5]

However, despite the sumptuous promises of Isaiah 40–55 about life after the return from exile, all was not well. The Jews had become so concerned with Torah-observance that never-ending supplementary rules had been invented just to make sure there were no infractions of the Sabbath.

As far as they were able, they had repented. They had forsaken their idols and become a people of the book. Yet, for all that, it was clear that they had never really returned from exile. Even those who had trickled back to the land found themselves living under one foreign oppressor after another: first the Persians, then the Greeks, then a brief but troubled period of independence under the Maccabees and Hasmoneans, and now the Romans. There was perplexity about the sufferings of the righteous:

> Has another nation known you besides Israel? Or what tribes have so believed your covenants as these tribes of Jacob? Yet their reward has not appeared and their labour has borne no fruit![6]

There was even a belief that God had withdrawn Himself:

> [God] remained unmoved, though He saw it, and rejoiced that they were devoured and swallowed and robbed, and He left them to be devoured in the hand of all the beasts.[7]

This despair resulted in a belief in two ages: this present evil age, which Wright correlates with "exile,"[8] and the messianic age to come, which Wright describes as the "new exodus."[9] Present sufferings and injustices would be resolved only by the coming of the Messiah in the age to come: "The Day of Judgment shall be the end of this age and the beginning of the eternal age that is to come."[10]

---

word "take" as Samuel describes the behavior of kings: see Klein, "Liberated Leadership," 285.

5. Brueggemann, "Ancient Israel on Political Leadership," 465.

6. 4 Ezra 3:32.

7. 1 En. 89:58.

8. Throughout his writings but most clearly and persuasively evidenced here in *Jesus and the Victory of God*, 268–74.

9. Wright, *Jesus and the Victory of God*, 268–74.

10. 4 Ezra 7:113.

Pictures of Atonement

It was believed that this coming of the Messiah would be cataclysmic:

> And in those days shall the earth give back that which has been gathered together in it and Sheol also shall give back that which it has received. . . . The Elect One shall in those days sit on my throne. . . . And he sat on the throne of his glory, and the sum of judgment was given to the Son of Man, and he caused sinners to pass away and be destroyed from off the face of the earth and those who have led the world astray.[11]

Thus it was that Jesus needed to reshape people's expectations of the Messiah in two ways. The first reshaping is exemplified by the incident of John the Baptist's messengers to Jesus asking, "Are you the Coming One or do we look for another" (Luke 7:18–23)? John seems to have been having a moment of doubt. He was disappointed that the Christ's cataclysmic judgement of the wicked, vindication of Israel, and final victory over evil had not come immediately. Similarly, in his teaching, Jesus tried to wean his disciples off the idea of an immediate in-breaking of kingly intervention, hence the dominant theme of the parables of the kingdom is *fulfilment without consummation*. This is the "mystery of the kingdom" (Matt 13:10–11).

The second reshaping of the messianic expectation was the way of the cross. Jesus seems to have been convinced that, not only was he the new David destined to reign at God's right hand, but that he was the new Moses who had come to lead people out of oppression. However, he saw clearly that the way from here to there, the way from "Egypt" to freedom, would be via a new sacrificial lamb, and that he himself would be that lamb. He saw his own impending death not just in martyrological terms—and there was plenty of precedent for that—but in redemptive terms.

It is interesting also to note that "redemption," especially in Luke-Acts with its heavy reliance on the Septuagint, is described in specifically nationalistic ways, avoiding any cultic sacrificial imagery. These two things: the deliverance of the nation, and the need for an offering for sin, are "two distinct divine salvific actions"[12] in Luke-Acts. History is invoked in order to convey God's redemption of his people from oppressors, whereas cultic categories are used when the need for atonement for sin is in view.[13] Israel is never pictured as needing to be redeemed from sin but only from external oppressors. Whereas, the language of atonement clusters around the

---

11. 1 En. 51:1–3; 69:27.
12. Carpinelli, "'Do This as *My* Memorial,'" 80.
13. Carpinelli, "'Do This as *My* Memorial,'" 80–81.

giving of alms, prayers, memorials, and temple sacrifices, all of which were deemed, in the Judaism of the day, to be able to atone for sins.

Redemption, then, specifically refers to liberation from oppressors. It celebrates that God is king and that he has asserted, and will again assert, his reign. He will deliver his people. What happens to this very nationalistic of concepts (which Luke preserves as it is) when it is cross-culturally communicated to the gentiles is something that will be interesting to note.

The Language of Redemption

We have painted a Jewish picture of the concept of redemption. Because of the centrality of the exodus trope to Jewish self-understanding, the very words "redeemed" and "Israel" seem to go together almost as synonyms. Even the most cursory glance at the Old Testament references in a concordance will confirm this, and the infancy narrative of Luke's Gospel takes its biggest cues from it (Luke 1:68; 2:38). Yet our access to the New Testament concept is via Greek words normally used in gentile contexts. In view of the fact, also, that a very sizable portion of the original recipients of the New Testament documents were gentiles to whom the Jewish writers were trying to make themselves intelligible, we will first look at the Greek words in their pagan settings.

There are two distinct Greek words that can underlie the English translation into the words "redeem" and "redemption." The first is *lytron*, ransom (Mark 10:45; 1 Tim 2:6: "who gave himself a ransom for all"), and *lytrosis*, a ransoming (Eph 1:7; Col 1:14: "in whom we have redemption"; Titus 2:14 "who gave himself for us that he might redeem us from all iniquity"; Heb 9:12: "having obtained eternal redemption"; 9:15: "a death has occurred that redeems them from the transgressions under the first covenant"; 1 Pet 1:18–19: "You know that you were ransomed from the futile ways inherited from your ancestors, not with perishable things like silver or gold, but with the precious blood of Christ"). The prominent concept whenever the *lytron* group is used is that of the freedom that results from the price that is paid, much as with the modern idea of ransoming a hostage. In Romans 3:24 *apolytrōsis* is used, "a ransoming from." This has much the same meaning as *lytrōsis:* to liberate by the payment of a price. The verb *lyō*, I loose, I free, as used in Revelation 1:5 "freed us from our sins by his blood," also carries much the same meaning. The emphasis is on the setting free of someone by some necessary action.

Some interesting examples of the use of *lytron* in inscriptions and papyri have been identified. Leon Morris seemed especially interested in the practice of sacral manumission, the freeing of slaves to supposedly serve a god or goddess for the rest of their lives in a temple. Whether this ever actually happened or was purely symbolic is open to question. Morris cites one of Deissman's examples:

> Apollo the Pythian, bought from Sosibius of Amphissa, for freedom, a female slave, whose name is Nicaea, by race a Roman, with a price [*lytron*] of three minae of silver and a half-mina. Former seller according to the law: Eumnastus of Amphissa. The price [*lytron*] he hath received. The purchase, however, Nicaea hath committed unto Apollo, for freedom.[14]

Besides the above extract, other ancient pagan documents might contain the words "Let no man hence forth enslave him" (compare 1 Cor 7:23), or as above, the phrase "For freedom" (compare Gal 5:1). The terminology could also be used in situations where prisoners of war must be freed.[15]

Many "confessional inscriptions" have been discovered in Asia Minor. In such cases *lytron* would be synonymous with *hilasterion*, propitiation.[16] It seems to have been a common practice in cases when, because of a misfortune, it was understood that the favor of a particular deity had been lost and their displeasure aroused. A stele (pronounced "steel"; plural: stela), was an upright stone slab engraved with a message addressed to the deity or deities whose favor is sought. Increasing numbers of these stela have been unearthed and they frequently include various forms of the *lytron* word group, in both noun and verbal forms. It seems that the act itself of setting up a monument was hoped to be enough to procure the release from calamity that was requested in the inscription. For Collins these stela are sufficient evidence for us to conclude that, in Mark 10:45, Jesus is describing the giving of his life as a "metaphorical ritual act of expiation for the offenses of many."[17] Even in cases of manumission, according to Collins, the

---

14. Deissman, *Light From the Ancient Near East*, 323.

15. See discussion, with references to the primary literature, in Collins, "The Signification of Mark 10:45," 377.

16. Collins, "Mark's Interpretation of the Death of Jesus," 549. Also Collins, "The Signification of Mark 10:45 among Gentile Christians," 371–82. My use of "propitiation" here is reflective purely of Collins' translation. A fuller discussion of the controversial term *hilasterion* will be given at various places in chapter 5.

17. Collins, "Mark's Interpretation of the Death of Jesus," 549.

notion of propitiating the gods was never far away since, in some cases, it is the god from whom the hapless victim must be symbolically freed.[18] We will discuss Mark 10:45 shortly.

The next term, also often translated by the English "redeem" is the Greek *agorazō*, "I purchase, I buy." This word had much stronger slavery overtones. With this word the leading idea is the price that was paid and the right of ownership that ensued. It is a purchase, a transfer of ownership. In contrast to *lytron*, *lytrōsis*, and *apolytrōsis*, the notion of being set free is not so much in the foreground (1 Cor 6:20: "For you were bought with a price; therefore glorify God in your body"; 7:23: "You were bought with a price; do not become slaves of human masters"; and Rev 5:9: "by your blood you ransomed for God people from every tribe and language and people and nation." Also Rev 14:3-4: the 144,000 have been redeemed "from the earth" and "from humankind"). In Galatians 3:13 (and 4:5), which we will come to shortly, the intensified form *exagorazō* is used, though it is not clear what the reason is for this.

The use of this term, based as it is on the noun *agora*, market place, may well have conjured strong images in people's minds of the slave markets that were such a common feature of first-century life. It was normal for human life to be on sale in the market squares with customers approaching to inspect teeth or muscles and barter for a price. The image is not one of freedom. Indeed, the slave has not even the most basic of rights but is always someone else's property. Levitical law (Lev 25) was critical of this and did not allow a slave to remain anyone's property indefinitely. A nation of freed slaves was not to become another slave-driving nation no better than the Egyptians. The Year of Jubilee, the Isaianic announcement of which Jesus appropriates in his Nazareth sermon (Luke 4:18-19),[19] made provision for the release of slaves every fifty years. Perhaps because of this inherent Jewish critique of slavery, it is only in 1 Corinthians 6:20 and 7:23 that the image of purchasing and owning a slave is being used without qualification. Paul, it seems, wants to put his proud Corinthian hearers in the position of the person without rights. He needs them to see themselves as the property of God and live accordingly. Even here, though, Paul is clear that the Corinthians have, by being purchased, been freed from a prior servitude to live for a new master who is incomparably better. Aside from these two references to God having bought and taken ownership of us, the tendency is to

---

18. Collins, "The Signification of Mark 10:45," 377.
19. It is even possible that the year of this sermon was a Jubilee year.

place the emphasis on what people have, by being purchased, been freed *from*, whether this be the curse of the law, life under the law, or simply the fate of the common mass of humanity that is coming under the judgment of God (e.g., Gal 3:13, 4:5, Rev 5:9, 14:3-4).

Mark 10:45, *Lytron*

> For the Son of Man came not to be served but to serve, and to give his life a ransom for many.

Scholarship has shifted in its interest in seeing Suffering Servant themes in the New Testament, with the pendulum swinging one way[20] and then the other, and Mark 10:45 has been at the heart of this. Currently the mood seems to be to allow back into the frame some limited echoes of Isaiah 53. The first but lesser difficulty for our purposes is the title "Son of Man," which Jesus here, as elsewhere, attaches to himself. Here, it appears after his third and final prediction of his death in Mark.[21] Yet, in the Jewish Scriptures the link between Daniel 7:13-14's Son of Man figure (the likely referent of Jesus) and any kind of violent death is not entirely obvious. The second and more significant difficulty, however, is the use of the word "ransom" itself since no similar terminology is to be found in Isaiah 53, indeed, if we assume it to be traceable to Jesus himself, it is hard to find a precedent for Jesus' use of it anywhere. But if we stay with Isaiah 53 for now, even the terminology of service is different in each case.[22] We are left, then, with only two verbal similarities: the phrase "his life," and the phrase "for many." In both passages a servant gives his life for many, though even here I am being generous as the terminology around the giving or handing over of his life[23] and the fact that this is for/on behalf of/in the place of many[24] differs

---

20. At the height of the negative view was Morna Hooker's *Jesus and the Servant* (1959).

21. The three are 8:31; 9:30-31; and 10:33-34.

22. Isa 52:13LXX introduces him as *ho pais mou* "my servant," Mark 10:45 has *ouk ēlthen dialonēthevai alla diakonēsai* "not to be served but to serve."

23. Isa 53:12LXX has *paredothē eis thanaton hē psychē autou* "his life was handed over to death." Mark 10:45 has *kai dounai tēn psychēn autou* "and to give his life."

24. Isa 53:12LXX has *hamartias pollōn anēnenke* "he bore the sins of many," plus references to the "many" at 52:14, 15; 53:11. In fact, the many are a significant character in the poem yet there is no terminology explicitly describing anything being done on behalf of or in place of the many. Mark 10:45 has *lytron anti pollōn* "a ransom for/in place of many."

in each case. Both Collins and Dowd and Malbon concur that the links between Isaiah 52:13—53:12 and Mark 10:45 "signify only that both the Servant and Jesus lost their lives for the benefit of many."[25]

More important than the possibility or otherwise of parallels with Isaiah's Servant is the theological meaning of the Markan passage since, on the face of it, this is one of the very few places where we are privy to Jesus' own understanding of the meaning of his death. The most distinctive word in the passage, *lytron*, is used widely both in the Septuagint and in pagan inscriptions. In the Septuagint it refers, for instance, to the ransom money that can be paid by the owner of a dangerous ox that has gored someone to death (Exod 21:29), or to the ransom money paid by individuals to ward off any plagues that might follow in the wake of the census they have just taken part in (Exod 30:11–16).[26] It is a word that certainly can be read as an ancient Isrealite cultic term.

Dowd and Malbon claim that the many for whom Jesus will give his life are "captives of the enemies of God."[27] These enemies include "human beings and spiritual beings."[28] Surprisingly, given their concluding emphasis on political powers,[29] they point out how the only human being successfully ransomed by Christ from the human enemies of God was Barabbas. The deliverances Jesus is mainly able to bring about are the exorcisms he performs. Christ's prediction points to a terrible price that will have to be paid before it will be possible for a great many more victims of demonic oppression to be freed.[30] Enemies did not let their captives go without payment. Dowd and Malbon also make the link to the "many" of the saying over the cup of Mark 14:24: "This is my blood of the covenant, which is poured out for many." With the obvious echoes here of the covenant inauguration of Exodus 24:8: "See the blood of the covenant that the LORD has made with you in accordance with all these words." Collins quibbles

---

25. Collins, "Mark's Interpretation of the Death of Jesus," 546; Dowd and Malbon, "The Significance of Jesus' Death in Mark," 283.

26. There seems to be some requirement for ritual purity as with conscription for military service—and the census was usually a way of counting the numerical strength of an army about to be mustered. See Collins, "Mark's Interpretation of the Death of Jesus," 547 and n12 for a brief discussion of this.

27. Dowd and Malbon, "Significance of Jesus' Death in Mark," 284.

28. Dowd and Malbon, "Significance of Jesus' Death in Mark," 284.

29. ". . . ransoming the majority from the tyranny of the elite." Dowd and Malbon, "Significance of Jesus' Death in Mark," 287.

30. Dowd and Malbon, "Significance of Jesus' Death in Mark," 284.

PICTURES OF ATONEMENT

with Dowd and Malbon over the fact that Jesus mentions his "poured out" blood whereas Moses "dashed it" on the people,[31] but more validly takes them to task over their curious insistence that the blood of the covenant procured liberation from oppressors and membership of the covenant but not the forgiveness of sins.[32] Matthew's version of the saying over the cup, of course, explicitly makes this link (Matt 26:28).

Brondos prefers to not see any kind of transaction born of any kind of legal or covenantal necessity.[33] He suggests: "the idea may simply be that, by surrendering his life (rather than seeking to preserve it), Jesus would obtain in exchange the promised redemption that he sought for the 'many.'"[34] Then, following his resurrection and exaltation, he is given the power and authority to carry out this very thing.[35]

The meaning, then, of Mark 10:45—and there probably is at least a faint allusion to Isaiah 53—is that, Jesus who was already locked in sporadic and localized combat with evil powers (human and demonic), was about to do something much more momentous than casting out a demon, healing a sick person, confronting misguided religious authorities or correcting misplaced ambitions in his disciples. He was now about to free a great many people from their distress and delusion, but this would be at the cost of his very life. The unexpected use of the word *lytron* to describe this, however, seems extremely mysterious.

Galatians 3:13, *Exagorazō*

Christ redeemed us from the curse of the law by becoming a curse for us—for it is written, "Cursed is everyone who hangs on a tree."

31. Collins, "Mark's Interpretation of the Death of Jesus," 549–50.

32. Collins, "Mark's Interpretation of the Death of Jesus," 549; Dowd and Malbon, "Significance of Jesus' Death in Mark," 292–93.

33. ". . . discussions of what God can and cannot do are foreign to the Jewish worldview, where it is constantly stressed that God is the 'Almighty' for whom nothing is impossible." Brondos, "The Cross and the Curse," 28. The only necessity of which the New Testament speaks in relation to the death of Christ, it seems, is the necessity that the Scriptures be fulfilled. Brondos lists: Matt 26:54; Luke 24:26–27; Acts 3:18; 17:2–3; 1 Cor 15:3–4. Brondos, "The Cross and the Curse," 28.

34. Brondos, "The Cross and the Curse," 20. In a similar vein on this point is Wright: "In Mark 10 Jesus insists that the power that overcomes the powers is the power of self-giving love." Wright, *The Day the Revolution Began*, 293.

35. Brondos, "The Cross and the Curse," 20.

Redemption

In *Atonement Theories* I identified Martin Luther's comments on this verse in his Galatians commentary of 1535 as the earliest unambiguous occurrence of the penal substitution doctrine I could find. Yet Luther is but one of a vast number of people who have looked at this verse, noted the missing logical link that ought to tie together cause (Christ dying under God's curse) with effect (we are set free), and have filled the lacuna with a theological idea that may or may not be supplied by the text itself. David Brondos has had a field day with such attempts, grouping them loosely under representative, substitutionary, or participatory ideas and writing them all off as wholly inadequate.[36] As Schwartz points out, the problem is with the "mechanics" of redemption: "How could such a death bring redemption?"[37]

We can start by saying that this passage very likely expressed something of the great reversal that we have explored; the shock of the new. It is quite likely that the verse in Deuteronomy 21:23 ("anyone hung on a tree is under God's curse") would have been quoted by the pre-conversion Paul as evidence that no one ought to be thinking so highly of a crucified man who was under God's curse, thus justifying his persecuting efforts. Since Damascus Road, Paul had begun to see that very fact as a redemptive fact. Christ's very bearing of the curse is precisely what saves people from it. All we need to do is supply what Paul must have supplied in his own reflections that gave him the mechanics of it.

Something that may be of help is to note the strong verbal resonances between Galatians 3:13 and 4:4–5: "But when the fullness of time had come, God sent his Son, born of a woman, born under the law, in order to redeem [*exagorasē*] those who were under the law, so that we might receive adoption as children." Schwartz points out that the Greek verb used in verse 4, "sent," is *exapostellō*, "sent forth," a word that (apart from 4:6, where the same word is used for the sending forth of the Spirit) Paul *never* uses. He prefers *pemptō* or *apostellō*. Yet this exact word *exapostellō* is the word used in the Septuagint of Leviticus 16:21 for the sending forth of the scapegoat.[38] At the time of writing, the scapegoats were routinely killed by being thrown off a precipice rather than being sent out into the desert. Schwartz also points to parallels with the Suffering Servant. In particular, both the scapegoat of Leviticus 16:22 and the Servant of Isaiah 53:12 are described as

---

36. Brondos, "The Cross and the Curse," 3–32.
37. Schwartz, "Two Pauline Allusions," 259.
38. Schwartz, "Two Pauline Allusions," 261.

bearing the sins of the people.[39] The language is unmistakably evocative of the Levitical language of the scapegoat bearing upon itself all the iniquities of Israel (Lev 16:22).[40] This parallel, if valid, introduces the thought of the bearing away of sin from the people, which in Galatians 4:4-5 is the means of release and could reasonably be read back into Galatians 3:13 also. The thought is that if sin, understood as a thing, a burden, is concentrated or loaded somewhere suitable then the people can be free of it. Luther's comments as he personifies the law as saying, "I see no sins anywhere else but in Him" might be on point here if we accept this concentration or loading of the burden in one place as the key to the mechanics of redemption. How is it that Christ bearing the curse frees everyone else from the curse of the law? It is that, like the scapegoat, everyone else's burden is reckoned to be his burden. The fact that Jesus overcame death and so could not have been bearing his own deadly weight of sin would have aided in the realization in Paul's mind of the nature of his death as a bearing of everyone else's sin.

It seems, too, we should avoid a purely individualistic interpretation of this passage. According to Deuteronomy 28, bearing the curse of the law for unfaithfulness would be something that would involve all Israel. A corporate interpretation seems to slide into a participatory and representative interpretation all by itself, hence Wright: "He *is* Israel, going down to death under the curse of the law, and going through that curse to the new covenant life beyond."[41] Likewise, in *Jesus and the Victory of God*[42] Wright supplies plenty of evidence that the forgiveness of sins was not some individual private blessing but was synonymous with redemption from exile. This exile had been warned of in such places as Deuteronomy 29:64: "The LORD will scatter you among all peoples, from one end of the earth to the other." This was, literally, the curse of the law, the curse pronounced on Israel's unfaithfulness. Return from exile would entail the forgiveness of this unfaithfulness.

Brondos suspects that penal substitution is the construct hiding behind even these more sophisticated interpretations. All we have is a

39. Schwartz, "Two Pauline Allusions," 262-63.

40. So Collins, "The Signification of Mark 10:45," 372.

41. Wright, *The Climax of the Covenant*, 152. Though see Ziesler, *Pauline Christianity*, 62-63 for a discussion around whether, in Judaism, the concept of a representative figure could ever have developed into a corporate figure, a corporate personality. Adam, the patriarchs, and kings were representative but the case that all Israel could be *included* in the one is yet to be made according to Ziesler.

42. Wright, *Jesus and the Victory of God*, 268-74.

"historicized" penal substitution.[43] I prefer to claim that in such ideas as the "sending forth" of the scapegoat bearing away the weight of Israel's curse, and in describing Christ in these sin-carrying, weight-bearing terms, and in claiming that he was doing this as a kind of Israel-in-person, we are getting as close as we can to painting the original picture. And not only is he Israel-in-person, he is every person, bearing the killing weight of failure of all of us so that we are freed from exile. Brondos' more martyriological interpretation of the death of Christ successfully demolishes all the atonement doctrines he does not like but sheds only a dim light on some of the most crucial passages for our understanding what it *did* mean.

Conclusion

With this concept we are sending a tap root deep into the soil of the story of Israel. We have arrived at Israel's most dearly held idea: that God, out of all the peoples of the earth, out of all the great civilizations and empires, chose little Israel. And this choice involved him in a costly and loving liberation of his people from cruel oppressors and the allocation of a promised land to dwell in. Unfaithfulness led to their disinheritance but with the promise of return and restoration. Hopes of the full realization of this began to center on a Messiah figure who would inherit the throne of David and even, according to Psalm 110:1, in some way share the throne of God himself. He would be Israel's redeemer and crush all her enemies.

Of all the New Testament writers, it is really only Luke who retains this flavor to the use of the redemption concept (Luke 1:68; 2:38; 24:21). He echoes the Septuagint's use of the concept of redemption as being specifically about Israel's nationhood. For all the other New Testament writers, the translation pressures of the mission to the gentiles seem to have channeled the concept into something slightly different. While still referring to the same basic ideas, the concept shed much of its nationalistic garb. Even the writer to the Hebrews does not use redemption terminology in ways that are conventionally Jewish (Heb 9:12, 15, where the references are to transgressions and sins rather than national liberation). The New Testament writers seem to be negotiating a compromise with Greco-Roman ideas about propitiating gods, the manumission of slaves, or the ransoming of prisoners of war. Gentile audiences, after all, would have been unable to hear redemptional terminology and *not* make these kinds of associations.

---

43. Brondos, "The Cross and the Curse," 8.

The New Testament writers work with this by often stressing what it is that believers have been freed *from*: whether sin, the law, aimless conduct, or humanity under judgment. In this way attention is drawn away from thoughts of angry deities or other demanders of a price on freedom, and the focus is subjective: our own helpless state from which we were freed.

It is also worth noting, if it is not already obvious, that the redemption metaphor is of a piece with the victory metaphor. Both are pictures addressing a situation of jeopardy under cruel and monolithic concentrations of power. Whether from within or without, these have impinged upon our lives to such an extent as to mean that we are not free. Christ the redeemer breaks their hold upon us. Where the victory metaphor focuses on what Christ has achieved by his incarnation, death, resurrection, and ascension—it is Christological, the redemption metaphor focuses on what this does for us—it is soteriological. We are freed by his victory.

Reflection

1. God has freed you, defeated your worst enemies (perhaps for you mainly an enemy within?). He has done what is necessary for this freedom to be real. So how free are you? Have there been any particular breakthroughs?

2. God has bought us with a price and we are not our own. What does this mean for discipleship? Would this be a helpful place to begin in a church discipleship course?

3. God has purchased us with the highest price conceivable. We could not be more valuable to God. In fact, both creation and redemption reinforce this: the individual attentiveness with which we were knit together in the womb on the one hand and then the ultimate price paid to fully own what was rightfully his on the other. Might this be a helpful way to address issues of low self-worth today?

CHAPTER 4

Dying and Rising with Christ

Introduction

A VICTORY SECURED BY what Christ has done which is then offered to us as a complete liberation from all the powers that seek to make us less human and less happy is now crying out for an answer to the question: but how does this actually work? How are we actually touched and transformed by this historic and long-awaited achievement? The earliest Christians answered this question by describing in various ways a new kind of relatedness to Christ. We call this "participation in Christ," but, despite the growing attention this has received from scholarship, it remains a rather elusive concept. Perhaps the main difficulty is that the underlying concept of a union with Christ is a genuine New Testament *novum*. Union with Christ in the Spirit was something completely new, it seems. It has no clear precedent anywhere. Be that as it may, there are some clues as to what participation in Christ entailed from the metaphors that were employed to describe it, especially the metaphor of the dying and rising with Christ.

In Christ and with Christ

You will have noticed the profusion of references in Paul to being "in Christ" and to having undergone something "with Christ." We are co-crucified, it seems, but also co-buried, co-risen, co-seated in the heavenlies, co-inheritors, and we even "appear with him in glory" when he returns.[1]

---

1. Gal 2:20; Rom 6:4; Eph 2:6; Rom 8:17; Col 3:4.

Pictures of Atonement

Doubtless both are related. It stands to reason that if we are *in* him we are also implicated in everything he has done, everything he has won, and everything he will do. In fact, maybe this is the best place for us to start as we try to figure what is, for me at least, a slightly baffling idea. We will try to test the suggestion that "in Christ" is the primary idea, with the "with Christ" assertions flowing from it.

A strong case could be made that Paul's *in*-Christ formulas come first, with his *with*-Christ formulas logically building upon them, on the basis of Romans 6:3, "Do you not know that as many of us as were baptized into Christ Jesus were baptized into his death." Here Paul builds upon a being in Christ that is assumed to be already understood and extends the concept to include the idea of having died *with* Christ. Then, of course, if being in Christ as a result of having been immersed into him is the primary idea, where does this come from? In what sense are we "in"? It is an apparently spatial idea,[2] though there has not been scholarly unanimity about this. For a start, the preposition *en* is the most common preposition in the New Testament and has such a broad semantic range (in, by, with, by means of, etc.) that, by the tenth century, its overuse had brought such imprecision to the Greek language that it actually fell out of use, sharing this fate with the whole dative case.[3] So, we cannot even be sure that "in" means literally "inside" or "within" or "in the sphere of." Many references to "in Christ" might mean the much blander idea of "by means of Christ," or even "by means of his example," though I hope not. This seems nowhere near as exciting as the thought of living a life that dwells and abides in him, and functions out of him.

Albert Schweitzer believed the exact opposite to what I suggested above: the "in Christ" occurrences, he said, are shorthand for the more fully expounded "with Christ" moments in Paul,[4] and the "with," according to Schweitzer, was a realistic physical union with the actual glorified body of Christ. Unlike the other metaphors of church, such as temple or bride, the body image was therefore a literal description.[5] This corporeal idea seems

---

2. The locative concept is a way of translating the slippery dative *en*. This way of translating it was especially advocated by Adolf Deissmann: "Just as the air of life, which we breathe, is 'in' us and fills us, and yet we at the same time live in this air and breathe it, so it is also with the Christ-intimacy of the Apostle Paul: Christ in him, he in Christ." Deissmann, *St Paul*, 140.

3. Harris, "Prepositions and Theology in the Greek New Testament," 1190–93.

4. Schweitzer, *Mysticism of Paul the Apostle*, 122.

5. Schweitzer, *Mysticism of Paul the Apostle*, 125–30.

Dying and Rising with Christ

unsatisfactory but cannot usefully be debated here. However, let us suppose, for now, that Schweitzer was right to intuit the priority of images of a dying and rising *with Christ* over the bald "in Christ" language, with the latter being derivative of it. Most would accept that Schweitzer at least has the chronology of Paul's letters on his side: the co-dying and co-rising occurs in the very earliest letters (1 Thess 4:14; 5:10; Gal 2:19–21); "in Christ" is commonest in the later Pauline and "deutero" Pauline letters (Colossians, Ephesians, Philippians, Philemon). If Schweitzer is right then all that needs to happen now is that the source for the dying and rising metaphor is identified, and this we will certainly do, even if we end up disagreeing with his suggestion.

Paul is working with two assumptions when he speaks of a dying and rising with Christ. The first is: "Everything about Jesus has something to do with me." This was because of a novel concept of faith that entailed more than mere assent, more than trust, and more even than faithfulness. Paul's concept of faith involved relatedness to a person. One believed "on" or "into" Christ. This was a new Spirit-given thing: a faith that was itself the "gift of God,"[6] and the search was on for a way of putting this in picture language that pagans could understand, bearing in mind that Paul was a cross-cultural missionary, not an academic theologian.[7] The other assumption of Paul's is "Resurrection is reversal."[8] Claims that Christ had made of himself had been radically called into question by the crucifixion, but were decisively vindicated by the resurrection. This great reversal, this "but now" moment, had been forcibly invading people's lives as an actual experience of reversal ever since Pentecost. All of this was crying out for picture language, and Paul, the missionary to the gentiles, found himself becoming a great painter of pictures. Specifically, he needed a picture of "everything about Jesus has something to do with me, especially the great reversal of resurrection." Against Schweitzer, being in Christ is never said to depend upon a prior dying and rising with him, rather dying and rising with him describes the dramatic about-turn of those that have experienced

---

6. A possible way of interpreting Eph 2:8.

7. "And if we are to do full justice to his own famous statement, 'I have become all things to all men that at all events I might save some,' we must recognize his willingness to put himself *en rapport* with men and women whom he sought to win for Christ. Hence it is of real value to understand something of the religious atmosphere in which his converts had lived as Pagans." Kennedy, *St Paul and the Mystery Religions*, 7.

8. See Galvin, "The Resurrection of Jesus in Contemporary Catholic Systematics," 123–45.

what it feels like to be "joined to the Lord" and "one spirit with him" (1 Cor 6:17). Hence Romans 6:3: if we are one with him ontologically, then we also participate in what he has been through and done. Tentatively, then, "in Christ" comes first. But we still need to try to get behind the imagery of dying and rising. Theologically it expresses the results of being in Christ, but it is clearly a metaphor: we have not literally died or risen. And all metaphors come from somewhere.

Paul and the Mystery Religions

I now want to imagine how this language of dying and rising was found, and how it is that it was needed as a way of expressing something for which no language yet existed. In other words, tracing the source of the metaphor might itself shed some light on the theology of it all. Paul was clearly trying to articulate something that could not be fully expressed with simple "in him" or "joined to him" language.

To do this I want to reconsider the once fanatically embraced, then widely criticized, and now largely ignored idea that Paul is making use of the mystery religions when he describes dying and rising with Christ.[9] Many scholars wish to advocate for a differentiated understanding of the mystery religions and are able to muster an armory of detail in support. There is, perhaps, a basic misunderstanding, though, about what commonalities we can expect to see between Paul and the mysteries. When closer inspection causes our parallelomania to vanish in a puff of differentiation, we conclude that all the advocates of such parallels—Nietzsche, Rénan, and Bultmann[10] being the most famous—were plain wrong.[11] It needs to be said that Paul is not building a system from these extraneous sources. He already has his system. It is encapsulated in the two premises offered above. Paul is not syncretistically borrowing from the mysteries in any way that would change his soteriological landscape. He is using the mysteries as a source for a metaphor, and metaphors are allowed to have strong dissimilarities as

9. One of the most recent substantial studies of union with Christ includes barely a mention of the mysteries: Macaskill, *Union with Christ in the New Testament*.

10. E.g., Bultmann, *Theology of the New Testament*, 297–98.

11. Gert Pelser is only really able to salvage the initiation rite of the Isis mystery as showing any definite likeness to Rom 6:1–11: "Could the 'formulas' dying and rising with Christ be Expressions of Pauline Mysticism?" 120. Wedderburn is skeptical even of this, however: Wedderburn, "The Soteriology of the Mysteries and Pauline Baptismal Theology," 57–62. Also Wedderburn, *Baptism and Resurrection*.

well as similarities. In fact, metaphors will always change the source into something else altogether in the process of being deployed as a pedagogical tool, as Ricœur observed.

In support of the mysteries as the source for Paul's dying and rising metaphor are three things. Firstly, *the mysteries were pervasive in the Greco-Roman world*. The emphasis on detail in the scholarship of those who are against the mysteries as a source has perhaps made us lose sight of how widespread adherence to the various mysteries was by the time Paul was writing Romans 6. By the second century, Justin Martyr was uncomfortable with the very strong similarities between the rites of the mysteries and the sacraments of the church, as was Tertullian in the century following.[12] Not only is this the case but, as Marvin Meyer has shown,[13] the roots of the mysteries run deep into the fertility cults of the ancient world involving, in many cases, the very same gods: Demeter, Kore, Dionysus, Adonis, Attis, Osiris, Cybele, Isis, and Mithras. The idea that most of these deities died with the winter and rose again with the spring (or with dry and wet seasons) was axiomatic, a universal "of course" that ran through all such devotions. The dying and rising narrative remained as the backbone of the mysteries by the time of Paul. Some of the literature emphasizes how common Mithraism was in Tarsus. There have even been claims that this mystery cult originated there,[14] where it made a profound impression on the young Saul.

The phenomenal growth of the mystery cults was symptomatic of a widespread disenchantment with the traditional Greco-Roman gods and their all-too human frailties. By the second century, Mithraea—places of Mithras worship—were at least as common as churches. There is one underneath the Vatican. Rénan famously remarked: "If the growth of Christianity had been halted by some mortal illness, the world would have become Mithraic."[15] The legacy of the mysteries can even be seen today in any painting of a Madonna and Child, the true origins of the Madonna and Child

---

12. All the literature repeats this, but see especially Morgan Rempel's discussion of Nietzsche's take on this: "Nietzsche, Mithras, and 'Complete Heathendom,'" 35: "Nietzsche, of course, shares Justin and Tertullian's suspicions that something diabolical lay behind such curious cases of correspondence. But the later Nietzsche, like so many researchers since, points to an altogether more mundane explanation: Paul's likely exposure to the language, teachings, and rites of the mystery cults."

13. Meyer, *The Ancient Mysteries*, 1–14.

14. Pfleiderer, *Christian Origins*; Angus, *The Mystery Religions*.

15. Rempel's translation: "Nietzsche, Mithras, and 'Complete Heathendom,'" 31.

tradition being Cybele, the Great Mother and Queen of Heaven, and Attis, her hero-son. Indeed, the very sacramentalism of such a huge portion of today's church probably took shape originally within the atmosphere of the ritualism of the mystery cults.[16]

Borrowing on the part of the first Christians from the mysteries, at the very least of a linguistic and metaphorical kind, was inevitable. Indeed, it is probable that Hellenistic religion had already strongly influenced the Judaism of the time, causing it to adopt some of its terminology and expectations.[17] Diaspora Judaism in particular is thought to have made use of some of the language and ideas of the mysteries.[18]

Secondly, *the mysteries showed strong similarities to early Christianity*. Mithras—known to Roman devotees variously as "redeemer," "savior," "light of the world," and "son of God,"—was said to have been sent to earth from heaven and born of a divine father and mortal virgin mother on December 25. He was characterized as a celibate miracle worker who, prior to his death, celebrated a final meal with twelve disciples. Worshippers of Mithras believed their redeemer died, was buried in a tomb, returned to life three days later, and ascended to heaven.[19] Indeed, the litany of parallels looks astonishing, but, as Wedderburn has pointed out, when we come to examine the evidence such claims have a habit of being difficult to verify from any sources actually *predating* or *contemporary with* the rise of Christianity. But my only point here is that, despite some excessive claims,

---

16. The history of religions school greatly exaggerated the role of the mystery cults in the formation of the Christian sacraments, e.g., Angus, *The Mystery Religions and Christianity*, viii. More recently, Klauck gives a more restrained view: "In my opinion, the Christian doctrine of the sacraments, in the form in which we know it, would not have arisen without this interaction." Klauck, *The Religious Context of Early Christianity*, 152.

17. John Levison, for example, has recently argued that the Judaism out of which Christianity arose was influenced by the Greco-Roman interest in ecstatic experience. The pneumatology of the period therefore incorporates the expectation of vivid mystical experience. This, claims Levison, is in marked contrast to the pneumatology of Israelite (i.e., Old Testament) religion, which sees the Holy Spirit as the giver of all life and only rarely attributes to the Spirit any invasive or ecstatic experiences. The New Testament fully adopts the Hellenized version. Levison, *Filled with the Spirit*. See also the considerable scholarly interest generated by his work, e.g., Waddell, "The Holy Spirit of Life, Work, and Inspired Speech," 207–12; Levison, "*Filled with the Spirit*: A Conversation with Pentecostal and Charismatic Scholars," 213–31.

18. Klauck, *Religious Context of Early Christianity*, 152.

19. Hempel, "Nietzsche, Mithras, and 'Complete Heathendom,'" 34, citing Burkert, *Ancient Mystery Cults*, 53; Clauss, *The Roman Cult of Mithras*, 62, 169; Nabarz, *The Mysteries of Mithras*, 48–49, and Angus, *The Mystery Religions and Christianity*, xi.

Dying and Rising with Christ

there is a good case to be made for the similarity of the mystery cults on some points, and these commonalities naturally allowed some borrowing of ideas and images.[20] A helpful moderate who was active while the history of religions school was finding parallels everywhere was H. A. A. Kennedy who, while skeptical about details, affirmed that the central conception that the mysteries were concerned with was "union with the Divine and attainment of undying life."[21] The mysteries offered salvation from fate, and in particular, death, through being born again, which happened by participating in the divine life. This participation seemingly transformed the initiate's essence.[22]

The search for any specific phrases that remind us in anyway of New Testament language yields meagre results. These would include parts of the Mithras Liturgy such as: "O Lord, while being born again, I am passing away; while growing and having grown, I am dying; while being born from a life-generating birth, I am passing on, released to death—as you have founded, as you have decreed, and have established the mystery."[23] Deities that were especially associated with seasonal dying and rising were Osiris, Attis, and Dionysus,[24] while Isis was famed for having resurrected Osiris.

---

20. Schweitzer's point, echoed by Macaskill, was that the main difference between the mysteries and the doctrine of union with Christ was that the mysteries offered an experience of some direct contact with and merging with the deity, whereas, in Paul's teaching, Christ has a strictly mediatorial function. Hence, the one system offers "deification" while the other offers "fellowship." Yet the Eastern Orthodox tradition has surely shown that both interpretations are at least possible. The Eastern fathers interpreted union with Christ precisely as deification. Besides, in the interests of creating a recognizable picture that involves dying and rising with a deity, such distinctions seem too subtle, notwithstanding the need to preserve strict monotheism in which the divine nature must maintain its separateness from humans. Schweitzer, *Mysticism of Paul the Apostle*, 16; Macaskill, *Union with Christ*, 22.

21. Kennedy, *St Paul and the Mystery Religions*, 35.

22. Kennedy, *St Paul and the Mystery Religions*, 70, though without necessarily any expectation that the initiate's lifestyle would henceforth be on a higher moral plane. Indeed, Adolf Van Harnack believed such antinomianism was what Paul was battling in Romans. The initiates of Christianity had assumed that their baptismal rite had worked *ex opere operato* with no need for any moral reformation thereafter. Again, such claims are looked upon today as a gross exaggeration of the evidence. Paul does not seem to be combatting a wrong conception of baptism as such, otherwise why would he not even mention it until chapter 6?

23. Lines 719–25, translation by Marvin Meyer in Betz (ed.), *The Greek Magical Papyri*, available at https://hermetic.com/pgm/mithras-liturgy.

24. Kennedy, *St Paul and the Mystery Religions*, 72. See also Meyer (ed.), *The Ancient Mysteries*.

PICTURES OF ATONEMENT

A ritual associated with the coming back to life again either of Attis or Osiris[25] reads: "Be of good cheer, initiates, the god has been saved: thus for you also shall there be salvation from your troubles."[26] Initiations into the cult of Osiris included mentions of a symbolic "voluntary death"[27] followed by a new birth. An initiation into the Isis cult is summarized by the comic playwright Apuleius whose protagonist Lucius, undergoes the ceremony:

> I have come to the borders of death and have set my foot on the threshold of Proserpina, I have travelled through all the elements and then returned, at midnight I have seen the sun shining in dazzling white light, I have come into the very presence of the gods below and the gods above, and I have adored them close at hand.[28]

Exactly what it is that the initiand experienced that would warrant such descriptions has been the subject of much speculation. Probably the best clue lies in the underground rooms that were discovered at a temple of Isis in Pompeii. These rooms, doubtless strangely lit and with music playing up above, would have been full of statues and frescoes of the gods and the devotee would have been shown around the rooms by a guide before emerging to face an adoring crowd of initiates.[29]

Devotees of Attis are in one place described as "condemned to death," probably symbolic of their state of spiritual death prior to being initiated.[30] The most notorious Attis-related ritual is the *Taurobolium*, in which the devotee would descend into a pit, possibly symbolizing their own burial, while on a platform above him or her a bull would be slaughtered and its blood allowed to trickle like rain through holes in the platform. The initiand standing beneath would be thus bathed in blood and emerge soaked in blood but born anew. It seems without question that no New Testament writer, even if we bear in mind the daring imagery of Revelation 7:14, would have been making any specific reference to so grotesque a ritual as this. Dionysiac-Orphic rituals may have involved the burying of the body

---

25. It is by no means certain which it is, as the ritual is being related by an outsider and critic: Firmicus Maternus, the fourth-century Christian converted from a background in astrology. A fuller extract from Maternus' description is in Klauck, *Religious Context of Early Christianity*, 126.

26. Kennedy, *St Paul and the Mystery Religions*, 72.

27. Kennedy, *St Paul and the Mystery Religions*, 209.

28. Klauck, *Religious Context*, 137, citing Apuleius, *Metamorphoses* Book 11, 23:8.

29. Klauck, *Religious Context*, 137–38.

30. Klauck, *Religious Context*, 125.

up as far as the head,[31] while those that have passed through their initiation drink milk as a sign of having become newborn.[32]

Thirdly, *the mysteries are the simplest explanation*. Schweitzer likened those who seek an explanation for Paul's mysticism in the mystery religions rather than in his Jewish eschatology to someone fetching water in leaky watering cans from far away to water a garden that turns out to be right next to a stream.[33] I would argue the same but in the exact opposite direction: why construct a more forced and cumbersome parallel with apocalyptic Judaism when Paul's metaphor of dying and rising in Christ lies right beside the stream of the pervasive presence of mystery cults everywhere Paul looked in his mission to the gentiles. Indeed, it takes a devout Jew to notice these things more than most, especially as the mysteries all involved the stench in his nostrils that was idolatry.

Pentecost and the Mysteries

The inundation of the Spirit in people's lives, which brought powerful experiences of a new birth and of a new creation, caused Christianity to display a mystical bent. This Christ-Mysticism, as Deissmann used to call it, meant that Christianity began to resemble the mystery religions far more than could ever have been anticipated. It is interesting to observe, as an aside, the way the charismatic movement, when it was at the height of controversy, was being likened to various mystical paths such as the New Age movement. The "cult watchers" busied themselves examining the off-the-cuff exclamations of over-heated preachers for evidences that the charismatic movement was at best highly syncretistic, at worst outright demonic. Christianity, they felt, ought to be more rational and, most of all, more solidly based on the doctrines of the Reformation. It should not keep running after miraculous and mystical experiences. The charismatic movement, its many shortcomings aside, perhaps gives us our closest modern equivalent to the pneumatic mysticism of earliest Christianity. And as with earliest Christianity, there has been rather little evidence of any deliberate borrowing from ideas outside of Christianity on the part of charismatic

---

31. Kennedy, *St Paul and the Mystery Religions*, 73. Attributed to a description by Proclus, though no reference is given.

32. "I hastened like a young kid to the milk," Klauck, *Religious Context*, 120, citing a funerary inscription from the fourth/third century BCE.

33. Schweitzer, *Mysticism of St Paul the Apostle*, 140.

teachers, but there is an almost inevitable resemblance.[34] And, like Justin Martyr, charismatic protagonists have tended to brush off resemblances in other spiritual movements as demonic counterfeits of the real thing.

In earliest Christianity, then, there was probably no deliberate borrowing, at least none that shaped doctrine and practice. Rather, what we have is an almost inevitable resemblance. And this resemblance was deepened by Paul's use of imagery taken from the mysteries in an attempt to create gentile-friendly language for the breathtaking new realities of life "in Christ."

Paul's Concept

As with all of the metaphors, it is helpful to make two distinct examinations: one of the source of the metaphorical language, and the other of the source of the underlying concept. By digging around for the source of the underlying concept we are hopefully not attempting to decipher or translate picture language into what it "really" means. As I explained at the start, I am completely on board with those who want to let the pictures be pictures. As Wittgenstein used to say about religious symbolism, sometimes the whole weight is in the picture.[35] The picture itself is enough, once properly appreciated. How could I not say this? I am an artist, albeit a failed one. Granted then that once a concept has taken metaphorical shape it has become something irreversibly new and revelatory, yet there is a concept, there is a tenor underlying it, and to this we now turn.

Robert Tannehill's *Dying and Rising with Christ* (1967, based on a dissertation of 1963) argued that the underlying concept that Paul is working with is that all humanity lies under the thralldom of two powers, or two lords.[36] These are pictured by Paul as asserting a "reign" or "dominion over" people.[37] The one is described in various ways evocative of the powers of death, flesh, sin, and law that we encountered in chapter 1, though, in Romans 5–6 the dominant descriptor is "sin." The power of sin is not simply a series of misdeeds with unfortunate results, but neither is it a wholly

---

34. See my *Bold Faith* for an attempt to trace where borrowing, for example from New Thought philosophy, has occurred: Pugh, *Bold Faith: A Closer Look at the Five Key Ideas of Charismatic Christianity*.
35. Wittgenstein, "Lecture on Religious Belief," 72.
36. Tannehill, *Dying and Rising with Christ*.
37. Tannehill, *Dying and Rising with Christ*, 14–20.

abstract principle or law. Rather, it is, according to Tannehill, "a demonic power, a world ruler who claims the obedience of men just as God does."[38] In Roman 5:14, 17 and 6:9, it is death that is the ruler, whose power to exercise dominion over Christ, and hence over all those who have been planted together with him in the likeness of his death, has been broken. In Roman 5:21, sin exercises dominion through death. In 6:12, the ruler is, again, sin, but this time pictured as reigning like a king, or rather, no longer having the power or right to reign in that way. Later on in the chapter, the imagery turns more militaristic, with the use of *hopla*, weapons, as a way of describing the way we should now use the members of our bodies under the new dominion (6:13), and the need to present ourselves like soldiers (6:13, and later, like servants: 6:16,19). Even the reference to the "wages" of sin at 6:23 may be an echo of the terminology used for a soldier's rations. In other words, Romans 6 may be presenting us increasingly with a picture of competing warlords.[39] The new power, of course, is Christ, with whom we are empowered to reign in life (5:17), but also "righteousness" (6:18, 19, 20) and "God" (6:10, 11, 13, 22), "grace" (5:21, 6:14), "obedience" (6:16), and a "pattern of teaching" (6:17). The two dominions are also correlate, according to Tannehill, with two aeons. Christ's coming has brought about the new age, but both ages are ruled by a master who lays absolute claim upon people's loyalty and service. The Christian, therefore, must choose only the new master to serve.[40]

Moving from Tannehill in 1967 to E. P. Sanders in 1977, we find that Sanders, while advocating for the absolute centrality of participation in Christ to the theology of Paul, confessed to not having the least idea about how it was understood to work, or in what it was supposed to consist.[41] Plenty of others since Sanders' epoch-making work, however, have taken up this challenge. In particular, the story of Israel: its election, exodus, and exile, seems to have helped many scholars to find a conceptual framework. Christ's story enacts the story of Israel and participates in it. Now, all those who belong to Christ also take part in this "narrative participation,"[42] ac-

38. Tannehill, *Dying and Rising with Christ*, 16.
39. Tannehill, *Dying and Rising with Christ*, 15–16.
40. Tannehill is probably indebted to Käsemann: "He . . . therefore summons Christians with inner necessity to confirm in their personal life the change of aeons that has been effected." Käsemann, *Commentary on Romans*, 159.
41. Sanders, *Paul and Palestinian Judaism*, 522–23.
42. Hays, *The Faith of Jesus Christ*.

cording to Richard Hays.⁴³ Michael Gorman builds upon Hays by borrowing the Orthodox term "theosis" to develop his concept of "cruciformity." This consists in a "transformative participation in the kenotic, cruciform character of God through Spirit-enabled conformity to the incarnate, crucified, and resurrected/glorified Christ."⁴⁴ He has been criticized, however, for not doing enough to pin down this terminology, both theosis and kenosis being words that are used in a huge variety of ways.⁴⁵

Participating in the history of Israel and the history of Christ is an idea that finds a ready home in the thinking of N. T. Wright, who also adds a concept from Israel's history that helps to give us language for the nature of the adhesive that joins us to Christ. The concept is "covenant."⁴⁶ To be in Christ is to be in the people of his covenant, it is a thoroughly corporate and relational experience. Indeed, if we are seeking to define the exact nature of the union with Christ expressed in the New Testament then covenant is, arguably, the only kind of union with the divine that Judaism knows of. No other precedents are to hand. Tantalizingly, though, there are a few pictures of that covenant relationship being extended to include something more fantastically intimate and personal. David writes of his one and only desire to dwell in the house of the LORD all the days of his life, beholding his beauty (Ps 27:4), and the author of Psalm 91 writes of the assurance that God can be a dwelling place, a secret place, a fortress, where we may find complete safety (Ps 91:1–2, 9–10. Also 90:1).

Wright deduces that Romans 6–8 contains an underlying exodus narrative, the baptismal imagery of Romans 6:2–11 being an image of the Red Sea crossing, as per the use of such imagery in 1 Corinthians 10:1–4.⁴⁷

> This death was like the passing of the Israelites through the Red Sea: those who pass through the waters of baptism are reminded that they have left behind the old world of slavery ('Egypt') and are on their way home to their inheritance.⁴⁸

---

43. Interestingly, this idea was anticipated in the theology of Karl Barth: "man in general . . . participates in the history enacted in him." Barth, *Church Dogmatics* IV, 1, 300.
44. Gorman, *Inhabiting the Cruciform God*, 7.
45. Macaskill, *Union with Christ*, 27–28.
46. Wright, *The Climax of the Covenant*.
47. Wright, *The Day the Revolution Began*, 276–94.
48. Wright, *The Day the Revolution Began*, 277.

Dying and Rising with Christ

The old slave master sin, as described in Romans 5:12–21 and as overcome in Romans 6:16–23, is likened to Pharaoh, "from whose grip one is freed by coming through the water."[49] And the Spirit leading us into our inheritance, as described in Romans 8, is compared by Wright to the pillar of fire and cloud that led the Israelites to their inheritance.[50] One wonders whether, at times, we are seeing the tyranny of a construct here. Nothing is permitted to lie outside the interpretational lens of Israelite history for fear, perhaps, of a return to the excesses of the history of religions school. New Testament scholarship has its pendulums and Wright seems at times to be hanging off the extreme end of one of these.

So, having looked at a few options, what do we have by way of a definition of the concept expressed in the dying-with and rising-with language that seems so natural to Paul, so strange to us? Does the union consist of allegiance a new master (Tannehill), or does it consist in what story we see ourselves as inhabiting (Hays, Gorman), or does it consist in an agreement we enter into, a covenant (Wright)? All of these seem to bring us to the edge of what we are looking at but cannot lead us inside the conceptual world of Paul. They fail to express adequately the radical termination of relationship to sin and death and the happy walking in newness of life that Paul presents as his answer to the antinomian misunderstanding.[51]

Besides Romans 6, there are three passages that speak of both a death and a resurrection with Christ as an accomplished fact: Galatians 2:19–20: ". . . I have been crucified with Christ; and it is no longer I who live, but it is Christ who lives in me . . . ," Colossians 2:20: ". . . buried with him in baptism . . . raised with him through faith . . . ," and Colossians 3:1–3: ". . . you have been raised with Christ, . . . you have died." Then there is a further co-crucifixion metaphor in Galatians 6:14, "the world has been crucified to me, and I to the world," and similar in Galatians 5:24: "those who belong to Christ Jesus have crucified the flesh."

Something we have not looked at so far is a word that features in two of the co-death and resurrection passages; it is the word "baptized/baptism." Martyn Lloyd Jones' famous series of sermons on Romans, which ran from 1955 to 1968, includes a novel interpretation of the idea of baptism in

---

49. Wright, *The Day the Revolution Began*, 277.

50. Wright, *The Day the Revolution Began*, 292. At this point I wrote a note in the margin: "Really?"

51. In Romans, the antinomian question recurs in 3:8: "Let us do evil that good may come"; 6:1: "Shall we continue in sin that grace may abound?"; 6:15: "Shall we sin because we are not under law but under grace?"; and 7:7: "What then shall we say? Is the law sin?"

Romans 6. Lloyd-Jones expresses the usual Reformed aversion to the idea of baptismal regeneration but extends this to the point of even claiming that water baptism is not being referred to here at all. On the basis of 1 Corinthians 12:13: "For in the one Spirit we were all baptized into one body ...," he interprets Romans 6:3-4 as a reference to the fact that we have been baptized or immersed *by the Spirit* into Christ, and only by the Spirit. This is in response to the question he poses: "What sort of baptism is this? What kind of baptism is taught in the New Testament which definitely says that it is a baptism that incorporates us into Christ and joins us to Him?"[52] He has already ruled out anything that would point to baptismal regeneration, as well as any kind of merely symbolic interpretation. It is clear that this baptism actually does something. Here in 1 Corinthians 12:13, the agent of our incorporation into the body of Christ is explicitly identified as the Spirit.

There is, however, a passage that is semantically closer to Romans 6:3-4 than this passage. Colossians 2:12 exactly echoes Romans 6:4 in affirming that we have been buried with Christ through baptism. Even here, however, it is not at all a given that Paul is referring to water baptism rather than Spirit-baptism or spiritual immersion. Lloyd-Jones may have been onto something. In Colossians 2:11 Paul is, here as elsewhere, at pains to distinguish between physical circumcision and spiritual circumcision. The same is not true of baptism. Water baptism, throughout Paul (and Luke for that matter) is allowed the closest of links to the more spiritual aspects of Christian beginnings, including Spirit-baptism.[53] The lack of a clear distinction between water baptism and Spirit-baptism is absolutely characteristic of Paul.[54] So, even if Lloyd-Jones is overstating his case by appealing to 1 Corinthians 12:13, a fallback position is the semantically much closer Colossians 2:12, which can be read as referring to water- or Spirit-baptism.

Moreover, even if Romans 6 and Colossians 2 refer *primarily* to water baptism, we have much support from Philip Esler's social-scientific analysis of Romans to say that even the rite itself was, for earliest Christianity, a profound experience of the Spirit. Indeed, any former adherents of mystery religions would have been disappointed with the rite had it not been. "It is all too easy for modern readers," says Esler, ". . . to overlook the dramatic

---

52. Lloyd Jones, *Romans: Exposition of Chapter 6*, 35.

53. Salter, "Does Baptism Replace Circumcision?" 18-20, 27.

54. Dunn, *The Theology of Paul the Apostle*, 443-45; Salter cites Anthony Cross, "Spirit- and Water-Baptism in 1 Corinthians 12:13," 120-48.

Dying and Rising with Christ

experiential aspects of receiving the Holy Spirit in the earliest period."[55] Baptism was a very memorable event, which involved being stripped completely naked and removing all jewelry and any other symbols of the old life and leaving them on the river bank. The candidate was then subjected to a hand pressing down upon the head until submerged. Sometimes this would be three times in the name of Father, Son, and Holy Spirit. Preferably, this would take place in "living water," that is, running water, which further symbolized the washing away of past sins. Only later as concessions were made to the lack of any large stretches of open water, did it begin to occur to anyone that pouring water over the head into a bowl might suffice. This, of course, then progressively evolved into a tiny sprinkle or the signing of a wet cross. Probably not all candidates had an experience of the Spirit but most would have had. They might have experienced the gifts of the Spirit for the first time, or emitted the cry of "Abba" or the heartfelt confession of "Jesus is Lord."

In fact, if the reference is primarily to water baptism, then there are some advantages. For one thing, the notorious problem of time is dealt with. My perennial question as I have poured over Romans 6 and Galatians 2:20 for the past twenty-eight years has been "How could I have been crucified with Christ?" The answer might be that it is in the very nature of a ritual such as water baptism "to bring past events into the present *in a socially and religiously significant sense*."[56] Rituals are there to help us recreate a holy moment by re-enacting it: "the redemptive death of Christ which happened but once in history is cultically made present in the shape of a visible rite."[57] We make present in baptism, perhaps, the vivid reality Barth describes: "For then and there, in the person of Christ taking our place, we were present, being crucified and dying with him."[58]

If Paul is referring mainly to water baptism in Romans 6 then it also becomes easier to understand the "do you not know?" rhetoric. He seems sure of a certain level of common knowledge. What was commonly understood was that the baptized are baptized into Christ. This was a closely related concept to being baptized into the name of Christ.[59] The additional element, that of the candidate's identity with Christ's death and resurrection

---

55. Esler, *Conflict and Community in Romans*, 206.
56. Esler, *Conflict and Identity*, 216, reflecting Lévi-Strauss, *The Savage Mind*, 237.
57. Baum, "Baptism," 143.
58. Barth, *Church Dogmatics* IV, 1, 295.
59. Beasley-Murray, *Baptism in the New Testament*, 129.

would have been obvious to some, less so to others, and practices would have varied from place to place. Hence, as we saw earlier, Paul says, "Do you not know that as many of us as were baptized into Christ Jesus . . ."— this is the familiar part—". . . were baptized into his death?" This is the big reminder and this forms the very striking basis for all that is to come.[60] Although he mentions baptism for the last time in verse 4, we can safely assume that this striking fact would have been assumed to have sufficient impact to remain in the minds of his hearers as he unfolded his argument.

So, in what does this union with Christ consist, such that it is a union not only with Christ enthroned in glory (a hard enough concept!) but also with his dying and rising? What is the nature of the joining? Do we merge with him, as in the mystery cults in which something of the very essence of the deity deifies the essence of the devotee? Or is the union a looser arrangement along the lines of an allegiance to a new master (in which case dying and rising imagery seems a bit dramatic), some kind of participating in Christ's history, who in turn is enacting Israel's history, or a signing up to a new covenant, leaving our discreet individualities largely untouched? The answer seems to be that we were symbolically, yet powerfully in the Spirit, crucified with Christ during baptism and died to sin with him there. It was both water and Spirit that saturated us and brought us into the realm of Christ's uncontested reign, into the realm where our rebellion against him goes to sleep because it has nothing more to rebel against. Risen with him, we enter the realm of *posse non peccare*, it is now possible *not* to sin. The powers of Satan, hell, death, flesh, sin, and the law no longer need have the last word, and we are not answerable to their claims: "the crucified are no longer subject to any man,"[61] as one ancient dream interpreter once observed.

And what is the nature of the adhesive by which we are joined? When he immersed us into Christ, the Holy Spirit, the bond of love within the Trinity, eternally bonded us to Christ in spirit. It is, perhaps, like the communication of the attributes in Christ: the human nature of Christ was neither swamped by nor at any time left helpless by the divine nature in Christ. It is the same with us: our individual souls do not become a drop of water in a vat of wine. We are not swamped by the one to whom we are joined, but, from the moment of our immersion and union, we are never left helpless by him either. It would take a much cleverer person than me to penetrate any

60. So Esler, *Conflict and Identity*, 213.
61. White (tr.), *The Interpretation of Dreams, Oneirocritica by Artemodorus*.

further than this into the mystery. All I can do is commend it in the form Paul assumes it to take: an *experience*. It is an experience by which we daily taste of the age to come if we will but present ourselves for service.

The Cross and Discipleship

> Mark's literary artistry underscores the importance of self-sacrificial cross imitation as the primary response of disciples to the unique self-sacrificial death of Jesus.[62]

When dealing with participation in Christ's dying and rising it would seem highly amiss not to pause at the mimetic aspect of this participation: the ongoing decision to pick up the cross, to die to sin, and to walk in newness of life. Tannehill was clear that, as well as the large number of passages that speak of our union with Christ's death as an already accomplished fact, there are also a significant number of Pauline passages that speak of this as a process.[63] The epistle of 1 Peter takes this call to suffering with Christ as the condition for participating in his vindication as its central theme (1 Pet 2:20–23; 3:9, 13–18; 4:1–2, 12–19). Easily the most fruitful place to study the role of the cross in discipleship has been the Gospel of Mark. New Testament scholars seem more or less unanimous in affirming that Mark's theology has two centers of gravity. One is the cross and the other is the call to discipleship. And the two motifs are very obviously intertwined. Gundry might have a point that Mark's entire Gospel is an *apology for the cross*.[64]

The cross informs every aspect of Mark's concept of discipleship. It means that humility and faith are front and center and the heroes are not the disciples but the marginal characters. The disciples themselves provide us mainly with negative lessons; they tell us how *not* to behave.[65] The disciples are very "fallible followers."[66] There is evidence that Mark draws in the reader initially through some positive portrayals of Christ's inner circle,

---

62. Hood, "Evangelicals and the Imitation of the Cross," 120.

63. The whole of Part II of his book is devoted to this aspect: *Dying and Rising with Christ*, 74–134.

64. Gundry, *Mark: A Commentary on His Apology for the Cross*, 1: "He writes a straightforward apology for the cross, for the shameful way in which the object of Christian faith and subject of Christian proclamation died, and hence for Jesus as the Crucified One."

65. Best, *Following Jesus*, 12.

66. Malbon, "Fallible Followers," 29–48.

causing the reader to identify with them. Then, very soon the weaknesses emerge, by which time the reader has already begun to identify him- or herself with the disciples. The result is that the reader identifies with both the successes and the failures of the disciples, forcing him or her to look at his or her own weaknesses. Tannehill takes this to be a very definite strategy: "The composition of Mark strongly suggests that the author . . . intended to awaken his readers to their failures as disciples and call them to repentance."[67]

Whether or not this is the case, it is clear from the examples that Mark selects that "Followership is not easy."[68] The best examples of the kind of faith that ought to underpin good discipleship come from Jairus (5:22–24a, 35–43), Bartimaeus (10:46–52), the scribe (12:28–34), the woman who anointed Jesus (14:3–9), the centurion (15:39), and Joseph of Arimathea (15:42–46).[69] Women stand out, especially during the passion narrative. They come the closest to Jesus during his hour of trial (15:40–41), they "continuously followed" *ēkolouthoun*,[70] and they lead the way at the resurrection (16:1–9). In fact, there seems to be a significant shift in the attention placed on the women from 15:40–41 onwards.[71] Gentiles also are prominent models of discipleship. It takes a Roman centurion to recognize the Son of God in a crucified man (15:39). The Syro-Phoenician woman is another outstanding example (7:24–30). Many of these serve as examples of the fact that successful discipleship is all about the humble willingness to accept God's help.[72] This continues to contrast sharply with the growing doubts, fears, and incomprehension of Christ's closest disciples as reflected in the three boat scenes (4:40; 6:52; 8:17–18—though a flash of insight eventually comes: 8:27–30).

The use of minor characters with outstanding faith and insight sets the scene for Jesus to open up the offer of discipleship to anyone who is

---

67. Tannehill, "The Disciples in Mark," 393. In contrast to this, Best is sure that the failures of the disciples would already have been known to the readers. The distinctive thing is the way the portrayal of these errors (e.g., Peter's denial) is followed by forgiveness and success in mission, which would have been "a source of great encouragement": Best, *Following Jesus*, 12.

68. Malbon, "Fallible Followers," 31.

69. Malbon, "Fallible Followers," 31.

70. Munro underlines the importance of this word. It describes total commitment: Munro, "Women in Mark's Gospel," 231.

71. Malbon, "Fallible Followers," 40, also Munro, "Women in Mark's Gospel," 227.

72. Best, *Following Jesus*, 12.

willing to take up their cross, deny self, and follow him (8:34).[73] And, as though to confirm this demanding side to the free offer, we are presented with a minor character who is a negative example: the rich young ruler (10:17–31), though Bartimaeus soon counterbalances this (10:46–52). The command to take up the cross brings judgment on everything we would take pride in. It is Mark's "theology of the cross."[74] For Mark, the nature of discipleship becomes apparent only in the light of this cross, and not in the light of Jesus' mighty acts.[75] The whole of the central section (8:27—10:52) is constructed as a journey from Caesarea Philippi to the edge of Jerusalem and is preceded by healing miracles in which blind men have their sight restored by Jesus.[76] This may well be symbolic of the spiritual blindness that must be miraculously cured.[77] It could be that Mark, like John, is expecting his readers to understand that spiritual blindness and its cure is the main significance of these miracles. Only to faith is the true identity and mission of Jesus revealed, but once our eyes are thus opened following him along the way becomes possible. There may well also be a symbolic significance behind Mark's use of *entē hodō*, "on the way" (8:27; 9:33; 10:32) in the all-important central section (8:27—10:52) where the three passion predictions occur. The journey to Jerusalem and to crucifixion is symbolic of the pilgrimage of discipleship, which leads there too.[78] This is all part of Mark's "narrative art" by which the reader is "drawn into the crucifixion account."[79]

Balancing Indicative and Imperative

My *Old Rugged Cross*, the second part of my three-part Atonement Project, explored atonement from the viewpoint of two millennia of Christian experience as recorded in sermon, song, and liturgy, in poetry, prose, and film. I concluded that the dominant theme was the "Participation Imperative."[80] This was perhaps more inevitable than surprising. Of course

73. Wiliams, "Discipleship and Minor Characters in Mark's Gospel," 339.
74. Tiede "Proclaiming the Hidden Kingdom," 325.
75. Best, *Following Jesus*, 13–14.
76. Best, *Following Jesus*, 134.
77. Hare, *Mark*, 7.
78. Best, *Following Jesus*, 15–16.
79. Bolt, "Feeling the Cross," 10. His ideas are developed further in *The Cross from a Distance*.
80. Pugh, *Old Rugged Cross*, xiv, 86

the atonement, when looked at from the viewpoint of the faithful rather than those who pontificate on their behalf, was going to be all about drawing personal succor from Christ crucified. But perhaps one of the most interesting contributors to that volume for our purposes here would be the preacher and teacher who did more than anyone I can name to take the content of Romans 6 and actually tell people what to do with it. That person is the Welsh revival chronicler and Keswick speaker Jessie Penn-Lewis (1861–1927). Of the twenty-one small books of hers I have collected, nine center on the theme of the believer's union with the death and resurrection of Christ. However, even those that don't have this focus shed important light on how she understands this union to work. For example, in *The Battle for the Mind* she highlights the importance of cognition: "The practical life is changed only in so far as we are 'transformed' by the 'renewing' of the 'mind'. Christ's 'mind' was to obey God, even unto the death of the Cross."[81] Being able to think in a cross-shaped way, however, involves a decision to give up ways of thinking that are too self-orientated and self-reliant. The crucial moment for her came when, after years of difficult and ineffective work as a leader within the YWCA, she experienced the Spirit whispering the words "crucified" to her during a night-time vision in which her own efforts were being shown to her as filthy rags. "I understood very quickly," she says, "the key to the full possession and outworking of the blessed Spirit in co-operation with our surrender, trust and obedience."[82] The key was precisely to see herself as "crucified." From that point there was a new life that was breathed into the Bible studies and prayer times that she would lead, as well as a growing number of invitations for her to speak at YWCA events across Europe and Russia. What then became her central message could be summarized as this: "Calvary means that Christ not only bore on that Tree your sins, but that He carried to the Tree the sinner—carried you there."[83] Hence, sin in our experience is not overcome by conquering it but

81. Penn-Lewis, *The Battle for the Mind*, 13–14.
82. Penn-Lewis, *The Leading of the Lord*, 12.
83. Penn-Lewis, *More than Conquerors*, 3.

Dying and Rising with Christ

by dying to it.[84] "In Him is the Fulness of God," she says, "In us—nothing! We have nothing to offer God but our *wills*."[85]

Robert Tannehill unwittingly endorses many of Penn-Lewis' insights in Part II of his *Dying and Rising with Christ*. In this part of his book he looks at Romans 8:10–13 where the Spirit ongoingly puts to death the misdeeds of the body, and various passages in 2 Corinthians (1:3–9; 4:7–14; 7:3; 12:9; 13:4) that speak of Paul's sufferings as a participation in the suffering and dying of Christ, which entail a renunciation of self-reliance and an enjoyment of the resurrection life and power of Christ. Further, 1 Thessalonians 1:5–8 and 2:13–16 set up a contrast between the merely human and the divine power that comes with suffering. Then there is Romans 8:17, in which suffering with Christ precedes glorification with Christ, and finally, Philippians 3:2–11, an especially outspoken and lyrical renunciation of all the things Paul could be self-reliant about in favor of being exclusively united to Christ. In the light of these passages, Tannehill says that, for Paul, the Christian faith involves a commitment to "life-in-death."[86] It involves rejecting all "boasting."[87] It is about "the end of trust in self."[88]

Paul's teaching about justification as being on the basis of not having one's own righteousness (Phil 3:9) and the decision to not go about seeking to establish one's own righteousness but submitting to the righteousness of God (Rom 10:3) is of a piece with this. This life-in-death approach to religion, ethics, and resilience in ministry absolutely permeates the Pauline corpus.

So much for the *imperatives* of dying and rising: the call to daily die and rise, but how does this work together with the equally important *indicatives* of a co-crucifixion and co-resurrection that is an already accomplished fact? As Tannehill points out, the one potentially cancels out the other. If

---

84. Penn-Lewis, *The Centrality of the Cross*, 3. Incidentally, this is the same basic insight behind 12-Step recovery. The addict stubbornly insists that he or she has the power to master a problem that has got out of control. To admit the inability to control oneself is frightening but necessary: Swora, "The Rhetoric of Transformation in the Healing of Alcoholism," 195. Hence the crucial word "higher." It is only a power higher and greater than ourselves than can rescue us. But first the addict must realize that what they are up against is bigger than they are and fighting it with their own resources will ultimately end in failure: Buker, "Spiritual Development and the Epistemology of Systems Theory," 143–53.

85. Penn-Lewis, *The Glorious Secret*, 4.

86. Tannehill, *Dying and Rising*, 77.

87. Tannehill, *Dying and Rising*, 76, 83.

88. Tannehill, *Dying and Rising*, 76.

we are already dead and risen what possible force could any call to now die and rise have? Conversely, if we must die and rise then this implies we have not in fact already died. Tannehill's answer is in the already-and-not-yet eschatology of Paul.[89] There is doubtless a lot of truth in this, but I wonder if Penn-Lewis' attentiveness to *the cognitive moment* might better serve as the hinge between the indicative and the imperative in Paul. Indeed, this is the way Romans 6 is structured. The insistence on a cognitive reckoning in verse 11: "So you also must consider yourselves dead to sin and alive to God in Christ Jesus," occurs at exactly the hinge moment between the accomplished facts and the life lived. This moment of recognition is then the gateway to a physical response in which there is a presenting of our bodies (6:13, 16, 19). We can take this mental reckoning as involving potentially all the renunciations of self-reliance that Paul enlarges on elsewhere: we reckon ourselves to be dead to it all and place the weight of our trust in Christ alone. Whether freely or by the constraint of circumstances we "hit bottom" and hand our lives over to the Higher Power of Christ. Yet this works because it is already the case that our union with Christ has involved us in his death and the power of his risen life is now available. The cognitive moment is what unleashes these new realities.

Conclusion

By the first century, popular religion had taken a mystical turn and was catering on a massive scale to a growing spiritual hunger after some dynamic and life-changing deliverance. Such popular religion helped to supply some of the language and concepts for the new thing that was now rocking Judaism and spilling over to the gentiles. Jesus had always insisted that entering the kingdom must involve losing one's life or humbling oneself. Mark illustrates this by his counter-intuitive use of heroes from far outside the inner circle of Christ's all-too fallible followers. And what do the marginal heroes display? Humble recognition of Christ as the only answer to their needs. Paul gestures towards the mystery religions as he seeks to find new language for a new thing. It results in the indicative that we *have* died and risen with Christ. This indicative is balanced by the imperative that we must let Christ's suffering and dying do its work in us. His risen life must be manifested. Our having died and risen is made effective by renouncing

89. Tannehill, *Dying and Rising*, 74–77.

self-reliance and leaning upon Christ alone. This is made possible by a mental reckoning of ourselves as dead to sin and alive to God.

This metaphor concludes a series of three that flow logically, one from the other. Victory is at the peak describing the achievement of Christ in vanquishing the powers. Redemption is a hill lower down which describes the liberty of those impacted by this victory. Then, the dying and rising metaphor describes how this victory and redemption touch our lives in the deepest possible way.

Yet there are twin peaks. The second interpretive peak is the sacrifice metaphor, an enormous monolith from which flow justification and reconciliation. The first peak is founded upon the most quoted Old Testament passage in the New: Psalm 110:1: the Messiah's victorious enthronement; the second peak is formed from the second most quoted Old Testament passage in the New: Isaiah 53: the sin-bearing Suffering Servant. To this second peak we now turn.

Reflection

1. Have you ever had a moment of recognition in which you finally understood your need to rely on Christ instead of self? Did new power and effectiveness flow as a result or are you still waiting for that part?

2. If Paul did tap into contemporary religious ideas about dying and rising with deities to help describe the new source of life for believers, are there examples within your culture that also supply a picture of this participatory aspect of the theology of atonement? What pictures are there of ending and starting, renouncing and taking up, severance and joining, retreat and advance?

3. Richard Hays writes of "Narrative Participation." When followers of a celebrity try to pattern their own lives after the rich and famous are we looking at the same concept? Someone might even justify and glorify their own failures by comparing themselves to a celebrity. They make their story fit someone else's story and doubtless feel some sort of union as a result. Does this, possibly, give us one angle on participation in Christ that might help us explain it today?

CHAPTER 5

Sacrifice

Introduction

Through his crucifixion, Jesus hammers the emperor-exalting, death-dealing instrument of cruel torture and imperial domination into the gospel-proclaiming, life-giving implement of God's reign of peace.[1]

TO THE DOMINANT CULTURE, death by crucifixion was the ultimate penalty. It acted as a deterrent directed primarily at all those who were of slave status. These made up as much as a third of the population of Rome and, were they to mobilize in revolt (which was not unknown), these presented a significant threat to the *Pax Romana*. It was "ultimate" in that, once Rome had exacted this penalty there was nothing more it could do to you. It was at the top of the list of the three modes of execution, atop burning and beheading, which came second and third respectively. It was the method most to be feared. It was not only slaves that were crucified. Insurgent Jews were also crucified but this was understood to be a slave's death. The association of crucifixion with slaves in people's minds was extremely close, hence to be crucified was effectively to have one's status lowered to that of a slave. It was a deterrent, but not in the sense that nuclear weapons are supposedly a deterrent. It was not a last resort but was used often, so often in fact that slaves had the threat of crucifixion hanging over them all their lives and could expect to meet such an end for even the most minor infringements. And the Roman criminal justice system could do little for those such as

1. Snyder-Belousek, *Atonement, Justice, and Peace*, 525.

Sacrifice

slaves who were not normally deemed to be fully human. No proper trial was needed.

Attitudes towards crucifixion within Judaism were just as irretrievable. As we saw in the chapter on redemption, the Jews even had a Scripture they could point to that supported the shamefulness of the cross: "for anyone hung on a tree is under God's curse" (Deut 21:23), and Paul, when he was Saul the persecutor, may have taken this verse upon his lips as justification for his actions. On Damascus Road, however, it was suddenly clear that the crucified Jesus was the glorified Lord. Paul saw the Scripture in a new light: "Christ redeemed us from the curse of the law by becoming a curse for us" (Gal 3:13).

Jesus appears to have been aware of and to have predicted his own death by crucifixion, and the Synoptic Gospels portray a Jesus who foresaw that his coming arrest, trial, and mockery by lawless hands would result in a resurrection and in a new exodus. His life, which all along had been a life lived for others, would culminate in a death "for many" (Mark 10:45). The fate of John the Baptist would probably have given Jesus a fair indication of his own likely end, but to this intuition is added some remarkably detailed prophetic foretellings.

But not only this, it appears that Jesus did certain things that were openly provocative of the religious authorities and were designed to expose their cynicism, corruption, and violence. In particular, a single event appears to have caused the career of Jesus to lurch from being merely problematic but tolerated to being problematic to the point of sparking a plot to kill him. It was the cleansing of the temple incident.[2] This appears to have sent matters beyond the point of no return. From that event onwards, things move very quickly towards the terrible humiliations of the passion. John 11:48 seems to capture the mood that led so easily to the condemnation of an innocent man. Caiaphas wanted to keep the Romans out of the temple and keep the peace. And tensions were running high at Passover season owing to the way Passover aroused renewed longings for liberation. Jesus added greatly to the tension by his symbolic prophetic act within the temple precinct.

The object of Jesus' act was not what we might assume. There was no obvious corruption in what the money-changers and dove-sellers were doing. The money changers, in deference to the Second Commandment,

---

2. Bond, "E. P. Sanders and the 'Trial' of Jesus" was useful here. See also Sandnes, "The Death of Jesus for Human Sins," 20–23.

enabled worshippers to exchange pagan coinage with graven images on for temple currency. The dove-sellers enabled the poor to fulfil the Levitical commandments: "a turtle dove or two young pigeons" (Lev 14:22). Mark frames the action with the cursing of the fig tree—again a deeply symbolic action pointing to the rejection of the temple system as barren. The temple incident seems to be in continuity with this: it is a symbolic prophetic assertion that the sacrificial system is about to be made redundant and to be replaced (Matt 12:6; Mark 13:1-2; 14:57-8; 15:29; John 2:18-22; Acts 6:14). Judging from the main piece of evidence that is brought by the only witnesses at his trial (Mark 15:29), the cleansing of the temple incident should be seen as the main catalyst behind the crucifixion.

Just before his trial and crucifixion, Jesus celebrated a last meal with his disciples, which may have been a Passover *seder* but was certainly a meal that was in perfect continuity with his habit of making table fellowship central to his mission. In two of the four accounts of this meal, there is the special instruction that his followers were to go on eating this meal after his departure as an act of remembrance (Luke 22:14-20; 1 Cor 11:23-25, as opposed to Mark 14:22-25; Matt 26:26-29). In a way that can only be a reflection of Exodus 24, Jesus gives a theological interpretation of the act, which is that it is a covenant inauguration. So, not only does Jesus see himself and his impending act as replacing the sacrificial system, he sees it as in some way replacing, fulfilling, or renewing the very covenant that God inaugurated with the children of Israel.

The Background to the Sacrifice Metaphor

In line with our manner of reasoning so far, let us suppose that the experience of Pentecost is the revelatory crisis that stimulates the need for new language. We have imagined that the first metaphors that were needed might have been those that helped to conceptualize the victory and freedom that the experience of participating in the risen life of Christ had brought. It may be that the next big issue to resolve was the fact that this glorified Christ died at all since he did not owe a death. It was concluded that his death was therefore in some way a death *for others*.[3] We can imagine Paul,

---

3. The simple logic of this is not without counterparts in Rabbinic Judaism, there being a saying by Rabbi Simeon b. Yohai (in *Leviticus Rabbah* 32.43) about the prophet who is killed by a lion in 1 Kings 20. Because the prophet was clearly a righteous man and did not deserve such a death, the reasoning was that his death must therefore be

in particular, thinking long and hard about this during his time in Arabia in the wake of his immensely unsettling Damascus Road experience.

Dying for Others

In contemplating Christ's death as a death that is affirmed in one way or another as simply for others without any elaboration, we have in mind such Pauline passages as these: 1 Thessalonians 5:10: "who died for us"; 2 Corinthians 5:15: "he died for all," as well as the Johannine theme of lovingly laying down one's life for others (John 10:11, 17-18; 15:13; 1 John 3:16).

Of particular note is 1 Corinthians 15:3, which does include a tiny theological elaboration: the insight that it was "for our sins": "Christ died for our sins in accordance with the scriptures." This passage is particularly significant because it preserves for us a tradition that predates Paul's apostolic ministry. Paul says it was a message that he passed on which he had received. It had been handed down to him from an already established body of teaching with its rudimentary creedal statements. Hence, it is "not the peculiar eccentricity of an apostolic lone ranger but the proclamation of the whole apostolic college."[4]

We will now look at all the possible sources for the simple concept that Christ's death was a death for others, and the basic extrapolation that it was for our sins.

The Fourth Servant Song

The source of some ten direct citations and thirty-two allusions in the New Testament,[5] as well as almost certainly a prophecy that Jesus saw himself as fulfilling,[6] Isaiah 53 is the most obvious place to go for the point of origin for "died for us/for our sins" language. This is the most obvious "scripture" that Paul can be referring to when he says that Christ's death for our sins

---

an atonement for Israel as a whole: Kim, "The Concept of Atonement in Early Rabbinic Thought and the New Testament Writings," 121. A similar logic infuses the Jewish martyr tradition: "Israelites killed by the Gentiles are an expiation for the world-to-come" *Sifre Deut.* 333[140a]: Kim, "Concept of Atonement," 126.

4. Gathercole, *Defending Substitution*, 58.

5. Hengel, *Atonement*, 60.

6. Taylor, *Jesus and his Sacrifice*, 48: Jesus "must have thought of His suffering as a sacrificial offering in which men might participate."

was "according to the scriptures" (1 Cor 15:3). There are no other canonical instances of human sacrificial vicarious death.[7]

The heart of the Isaiah passage is the "drama of delayed recognition."[8] We thought X, but, to our surprise, Y was the case. The onlookers thought this pathetic figure was suffering for *his own* sins, was deservedly stricken *by God*. And there was nothing, in any case, to make us want to give him a second glance. He was despised. But something startles the onlookers into thinking again. A report has come (53:1) which seems to compel a reassessment: it turns out he was suffering on account of and instead of the onlookers. He might even be described as an "offering for sin" (Isa 53:10). And it is precisely this note of reversal, of radical reassessment, that would have struck a chord with Paul himself. Following his encounter with the risen Christ on the road, he had had his own remorseful reassessment to make. The same could be said of James, the Lord's brother, who gets a mention by Paul at 15:7 as having had a post-resurrection encounter with Christ. Along with Joses, Simon, and Jude, he had been dismissive of his brother's ministry (John 7:1–5; Mark 3:21) yet all the brothers end up being present in the upper room just before Pentecost, praying together with Mary and 115 others (Acts 1:14). One could surmise that similar dramas of delayed recognition were a feature of many early conversions to faith in a crucified Christ.[9] The surprise factor is only strengthened by the fact that, in Israelite religion, it was understood that each person should die for their own sins: "The default Old Testament position would be '*he* died for *his* sins' or '*we* died for *our* sins.' The miracle of the gospel, however, is that *he* died for *our* sins."[10]

There are, of course, other passages besides 1 Corinthians 15:3, with a far closer verbal similarity to Isaiah 53. In particular, Romans 4:25: "who was delivered up (*paradothē*) for our transgressions" (parallel with Isa 53:12LXX) and Romans 8:32: ". . . but delivered him up for us all" (parallel with Isa 53:6bLXX). It is clear then that Paul, not only when citing the tradition handed down to him, but also when reaching for passages that helped picture the atonement, went very readily to Isaiah 53 for resources.

---

7. Gathercole, *Defending Substitution*, 61.

8. Janowski, "He Bore Our Sins," 48–74.

9. So Gathercole, *Defending Substitution*, 63: "The delayed recognition by Israel in Isaiah 53 thus corresponds very well to the delayed recognition by Jewish Christians like Paul himself."

10. Gathercole, *Defending Substitution*, 73.

Sacrifice

The Greco-Roman Heroes

Not all of Paul's "died for us" passages can be accounted for very easily by way of Isaiah 53, however. Paul was, after all, the apostle to the gentiles and would have employed any images he knew of that would be familiar to his hearers. It is just such an image that seems to be the focus of Romans 5:6–8. Here Paul is comparing and contrasting familiar ideas of heroes being brave enough to die for good or deserving people, with Christ dying for weak people, for sinners, for the ungodly. As Gathercole has pointed out, the image is specifically of a hero dying for a *person*, not a martyr for a *cause*, so that rules out the superficially similar ideals involved in the Maccabean martyrs who were described as dying "for piety" (4 Macc 6:22) or "for the covenant of our fathers" (1 Macc 2:50).[11] Even with the instances of dying for a cause ruled out the examples to choose from within Greco-Roman literature of people dying for people are vast.[12] People-dying-for-people was a recurring Greek tragedian theme. Scholars often single out the story of Alcestis because this one was so widely discussed and referenced in the ancient world that it was sure to have been widely known at the time Paul wrote to the Romans.[13] The story is in a play by Euripides in which King Admetus has been promised by the god Apollo the power to live longer than his allotted time. This is in gratitude for hospitality shown to the god, but there is a condition: Admetus must nominate a volunteer to die early in his place. His father is approached but is unwilling. Finally, Admetus' devoted wife Alcestis proves willing to die instead of her husband. However, so "stereotyped"[14] was the Greek expression *apothnēskein hyper*, "to die for," that there seems little need to analyze particular instances. It was an ideal that was at least as widely held aloft as it is today, and the idea of noble self-sacrifice was as frequently reiterated on the Greek stage then as it is on the big screen today.

---

11. Gathercole, *Defending Substitution*, 90.

12. Probably the most complete recent survey would be that by Versnel, "Making Sense of Jesus' Death: The Pagan Contribution," 215–94. See also Hengel, *The Atonement*, 4–15, and Seely, *The Noble Death: Graeco-Roman Martyrology and Paul's Concept of Salvation*.

13. Gathercole thinks it just possible that Alcestis might even be the one Paul has in mind when he writes Romans 5:6–8: Gathercole, *Defending Substitution*, 97.

14. Hengel's word for it. See Hengel, *The Atonement*, 9.

PICTURES OF ATONEMENT

The Akedah *Hypothesis*

By the first century a tradition had arisen around the binding (Hebrew *Akedah*) of Isaac by his father Abraham, who was obediently willing to offer up his one and only son as a human sacrifice. Within the *Haggadah*, the devotional literature of Judaism (especially the recently discovered *Poem of the Four Nights* in the Palestinian Targum) a version of the story circulated in which Isaac, not now a boy but a fully consenting man of thirty-seven, was actually sacrificed and not spared by the discovery of a ram caught by its horns. Importantly, the *Poem of the Four Nights* places the incident within the Passover narrative, the third "night" or episode in the history of Israel's redemption. The Passover night follows the second night which is the covenant with Abraham. This covenant-with-Abraham night includes a conflating of Genesis 15 and 22, foreshadowing what we see in James 2:14–26.[15] The self-offering of Isaac was what made possible the Passover. He was the true firstborn who was sacrificed to deliver Israel from Egypt.[16] The merit of his sacrifice is so great it lasts from the second night of salvation history until it is time for the third night, the Passover night. The last night is the end of the world.[17]

Some argue that this *Akedah* tradition is one of the most important precursors we have to the New Testament teaching that God did not

15. In 1 Macc 2:52, too, there is a midrash of Genesis 15 and 22. This one goes as far as reversing the chronology so that, in Genesis 22, Abraham is tested and found faithful, then, in the light of this, Abraham is reckoned as righteous as per Genesis 15. The effect is that, in 1 Maccabees, Abraham's virtuous act is treated as though it were the basis of God's justification. In James 2:21–23, the same two episodes from the life of Abraham are exegeted, but the right way around, this time to demonstrate that the faith which was recognized in Genesis 15, was demonstrated as real in Genesis 22. In Romans 4, Genesis 22 does not even feature. Instead, the priority of faith is emphasized by exegeting Genesis 15 and then Genesis 17, the circumcision. Paul could have gone on to use Genesis 22 to show that this faith results in a reformed life (and this might have saved him from the accusations of "let is to evil that good may come") but he chose instead to deal with the most prized ethnic boundary marker: circumcision: Talbert, *Romans*, 118.

16. Schwartz finds the *Akedah* explanation of Rom 8:32 insufficient. He asks: "How does God's 'giving up' His son help mankind?" He seems to have ignored the developments within the *Akedah* tradition about Isaac actually laying down his life and how this has atoning merit. Biblically, he quite correctly says: "he [Isaac] did not die . . . and his death would not have been *for* anyone." Schwartz, "Two Pauline Allusions," He offers David's sparing of Saul's son Mephibosheth in 2 Sam 21:1–14 as a more likely background because this accounts for the "not sparing" terminology of Rom 8:32: Schwartz, "Two Pauline Allusions," 263, 265–66.

17. See also Rosenberg, "Jesus, Isaac, and the 'Suffering Servant,'" 381–88.

SACRIFICE

withhold his own Son but gave him up for us all, that God so loved the world that he gave his one and only Son, and sent his only begotten Son into the world to be the sacrifice for our sins so that we might live through him (Rom 8:32, John 3:16; 1 John 4:9-10). It is also notable that Hebrews 11:17-20 itself seems to follow the *Akedah* tradition by strongly implying that Isaac was actually sacrificed, yet because we assume he is referencing Genesis 22 and not the Jewish *Haggadah*, we tend not to believe what our own eyes are telling us when we read the Hebrews version of the account.

The Maccabean Martyrs

The martyr theology of 2 and 4 Maccabees is a version of the widely held reverence for heroic deaths within the surrounding Greco-Roman culture that we have already briefly looked at. There has been a steady undercurrent of interest in Jewish martyr theology as a background for Paul's understanding of Christ's death for others, and its atoning or propitiatory value.[18] Interest centers on 2 Maccabees 5:20, 7:30-38, and 8:29, and 4 Maccabees 6:27-29 and 17:21-22. These passages use the language of taking the place of others to assuage divine wrath and secure God's reconciliation to his people. Jarvis Williams includes extensive exegesis of both 2 and 4 Maccabees. These books retell the story of the wicked Antiochus Epiphanes IV who, under the pretense of wanting peace with Israel proceeds to invade and desecrate the temple. Jews who, in deference to their consciences, refused to obey him were executed. The civil disobedience of the martyrs mainly consisted in their refusal to eat swine's flesh and these acts were emboldened by a sure and certain hope of ultimate resurrection from the dead.

There are especially strong verbal similarities between 4 Maccabees 17:21-22 and Romans 3:25. 4 Maccabees 17:22 even includes the word *hilasterion*, "means" or "place" of propitiation,[19] and is the only other viable

---

18. Particular advocates have been Lohse, *Märtyrer und Gottesknecht*; Williams, *Jesus' Death as Saving Event*; Hengel, *The Atonement*; van Henten, *The Maccabean Martyrs as Saviours of the Jewish People*, and many others works; Williams, *Maccabean Martyr Traditions in Paul's Theology of Atonement*.

19. Van Henten is so taken by the parallels between the uses of faith, blood, and *hilasterion* that he even makes the claim that by the time of Paul's writing there was a known formula arising from the Maccabean martyr tradition: van Henten, "The Tradition-Historical Background of Rom 3:25," 126, cited in Finlan, *Problems with Atonement*, 55, n53. Williams is more cautious, concluding that Paul used martyr theology in

background for the use of the word in Romans 3:25 other than the Septuagint of Leviticus 16:2, 13, 14, 15. In Leviticus it rather awkwardly[20] refers to what Tyndale translated for us as "Mercy Seat," the rectangular gold-plated lid of the ark within the Most Holy Place.[21] It was, of course not a seat though it did have a lot to do with God's mercy, and we will have reason to return a few times to this marvelous meeting place between heaven and earth before the end of this chapter.

Against the use of 4 Maccabees 17 as the background, Paul opens the whole passage with a reference to "the law and the prophets" (Rom 3:21). This would seem to tip the scales in favor of a use of *hilasterion* by Paul that is inspired by the Torah, not 4 Maccabees. There is also some doubt about the date of 4 Maccabees, with some scholars dating it as a second- or even third-century document (AD 135–235 is suggested by Schreiner),[22] which potentially writes it off as a source for Paul. Williams, however, reckons that, even if the late date is ever proven, it merely shows that the ideas expressed in 4 Maccabees were at large within Second Temple Judaism and therefore Paul's environment.

Which Is It to Be?

So, with these backgrounds: the Servant, the heroic death, the *Akedah*, and the Maccabean martyrs, we are looking at sources for what we might call sacrifice-lite language. Such language is not freighted with much cultic

---

combination with Greco-Roman ideas about heroic deaths, the Levitical cult, and Isaiah 53. Yet still the advantage of the martyr theology of Maccabees is that it presented a ready-made example of humans atoning for sins and thus saving others from their sins through their own sacrificial deaths. This only then needed extending to include gentiles as well as Jews as the beneficiaries, and applied to Jesus. A strong supporting argument is that this picture would have resonated with Greco-Roman audiences with their own already strong heroic death ideas. Whereas too often scholars assume that Paul's audiences would have been much more conversant with parallels from the Old Testament than they probably were: Williams, *Maccabean Martyr Traditions*, 120–24. See also Bailey, "Jesus as the Mercy Seat," 158 for the strong notes of "Greek heroic and athletic imagery" throughout 4 Maccabees, including at 17:22.

20 Awkward because the word, in this form, was always used to refer to a thing, never an idea or action. In 4 Maccabees and Romans 3, a concrete object is given rare metaphorical meaning: Bailey, "Jesus as the Mercy Seat," 155–56.

21. Williams helpfully summarizes the literature: *Maccabean Martyr Traditions*, 6–26.

22. Schreiner, *Romans*, 192 n24.

terminology. In the "died for us" passages we are not necessarily being asked to reimagine Levitical laws and what these would look like if applied to a willing human victim. We are simply pondering the wonder of one person being willing to give up his life for the sake of others. It is the laying down of a life for others that is rightly described as the greatest act of love conceivable (John 15:13).

This act is always described as an act of love for other people rather than a martyrdom for a principle. This seems to hint strongly that a generalized awareness of and reverence for such acts within Greco-Roman culture is what is being appealed to. Where the cultic element intrudes, such as "for our sins" in 1 Corinthians 15:3, we go beyond sacrifice-lite into something more developed, which would seem to require us to look at Isaiah 53, as well as possibly the *Akedah* tradition and the 4 Maccabees, but certainly Leviticus. To this more developed concept and its background we now turn.

A Sacrifice for Sin

It was known that Jesus had always emphasized the forgiveness of sins, even the forgiveness of those who were hardened sinners. He had controversially assumed the power to pronounce such forgiveness as though he himself were God, the one sinned against. It is likely that this coalesced in the minds of his followers with stories of his equally memorable and even more controversial acts of overturning the sacrificial system and inaugurating a new covenant. The two elements: forgiving sinners and setting aside the sacrifices, combined to produce a view of him as in some way embodying and bringing to final consummation the whole bloody litany of offerings that had been central to Israelite spirituality for well over a thousand years.

The readiness of people to accept Christ's anti-temple message is evidenced by Mark's comment that the scribes and chief priests could not find a way to "destroy" him because all the crowds were astonished at his teaching (Mark 11:18). It could be that Jesus was tapping into some popular feeling.[23] Such feelings would have been shaped by a long history of prophetic critique of the sacrificial system within Israel.[24] Such prophetic critique was part and parcel of what biblical scholars have long described

23. Finlan, *Problems with Atonement*, 20.
24. E.g., Pss 40:6; 50:12–13; Amos 5:21; Hos 6:6; Mic 6:6–7, theses latter two are, tellingly, quoted by Jesus: Matt 9:13; 12:7; 23:23.

as the trend towards the "spiritualization" of sacrifice.[25] The spiritualization of ritual meaning away from actual sacrifices and towards symbolic alternatives is a phenomenon that has been noticed in other traditions too, including the Greco-Roman religions. Plato, Heraclitus, Euripides, and Plutarch all joined the chorus rejecting the very idea of sacrifice as absurd and unbecoming of God.[26] Philo also added his insistence that what mattered was not what was given in sacrifice but the disposition with which it was given.[27] Biblical examples such as Psalm 141:2: "Let my prayer be *counted as* incense before you, and the lifting up of my hands as an evening sacrifice," involve the right attitude serving as, or replacing, the ritual.[28] The New Testament builds upon the spiritualization process[29] by affirming in many places that the church is now the temple, a development that must have been even further bolstered by the actual destruction of the Jerusalem temple in AD 70.[30] Paul exhorts that each person must respond to God's mercy and grace by the presentation of oneself to God in the manner of a sacrifice (Rom 12:1).

A net result of this spiritualizing of sacrifice is that the way is opened for Jesus' death to be interpreted in sacrificial metaphors, which, having been already freed of purely concrete associations, can intermingle and interpenetrate,[31] can switch happily between Christ's actual physical death and metaphors taken from cultic practices. And this switching between the two does leave some questions unanswered. Ian Bradley shows a keen

25. See Daly, *Sacrifice Unveiled*, 69–74 for a credible narrative of this process.
26. For details, see Finlan, *Problems with Atonement*, 23–24.
27. Daly, *Sacrifice Unveiled*, 29.
28. Finlan, *Problems with Atonement*, 22.
29. An earlier generation of scholars would have claimed the opposite, namely, that, after centuries of a refining spiritualization process, suddenly the New Testament hurls us back into the blood-soaked barbarity of a fully visceral offering: "In Christianity the age-long Jewish process of sublimation disappears as if in a sudden bout of psychosis. We are back at the primitive level at which the abyss opens and panic requires a victim." Maccoby, *The Sacred Executioner*, 105. Long before him William James was claiming the same: *Varieties of Religious Experience*, 462. Much of the twentieth century seems to have been bewitched by Darwin-inspired notions of inexorable progress upwards, making even biblical subject matter susceptible to being viewed through only that lens. Nothing other than the neat trajectory was visible, except, as here, when it proved useful to draw attention to a particularly heinous variation in the trajectory.
30. The process develops from spiritualization into christologization at this point according to Daly, *Sacrifice Unveiled*, 34–35.
31. Finlan, *Problems with Atonement*, 55.

Sacrifice

eye for the incongruences. For a start, he asks, "Who exactly is doing the sacrificing?"[32] Those who executed him were not conscious of presenting any kind of sacrifice. They were not priests, and the location was not an altar but an instrument of torture. And what sense does it actually make to speak of Christ as both "priest and victim"? Are we saying that God "sacrificed himself to himself?"[33] These incongruencies, perhaps too conveniently some would argue, can be set aside using the "is/is not" dynamic of metaphor. The New Testament writers, while being conscious of the dissimilarities between the crucified Christ and, say, a sin offering, seemed to believe that the similarities were striking enough to warrant the sacrificial language nonetheless.

But there are further problems: Christ's willing self-offering is presented in atonement theology as the factor that safeguards the moral status of the sacrifice of Christ, preventing us from sinking to language that could be construed by others as descriptions of "cosmic child abuse." A freely willing, not to mention fully adult, Jesus cannot be described as the Father's abused victim. Yet Bradley undermines this safeguard by pointing out that Christ's resignation, his submission to his fate, is at least as strong an emphasis in the New Testament as willing self-offering. Alongside the setting of his face like flint to go to Jerusalem, where he knew what awaited (Luke 9:51), there is clearly a sense of him bowing to a "dark necessity,"[34] finally enshrined in the words "not as I will, but your will be done" (Luke 22:42). And Christ describes, after his resurrection, how "necessary" it had all been (Luke 24:26). "[T]his stress on inevitability and necessity," claims Bradley, "surely invalidates a portrayal of Jesus' suffering and death simply in terms of a free and voluntary self-sacrifice."[35] Bradley is building up to the introduction of his concept of the "power of sacrifice," which is the life-force of the cosmos and to which Jesus must submit. Yet, cosmic forces aside for now, it is surely possible to see the element of resignation and surrender as being entirely of a piece with the notion of free and willing self-offering. Indeed, suffering and death, by definition, were things that Christ needed to allow to be done *to* him. If suffering and dying had been things he did *to himself* we would find ourselves with far worse moral questions to answer.

---

32. Bradley, *The Power of Sacrifice*, 106.
33. Bradley, *Power of Sacrifice*, 106.
34. Bradley, *Power of Sacrifice*, 112.
35. Bradley, *Power of Sacrifice*, 113.

It is time to see if we can break down the possible elements that make up the metaphor of Christ's death as a sacrifice for sin. We now move from sacrifice-lite to a more fully described designation of Christ's death using words that paint the picture of temple courts, blood-letting, and smoke ascending, a dark and mysterious place for us to go these days, but we will try to imagine what it was like and what it meant.

Offerings in General

It has proven nearly impossible to simplify the meaning of the sacrificial system as a whole by the use of a single motif. As far back as 1959, Vincent Taylor, in his classic work *Jesus and His Sacrifice*, explored all these as possible options: fellowship and communion, gift, propitiatory offering, self-expression, and participation, before concluding that the concept that Jesus would have assumed was "a representative offering to God in which men might share."[36] For all the difficulty of defining in a scholarly way what the sacrificial system actually was, it has been remarkably easy for Christians to impose upon the sacrificial offerings an interpretation involving penalty-bearing and substitutionary death. This tendency has now been corrected to the point where Daly now applauds the caution of much scholarship around explaining the sacrifices with any unified concept. He himself reluctantly chooses the word "gift" as the best word to describe what was going on.[37] Whether of cereal, drink, or meat, the people were bringing a present to God. John Goldingay even thinks the analogy of a man who comes home holding a bunch of flowers for his wife is of some help.[38] Perhaps this is another case of the "is/is not" tension inherent in any metaphor!

If anything there has now probably been an over-reaction against penal substitutionary interpretations of the Levitical sacrifices. Conservative scholar Emile Nicole expresses frustration with "a priori opposition to the concept of substitutionary atonement" too often being allowed to drive the scholarship on the Levitical sacrifices.[39] However, even if we grant that some of the sacrifices entailed a death *in place of* the offerer, Nicole himself admits that we then have a problem of a disproportionate implied penalty. The sin offerings were always to atone for a relatively minor and

36. Taylor, *Jesus and His Sacrifice*, 75.
37. Daly, *Sacrifice Unveiled*, 28.
38. Goldingay, "Old Testament Sacrifice and the Death of Christ," 3.
39. Nicole, "Atonement in the Pentateuch," 37.

SACRIFICE

unintentional infringement; what Wright calls "unwitting" and "unwilling" sins:[40] sins of inattentiveness and ignorance such as failing to speak out as a witness in a trial or mouthing careless oaths (Lev 5:1, 4). If we maintain that the death of the sacrificial victim is central to the ritual and that this animal somehow dies the death that its offerer deserved, we end up with a God who apparently demands death for small mistakes but can be persuaded to accept the slaughter of prized livestock instead of your own death. To resolve this, Nicole points out that offering sacrifices for sin was a human instinct from the start, from the time of Cain and Abel. The Levitical laws were not so much prescribing as directing that human instinct: "the purpose of sacrificial regulations in the Pentateuch was not to impose sacrificial practice upon a people who previously ignored it but to submit an already existing practice to the proper understanding of the relationship between God and his people."[41] I am aware, though, that we have not here resolved the problem of disproportionality: death for minor mistakes. We will return to it.

One last important observation needs to be made before we consider some specific types of sacrifice. Although the sacrifices do differ in the degrees of importance given to atonement and forgiveness, yet some atoning significance, leading to the forgiveness of sins, seems to be woven in from as early as Leviticus 1:4 and its prescriptions for the burnt offering: "He [the worshipper] is to lay his hand on the head of the burnt offering and it will be accepted on his behalf to make atonement for him." The manipulation of blood is common to the burnt offering (Lev 1:5, 11, 15), the fellowship offering (Lev 3:2, 8, 13), the sin offering (Lev 4:30), and the guilt offering (Lev 5:9) and we are explicitly told in Leviticus 17:11 that this offering of blood was "to make atonement for your souls."[42] So, reparation, covenant repair, compensation, these are the kinds of words and phrases we may use to describe a big part of what was going on, even though this would not extend to everything and plays only a minor part in the fellowship offering, for example.

It seems then that the purpose of the Levitical sacrifices was to do something good with an already existing sacrificial instinct, an instinct that we can assume already included both the urge to give a gift and the need to repair covenant relations with God. The Levitical laws ensured that, when

40. Wright, *The Day the Revolution Began*, 290.
41. Nicole, "Atonement in the Pentateuch," 42.
42. Nicole, "Atonement in the Pentateuch," 43, and n30.

giving a gift, those of slender means would not feel obliged and manipulated into giving more than they could afford, and when wanting to cover a mistake and repair relations with God, offering a slain animal could not be allowed to cover, and thus cheapen, very serious infringements (such as murder) which damage community life. Serious mistakes required more drastic action but, even then, could take the offender on a path to restoration. It is perhaps for this reason that the New Testament writers seem to gravitate especially to the Day of Atonement ritual, when Israel as a whole entered into a comprehensive cleansing of the sum of all the mistakes of all ranks. The point seems to be: Christ's sacrifice surpasses even that.

The Sin Offering

In Second Temple Judaism, with its post-exilic awareness of the power of sin—it was the power that had disinherited the nation—the sin offering appears to have taken on a more central significance than before. Further, as a result of the deliberations of the rabbis about the role of blood, the offering up of the *blood* of the sin offering had become the defining atoning act,[43] which may help to explain the ease with which the New Testament writers could abbreviate Christ's sacrifice by using the word "blood."

The role of the animals offered in sin offerings is variously described. Some scholars insist that the animal could not have been understood as bearing sin since this would have rendered it unacceptable to God; it would be rendered unholy and unclean. Others go so far as to say that, even in the case of the cereal offering, sin-bearing took place: it was the priests who took upon themselves the sins of the offerers when they ate their portion of it (Lev 10:17).[44] The hand that is pressed onto the head of the animal (and on the Day of Atonement both hands are pressed: Lev 16:21) while the sins of the people are confessed over it seems hard to explain if the sin offering is not bearing sin at all. To explain this laying on of hands as solely expressing ownership or identification with the animal is perhaps another instance of the effort to avoid substitutionary interpretations.[45] However, some sin offerings cannot be about sin-bearing. For example, at the dedication of the altar the blood of a "sin offering" would be applied to the horns of the altar (Lev 8:14–15). In such cases a translation of "purification sacrifice"

43. Daly, *Sacrifice Unveiled*, 35, 37
44. Romerowski, "Old Testament Sacrifices and Reconciliation," 13.
45. Romerowski, "Old Testament Sacrifices and Reconciliation," 16–17.

rather than "sin offering" seems preferable, both on the basis of grammar and context.[46]

Further evidence, however, that the sin offering was understood to be in some way bearing away the sin of the worshiper is in what seems to be an expectation that there would be an afflicted conscience in the one bringing a sin offering. Since the sin offering was very often for sins committed in ignorance, some moment of realization is strongly implied, or even required (Lev 4:13, 22, 27). In these places Milgrom likes to translate "feel guilt" instead of "incur guilt." "It denotes," he says, "the suffering brought on by guilt."[47] It is about being "torn by grief and remorse,"[48] and this is half the process of atonement, according to Hayes.[49] The second half of the process is the purging of the relevant holy places that make up the sanctuary, God's space. This is what restores the offender to a right relation to God. It is this restoration that is the goal, rather than punishment, whether of the worshipper or of the animal.[50] Restoration is possible even for deliberate and flagrant sins (as in Num 15:30–31), according to Milgrom, so long as the all-important first stage of repentance is fulfilled. This has the effect of downgrading a deliberate sin that ought to result in being cut off from the people, to an unintended infringement that qualifies for the sin offering remedy.[51]

In many ways, any difficulties in defining what the sin offering was, in and of itself, are softened by the fact that the New Testament writers seem shy of identifying explicit links between Christ's death and this Levitical rite. Where it does occur it comes to us encased in something else. It greets us in the book of Hebrews, but only as an offering that was part of Yom Kippur (Heb 9:13 "For if the blood of goats and bulls . . ."). In 1 Peter 2:24 ("He himself bore our sins in his body on the cross") and 2 Corinthians 5:21 ("For our sake he [God] made him [Christ] to be sin who knew no sin"), sin offering language comes to us wrapped in allusions to Isaiah 53. In particular, it is this filtering of Levitical cult through the Fourth Servant Song (which itself makes an explicit reference to the sin offering in 53:10) that we will see is a hall mark of the sacrifice metaphor in the New Testament.

46. Hayes, "Atonement in the Book of Leviticus," 8.
47. Milgrom, *Leviticus 1–16*, 343.
48. Milgrom, *Cult and Conscience*.
49. Hayes, "Atonement in the Book of Leviticus," 10.
50. Hayes, "Atonement in the Book of Leviticus," 11.
51. Milgrom, *Leviticus 1–16*, 373.

PICTURES OF ATONEMENT

The Whole Burnt Offering

The *'ōlāh* or burnt offering has been described as "representative of Israel's worship, shaping the religious imaginations of Jews and Christians."[52] The claim has recently been made that Christ's crucifixion was viewed as simply the "ultimate burnt offering." Morales applies to it the term "ascension offering," a reference not only to its original theological meaning as a soothing or "restful" aroma[53] that would ascend to God, literally "softening" his face, but also the wider implications of the work of Christ as completed by his ascension to heaven, the true locus, in Hebrews, of the offering up of Christ's blood.[54] In the temple of the times of Jesus, the whole burnt offerings bookended each day, "subsuming all of the day's other sacrifices."[55] The offering was an act of consecration.[56] Its logic lay in the vaporization of the animal, its transformation into smoke, which could hence be carried up into heaven. In the whole burnt offering the animal is "etherealized,"[57] in an act of love towards God. It is transported into the "ownership of God,"[58] in Israel's stead.

Ephesians 5:2 makes this link explicit: ". . . and live in love, as Christ loved us and gave himself up for us, a fragrant offering and sacrifice to God." The fact that lambs were the most frequently offered species also helps us to draw some tentative lines from the holocaust offerings to the Lamb of God imagery of the New Testament.[59] For Morales, Gethsemane

52. Morales, "Atonement in Ancient Israel," 27. See also the much older article: McCarthy, "The Symbolism of Blood and Sacrifice," 166–76 from which Morales seems to draw some inspiration.

53. Kidner includes "soothing," "pacifying," and "propitiating" as ways to explicate the Hebrew *nichoach*. Kidner, "Sacrifice," 123.

54. There is even an anticipation of this in the ascension of the angel of the annunciation scene of Judg 13:20, who ascends to heaven in the smoke of the burnt offering: Morales, "Atonement in Ancient Israel," 36.

55. Morales, "Atonement in Ancient Israel," 29.

56. Keil and Delitzsch, *Biblical Commentary on the Old Testament* vol. II, *The Pentateuch*, 91. The alternative is that these were meals to which God was invited (Num 28:2), which is the view of Alfred Marx, *Les Sacrifices de l'Ancien Testament*, 12, 24–27. See Romerowski's summary of the views: Romerowski, "Old Testament Sacrifices and Reconciliation," 15.

57. Hicks, *The Fullness of Sacrifice*, 13.

58. Morales, "Atonement in Ancient Israel," 35.

59. A. F. Rainey, draws up a list: Rams are stipulated thirty-two times, bulls 113 times, and male lambs 1,086 times in Numbers and Leviticus: "The Order of Sacrifices in Old Testament Ritual Texts," 492.

SACRIFICE

provides a way into the cross as an act of total consecration analogous to the whole burnt offering:

> Jesus's tormented night of prayer in Gethsemane's garden, therefore, was not only the counter to Adam's self-willed failure in Eden's garden, but also the fulfillment of the Levitical cult, as out of his deep sorrow and distress he cried, "Nevertheless not as I will, but as you will—your will be done" (Matt 26:36–46).[60]

It could be, therefore, that when the writer to the Hebrews emphasizes the obedience of Christ (e.g., Heb 10:1–10), he may not be simply highlighting the qualitative difference between a dumb animal that has not willingly offered itself and the element of voluntarism that enters in when the man Jesus Christ offers himself. He might be using the obedience of Christ to describe the total consecration that qualifies Christ's sacrifice as the ultimate and final sacrifice, the definitive whole burnt offering perfected by his ascension to the right hand of God.[61]

The designation of the whole burnt offering as an ascension offering and linking this to Jesus may be part and parcel of the ascension-eye-view of atonement, which is presented to us by the writer to the Hebrews throughout his letter: "The central theme of the Epistle . . . is the perpetuation in the eternal world of the perfect sacrifice once offered on the Cross in time and space."[62] The South African revivalist Andrew Murray drew much inspiration from this unique teaching in Hebrews: "Our Lord is a High Priest 'in the power of an endless life,' and thus the cleansing power of the blood of the Son of God is unceasingly conveyed to us."[63]

A question the writer to the Hebrews seems to address as a central concern is that the earthly Jesus, being of the tribe of Judah and not of Levi, is not qualified to serve as high priest, so any claims that Christ had superseded the earthly office of the high priests were null and void. The writer basically agrees with this assessment: he is qualified to be a king in David's line but not to be the fulfillment of the priesthood (Heb 7:14; 8:4). However, it is not an earthly priestly ministry that he performs, the writer argues, but a heavenly one, carried out within the original heavenly tabernacle, which, under the direction of Moses, was copied in the form of the earthly one.

---

60. Morales, "Atonement in Ancient Israel," 27.
61. Morales, "Atonement in Ancient Israel," 37–39.
62. James, *Sacrifice and Sacrament*, 54–5.
63. Murray, *The Blood of the Cross*, 131.

And, according to the writer to the Hebrews, it is there in that heavenly sanctuary that Christ offers his own blood, a fact that underlines the near consensus now that, in the Levitical sacrifices, it was never the death of the victim that was the definitive element in the ritual[64] but the manipulation of the blood. "If one only slaughtered a victim, even at the temple," observes Moffitt, "but did not bring the body and blood of the victim to the alters and offer them to God, no sacrifice has occurred."[65]

The writer to the Hebrews might be alluding to the whole burnt offering when he speaks of "the blood of bulls and goats" (Heb 9:13), a possible reference to Numbers 7:15–16, where the bull is a burnt offering and the goat is a sin offering,[66] and might also be referring to it when he discusses the repetitious nature of the sacrifices, not just the annually repeated Yom Kippur (Heb 9:25—10:3) but the daily repeated burnt offering (Heb 10:11). However, it must be noted that the writer to the Hebrews is intermingling cultic imagery, at times very tightly. He can speak in the same breath of the sin offering, the whole burnt offering, Yom Kippur, and the red heifer (Heb 9:12–13). This would seem to limit the amount of hard evidence that could be gathered for a view of Christ's death that was significantly informed by the whole burnt offering in and of itself. The same could not be said, however, for Yom Kippur. For the writer to the Hebrews this is a dominant Levitical image. To this we now turn.

The Yom Kippur Rituals

When describing both of the main stages of the Yom Kippur ritual of Leviticus 16, scholars like to use contemporary terms, like decontamination, men dressing in special clothes as though in a nuclear power station,[67] airborne contaminants magnetically attracted to the sanctuary,[68] pollution which "attacked the sanctuary,"[69] necessitating blood that acted as "ritual detergent."[70] This was the day on which even the most flagrant and unrepen-

---

64. E.g., Daly, *Sacrifice Unveiled*, 26: "*No significance is attached to the death of the animal. Its death, in itself, effects nothing*" (italics original).
65. Moffitt, "It Is Not Finished," 163.
66. Lane, *Hebrews 9–13*, 239.
67. Nicole, "Atonement in the Pentateuch," 48.
68. Hayes, "Atonement in the Book of Leviticus," 6.
69. Hayes, "Atonement in the Book of Leviticus," 8.
70. Hayes, "Atonement in the Book of Leviticus," 8. He translates *kipper* with the

tant sins could be removed from Israel and sent away with the scapegoat. It was a day of cleansing, a day of clearing out.

However, it is also worth noting the other theological emphases, such as the element of self-humbling and confession (Lev 16:21, 31), which came to dominate the festival in later Judaism, and the element of compensation offered to God.[71] God accommodates himself to this compensation and chooses to accept it as an act of clemency. The implied quantifying of the amount of divine offense by means of a suitably large-scale, violent slaughter which buys him off seems distasteful. And efforts to eliminate the compensation element can end up mired in the opposite problem: we still have a large-scale slaughter but now it is totally gratuitous and no longer linked in any way to a specified and limited compensation.[72]

Yom Kippur plays a central role in Hebrews 8:1—10:18 and its role there has attracted a small body of literature.[73] Less widely acknowledged is the possible allusion to it in Luke 24:50-53, the ascension scene where Jesus lifts up his hands to bless the disciples before being lifted up. This may be an echo of the lifting up of the hands of the High Priest to bless the congregation once the blood rite of Yom Kippur had been completed.[74] It is possible that Luke is picturing Christ as dispensing the Aaronic blessing before ascending, the atoning blood rite having already been performed in the sharing of the cup.[75] Allusions to Yom Kipper have been detected elsewhere too. Daniel Stökl ben Ezra's study,[76] which includes important

---

cleansing motif dominant and renders the Day of Atonement, defensibly on that basis, as the "Day of Purgation": "Atonement in the Book of Leviticus," 12.

71. "[I]n *kippur* rites, purification cannot be disconnected from compensation: through compensation given to God, purification and forgiveness were granted." Nicole, "Atonement in the Pentateuch," 48.

72. Nicole, "Atonement in the Pentateuch," 50.

73. See Cortez, "From the Holy to the Most Holy Place," 527 n1 for an overview.

74. Carpinelli, "'Do This as *My* Memorial,'" 83. It is also an echo of Ben Sirah 50:14–15, 20-21: "Finishing the service at the altars, and arranging the offering to the Most High, the Almighty, he held out his hand for the cup and poured a drink offering of the blood of the grape; he poured it out at the foot of the altar, a pleasing odor to the Most High, the king of all. . . . Then Simon came down and raised his hands over the whole congregation of Israelites, to pronounce the blessing of the Lord with his lips, and to glory in his name; and they bowed down in worship a second time, to receive the blessing from the Most High."

75. Carpinelli, "'Do This as *My* Memorial,'" 90.

76. Ben Ezra, *The Impact of Yom Kippur on Early Christianity*.

non-canonical sources such as the *Epistle of Barnabas*,[77] as well as the New Testament, concludes that early Christianity made use of Yom Kippur in a number of ways. The *Epistle of Barnabas* is a case of typological over-kill in which an absurd range of elements from the passion narrative are brought into relationship with elements, not from Leviticus 16, but from the Yom Kippur rituals as they had developed by the time of Barnabas' writing. These included spitting on and goading the scapegoat and making it wear scarlet wool about its horns before being driven out into the wilderness. According to ben Ezra, Yom Kippur is central to Hebrews in that Christ is high priest (9:6–8), veil (6:19–20, 10:19–21), and sacrifice (9:12; 9:24—10:4, 12), and central to Romans 3:25, where the use of *hilasterion* is translatable as the *kipporet* or lid of the ark, the mercy seat, which we have mentioned already and will discuss more later.

The most notable thing about the use the writer to the Hebrews makes of Yom Kippur imagery is precisely *not* the kind of typologizing that we find in *Barnabas* but instead an emphasis on contrasts. The writer, after all, is seeking to set up, not a likeness, but a contrast between the two covenants because God "finds fault with" (Heb 8:8) the elements of the former covenant. The new and better covenant is based on a qualitatively different sacrifice. Yom Kippur was the ultimate day of cleansing for Israel yet even that was never enough. Christ's self-gift surpasses even the greatest remedy for sin available under the old covenant.

Speaking of covenant, now seems as good a time as any to turn our attention to this concept that had shaped the Jewish faith into which Christianity was born.

Sacrifice and Covenant

> Covenant fellowship with God is the goal for which humanity was created and which it has lost as a result of its fallenness. The key question for all atonement theories, then, is how this alienation from God can be overcome and the covenant relationship restored.[78]

Covenant is a concept that is about as far from being a metaphor in the New Testament as any concept can be. There is no sense in which the New

---

77. Barnabas discusses the two goats at length at *Barnabas* 7:4–11.
78. Shelton, *Cross and Covenant*, 20.

Sacrifice

Testament writers are saying: "the atonement is *like* a sort of new covenant," the New Testament witness is that what resulted from the death of Christ *is* the new covenant. So, although covenant will not be dealt with in depth in this volume, we need to register that there have been some recent attempts at defining the atonement as the birthing of the new covenant. Most notably, Michael Gorman who, in *The Death of the Messiah and the Birth of the New Covenant* is mainly restating his "cruciformity" theme, which can be found in a great many of his other publications.[79] In this work he is also building interestingly on the work of three previous scholars who have placed covenant at the center of their atonement theology: T. F. Torrance,[80] Kevin Vanhoozer,[81] and Larry Shelton.[82]

That a biblical case can be made for a fundamentally covenantal understanding of the atonement is clear from the Last Supper sayings in:

- Mark 14:24: "This is my blood of the covenant, which is poured out for many."
- Matthew 26:28, which makes a link to the forgiveness of sins: "This is my blood of the covenant, which is poured out for many for the forgiveness of sins."
- Luke 22:20b, which uses the term "new": "This cup that is poured out for you is the new covenant in my blood."
- 1 Corinthians 11:25a, which shares the term "new": "In the same way he took the cup also, after supper, saying, 'This cup is the new covenant in my blood.'"

The Lukan and Pauline versions include the instruction: "Do this in remembrance of me"; Mark and Matthew do not. Aside from these, there is the fact that the promises of a new covenant in Jeremiah and Ezekiel[83] are frequently alluded to and quoted, the Jeremian one forming the longest continuous quotation from the Old Testament in the New: Hebrews 8:8–13 (and the writer to the Hebrews quotes it a second time at 10:16–18). It is

---

79. Gorman, *Cruciformity*; Gorman, *Inhabiting the Cruciform God*; Gorman, "Cruciformity According to Jesus and Paul," 173–201; Gorman, "Paul's Corporate, Cruciform, Missional Theosis in Second Corinthians," 181–208; Gorman, *Becoming the Gospel*; Gorman, *Apostle of the Crucified Lord*; Gorman, *Participating in Christ*.

80. Torrance, *Atonement: The Person and Work of Christ*.

81. Vanhoozer, *The Drama of Doctrine*, and Vanhoozer, "The Atonement in Postmodernity," 367–404.

82. Shelton, *Cross and Covenant*. See also Burnhope, *Atonement and the New Perspective*.

83. Though, strictly speaking, the term "new covenant" only occurs in Jer 31:31.

probably no exaggeration to say that covenant is "the central theological concept" in Hebrews.[84] That it is also important to Paul is clear from his discussion in 2 Corinthians 3, with its allusions to the original covenant inauguration ceremony of Exodus 24:29–35.

What is less clear is *how* the death of Jesus brings about the new covenant.[85] Gorman affirms that "it is Jesus' death that is the covenant-creating and community-creating act," but *why* is it? In fairness, the New Testament itself does not answer this question. The throwback to the first covenant inauguration of Exodus 24, with its sprinkled blood (1 Pet 1:2), together with the covenant's wider setting of Passover and exodus from Egypt is assumed to be perfectly adequate. The rich associations with deliverance were enough, it seems. It is noteworthy, too, that Jesus chose Passover, not Yom Kippur, as the feast during which to inaugurate his new covenant, replete as Passover was with the imagery of a second exodus.[86] Jesus chose Passover as the "explanatory setting for what he had to do."[87]

A case can be made that, in extending the call to the gentiles, God was, through the atonement, making a way to extend an election that had once been specific to Israel. The atonement is a "universalized and radicalized version of Israel's election."[88] God, in creating the new covenant has simply extended the "boundary rope" around all the nations.[89] This requires an individual response just as it always did.[90] The main difference is that remaining "in Christ" replaces being "in Torah" as the main covenant obligation.[91] What I have just related is very much the "new perspective on Paul" way of seeing things: maximizing the continuities, minimizing the discontinuities, yet the angle is illuminating.

---

84. Gorman, *Death of the Messiah*, 16.

85. Gorman is helpful here and seems to represent a significant consensus among New Testament scholars today: "The appropriate perspective of Christian faith, therefore, is that the new covenant in which it claims to participate is not a *replacement* covenant but a *renewed* covenant, . . . the old has *become* the new for those who believe Jesus to be God's Messiah." Gorman, *Death of the Messiah*, 23. A useful resource discussing Israel and the church in relation to the phrase in Rom 11:26, "and so all Israel will be saved," is Zoccali, "'And so all Israel will be saved,'" 289–318.

86. Burnhope, *Atonement and the New Perspective*, 200.

87. Wright, *The Day the Revolution Began*, 277.

88. Burnhope, *Atonement and the New Perspective*, 174.

89. Burnhope, *Atonement and the New Perspective*, 175.

90. Burnhope, *Atonement and the New Perspective*, 174–78.

91. Burnhope, *Atonement and the New Perspective*, 182.

SACRIFICE

There is one place where covenant might have a metaphorical role in relation to atonement. It is Hebrews 9:16–17. Here, in the middle of a passage otherwise rich in vivid imagery from the cultus of ancient Israel, the writer seems to quite suddenly resort to an everyday non-religious use of *diathēkē*, covenant:[92] "Where a will [*diathēkē*] is involved, the death of the one who made it must be established. For a will [*diathēkē*] takes effect only at death, since it is not in force as long as the one who made it is alive."

Translators often intuit a change in the sense of *diathēkē* from what precedes and follows and use the words "will" or "testament" for verses 16–17, but "covenant" for all the other occurrences of the same word. If this change in the sense is supportable then it would primarily be about evidence of death being needed to activate the will and, secondarily, the release of the deceased's inheritance. Homiletically this inference has been easily drawn and can lead to some kind of allowable celebration of the death of the will-maker, which would, under normal circumstances, be completely unacceptable.[93] Even when inheriting a large estate from a relative, it is rare for the recipient to be openly glad about the relative's death. However, we may not even need to grapple with any of this. For a start, there is no evidence that Hellenistic wills and testaments could only come into effect after the death of the testator. There are plenty of examples of wills coming into effect while the testator was still alive. Secondly, there is a good case to be made for translating *diathēkē* in exactly the way the writer has been using it in the preceding verses. For reasons too involved to go into here, there is a lot of technical terminology in these two verses that is drawn from the Septuagint rather than from pagan Greek. There is strong evidence that the general principle the writer is referring to is a specifically *Old Testament* general principle. There, covenants were ratified by the subordinate party presenting an animal sacrifice. The death of the animal (evidenced by the sprinkling of blood on the people in the most important of them: Exodus 24) was understood to stand in for the death of the subjugated party. Death was implicitly acknowledged to be the penalty for breaking the stipulations of the covenant. It was a way of making the agreement binding in as serious a way possible. Hence, in an astonishingly thorough article of 1979, John

---

92. Paul does something very similar in Gal 3:15, though without any direct link being made to atonement themes.

93. E.g., Andrew Murray: "we may now claim and take the promise of the eternal inheritance. *A death having taken place!* Now *the testament avails.* The maker of the testament has died to put us in complete possession of all He had and all He won for us." *The Holiest of All*, 333.

Hughes offered the following translation of Hebrews 9:16–17: "For where there is a covenant, it is necessary to bring forward (i.e., to represent) the death of the one who ratifies (it). For a covenant is (made) legally secure on the basis of (or, 'over') the dead."[94]

Systematicians have wanted to confirm whether there is an absolute or relative necessity for the death of Christ, or even no necessity at all. The writer to the Hebrews affirms that the death of Christ was absolutely necessary within the logic of his argument. It was necessary so that Christ could bring to full consummation the old covenant, bearing in his own person the consequences of its having been so repeatedly and comprehensively broken. We could think also of Galatians 3:13: Christ takes upon himself the curse of breaking the covenant, curses so clearly spelled out in Deuteronomy 28:15–68 and centering on the punishment of exile. But, not only that, it was necessary for him to be, on behalf of humanity, the ratifier of the new covenant. This role prompts the writer to the Hebrews to use the title "mediator" of the new covenant (Heb 9:15), as though Jesus were the new Moses representing the subordinate party in the agreement. And the death brought forward to ratify this covenant is not the blood of a sacrificed animal but his own blood, as symbolically explained at the Last Supper.

There is just one more world of sacrifice to peer into before we move on: the sacrifices of the pagan world.

Greco-Roman Sacrifices and Propitiation

It has been long accepted that, in contrast to the God of Israel, pagan gods could be capricious and unpredictable. The gods and goddesses of the Greco-Roman pantheon, in particular, possessed all-too-human qualities of jealousy, petulance, and rage. The immense gulf between the behavior of the gods of the ancient world and the God of Israel has, understandably, been at the heart of discussions about the *hilaskomai* word group traditionally translated with words like "propitiation" or "sacrifice of atonement." The difficulty lies in the fact that this terminology seems to have been borrowed from pagan sacrificial rites.

It is well to note, first of all, that there is another side to the Greco-Roman picture. It has perhaps been assumed that great fear would have

---

94. Hughes, "Hebrews IX 15ff. and Galatians III 15ff," 42–43. For a balanced and more up-to-date discussion of the scholarly debate around Heb 9:16–17 see Hahn, "A Broken Covenant and the Curse of Death," 416–36.

filled the minds of the Greeks and Romans, fears that perhaps, out of all the many gods they worshipped, one had been left out, hence the altar in Athens entitled, "'To the Unknown God'" (Acts 17:23). However, it seems that, by the first century the Greco-Roman gods were in fact mostly understood to be passionless.[95] Further, and not unrelated to that, there is no evidence that the devotees felt any fear or guilt as they approached.[96] Just a glance at the art work on a Greek vase will show that easy-going festivity and indulgent celebration were meant to accompany the sacrifices. The gods too were assumed to be enjoying eating the meat of the sacrifice and joining with the worshippers in fellowship.[97] There also seems to have been an almost total absence of the very concept of forgiveness and in particular, no relationship was understood to exist between an animal having been sacrificed and forgiveness being procured for the offerer's sin, except in extreme cases, such as parricide or incest. Greco-Roman polytheists would have been completely nonplussed by the statement in Hebrews 10:18 that where transgressions have been forgiven there is no longer a need for an offering.

It may well be that the first Christians simply ignored all the pagan sacrificing that was going on all around them, with no connection understood to exist between pagan rituals and Christ's saving work.[98] Yet it is significant that both Paul (in Rom 3:25) and John (in John 2:2 and 4:10) associate Jesus ontologically with propitiation. He *is* the propitiation, the *hilasterion*, the *hilasmos*. These words all belong to what we call the *hilaskomai* word group and convey ideas about the pacifying or soothing of anger and its transformation into joy. The origin of the word group is *hilarotēs*, meaning "cheerful," literally "hilarious" (e.g., 2 Cor 9:7, God loves a "hilarious" giver). In *Atonement Theories* I briefly covered the debate about propitiation sparked by C. H. Dodd's decision that *hilaskomai* words should be translated into words about expiation, the removal of guilt, rather than propitiation, the removal of wrath.[99] The debate was fueled by the distaste that many scholars felt about attributing to God the kind of rage that must be soothed or

---

95. Braund, "The Anger of Tyrants and the Forgiveness of Kings," 96; Várhalyi, "'To Forgive is Divine,'" 130–31, both cited by Schnabel, "Jesus's Atoning Sacrifice," 72, 80.

96. Bremmer, "Greek Normative Animal Sacrifice," 139. See also, Faraone and Naiden (eds.), *Greek and Roman Animal Sacrifice*.

97. Schnabel, "Jesus's Atoning Sacrifice," 66–67.

98. Schnabel, "Jesus's Atoning Sacrifice," 79.

99. Pugh, *Atonement Theories*, 108–11. Dodd, *The Bible and the Greeks*, 93.

bribed by means of a violent death before God could then become cheerful enough to forgive us. Leon Morris' magisterial *Apostolic Preaching* was a happy byproduct of this debate. Though full of the attention to detail we would expect of Morris, the book is used repeatedly as a platform for sniping at anyone who wants to deny that God is a God of wrath and judgment, and who satisfies his wrath through the sacrifice of Christ.

There is perhaps some way of speaking of God being propitiated if the pagan gods' readiness to be bribed, to be bought off, is replaced by God's readiness to be persuaded, a wonderful quality seen throughout Scripture and in Christ himself.[100] Moreover, if, as we find in Anselm, agency is ascribed mainly to Christ rather than the Father—Christ freely offering rather than the Father cruelly punishing—there is a place for seeing the sacrifice of Christ as a propitiation.[101] It is a propitiation in the sense that, by Christ's free self-donation on behalf of humanity, judgment is averted. This was the crucial difference between Anselm and the Reformers. In the Reformers someone *must* be punished, and Christ steps in to take this undeserved judgment upon himself. In Anselm, judgment never needs to happen because the thing incurring the judgment has been more than compensated for in Christ the representative human. We will return to these reflections shortly.

Abbreviated Forms

We now come to the last stage in the development of a metaphor: the point at which it becomes abbreviated and incorporated into everyday language. We began with sacrifice-lite language: not yet very adventurous, and very much in line with everyday understandings about heroic deaths for others. But then we have, in the writer to the Hebrews, a burst of elaborate descriptions of priesthood, holy place, and sacrificial animals. The superficially improbable likeness drawn between animal sacrifices and the death of Christ is given credibility by the use of the word "obedience," which acknowledges and proclaims the very real *difference* between the source and the target of the metaphor. The metaphor is thus strengthened by the fact that, in Hebrews, its *dis*similarity is openly and yet edifyingly explored as

---

100. Derek Kidner cites the example of Christ's interactions with the persuasive Syro-Phoenician woman: Kidner, "Sacrifice," 121. See also Bailey, "Jesus as the Mercy Seat," 155–58 and his Cambridge PhD thesis of the same title.

101. See my defense of him in *Atonement Theories*, 45–62.

SACRIFICE

well as its similarity. This happens for none of the other metaphors. Now, the final phase is the reduction to little phrases exclaimed in worship and seasoning theological discourse. The journey from simple sayings to fully expounded metaphor to little phrases and words is the result of the success of a metaphor. It becomes language. It becomes symbol and sign. In our case, it becomes "Lamb of God" and "the Lamb" and it becomes "blood of Jesus" and "his blood."

The Lamb

When New Testament writers use "Lamb" as an abbreviated metaphor no elaboration is thought necessary. Christ is referred to as the Lamb or the Lamb of God numerous times in the book of Revelation,[102] as well as by John the Baptist in John 1:29. In only two places is Jesus referred to as a lamb with the referent made explicit: there is 1 Peter 1:18–19 where Jesus is the lamb without blemish, a clear echo of the Levitical requirements that applied to all the offerings. And there is 1 Corinthians 5:7: "Christ our Passover Lamb has been sacrificed for us." These are the only passages that tell us where the image came from.

Most discussion has centered on the vaguest of them all: John 1:29: "Behold, the Lamb of God who takes away the sin of the world." Of the many options, the four most likely ones are, firstly: it is a reference to the Servant of Isaiah 53, especially his having been led away like a lamb (Isa 53:7; also Acts 8:32),[103] or it could be a reference to the Passover lamb as per Paul's usage and the heavy allusions to Passover in John's crucifixion narrative (John 19:14, 29, 31, 33–36, 42),[104] or it could be a reference to the

---

102. Twenty-eight times, according Daly, *Sacrifice Unveiled*, 67.

103. This is favored by Daly who asserts that, "only here do we have a personal title capable of carrying the full breadth of Christological meaning associated with the title: the Lamb." Daly, *Sacrifice Unveiled*, 67. It also had former Archbishop George Carey's cautious and not exclusive backing: "Lamb of God and Atonement Theories," 120. Also Taylor, *Jesus and His Sacrifice*, 227.

104. An interesting aside here is John's reference to blood and water flowing from the side of Christ (19:34), which is given particular stress in the verse following: "(he who saw this has testified so that you also may believe. His testimony is true, and he knows that he tells the truth)." Rabbinically, it was important that the blood shed from the Passover lamb was not allowed to congeal—even to the point where the bowls for collecting the fresh flowing blood did not have a flat bottom and so could not be rested on the ground. The blood was to be tossed at the altar while still fully liquid. Such blood was described in the Talmud as blood that was "as water." Josephine Massingberd Ford

lambs that were sometimes offered as sin offerings (Lev 4:32–35), the lamb standing in symbolically for all other animals (bulls, goats) that could be offered. Similarly, some have claimed that it refers to the daily burnt offerings.[105] Fourthly and lastly, a reference to gentleness is thought possible by some, owing to the precedent in Jeremiah: "But I was like a gentle lamb led to the slaughter" (Jer 11:19). However, it is unlikely that this one reference was well known enough to have awakened this kind of recognition in John the Baptist's hearers, and neither is there, in this passage, a reference to the taking away of sins. This is not to say the previous three options: Servant, Passover, sin offering/burnt offering are without their problems too.[106]

Probably the wisest solution has been that offered by Leon Morris in his *Apostolic Preaching*. The reference must be to a sacrificial lamb, otherwise the reference to taking away sins would seem out of place, yet to be more specific than that seems to run against the grain of John's literary style. John often leaves phrases susceptible of more than one meaning. He wants us, it seems, to be able to hold together a wealth of meanings.[107] To go with the grain of John would be to allow "Lamb of God" to stand for the whole sacrificial system that Christ came to fulfil and supersede, and, within that, the picture of Isaiah's sin-bearing Servant, who is led away like a lamb, is not impossible.

---

put forward the suggestion that the "blood and water" flowing in John 19:34 is actually reflecting a Jewish idiom relating to Passover: "blood as water." In a tiny little study for *New Testament Studies*, she offered this translation: "And there came out immediately blood even fluid," concluding then that John 19 contains three allusions to Passover: the hyssop of v. 29, the unbroken bones of vv. 33, 36, and the watery flowing blood of v. 34: Ford, "'Mingled Blood' from the Side of Christ," 337–38.

105. Hoskyns, *The Fourth Gospel*, 169: "Salvation from sin depends upon that sacrifice of which the lambs, consecrated morning and evening in the Temple to be the possession of God, provide the proper analogy."

106. Carey discusses these very diligently: Carey, "Lamb of God and Atonement Theories," passim.

107. Morris gives the "In the beginning" of John 1:1 and the "Born again/born from above" of John 3 as examples of this Johannine habit: *The Apostolic Preaching of the Cross*, 129–30. Carey makes a similar point about John's use of OT imagery in a way that is fluid and often cannot be tied down to a particular passage: Carey, "Lamb of God and Atonement Theories," 107–12.

Sacrifice

The Blood

References to the "blood" are the most common New Testament way of speaking in shorthand of the atoning value of the death of Jesus. To make sense of this use of blood language it is important to give attention to the interpretation we might place upon the prohibition on the eating of blood in Leviticus 17:11 and 14 since whatever we agree on here will have a profound effect upon what we then take the sacrificial system as a whole to mean. Historically, there have three main developments:

Evidence of Death and Divine Convention

On this view, the places where blood was smeared or sprinkled were almost always places within God's space, God's domain. For ordinary Israelites blood would only come as far as the horns of the altar of burnt offering in the Outer Court. For priests it would be brought into the Holy Place. Then, once a year, the blood would be taken all the way into the Most Holy Place by the high priest to be sprinkled on and in front of the *kipporeth*, the *hilasterion*, the lid of the ark of the covenant. The blood could enter as far as the person being atoned for could enter.[108] Only in cases of cleansing "lepers," the consecration of priests, and in the once-only inauguration of the covenant itself in Exodus 24, is blood sprinkled upon the people. This would seem to suggest that the blood was not so much a life-force to be applied *to* the people, but a token of life that has been given *for* the people. It is brought into God's spaces as evidence of death,[109] or of life given rather than as life released.

Another angle, which need not entirely contradict the "evidence of death" approach, is that blood was used simply because of divinely ordained convention. If so then we can see how the blood stands *for* the life taken (Lev 17:11, 14). It stands for it because God declares it so and when blood is offered it represents life offered.[110] In that case, a translation of Leviticus 17:11 such as the following would be apt: "For the life animating the creature is represented by the blood and I have reserved the blood for

---

108. Romerowski, "Old Testament Sacrifices and Reconciliation," 20.

109. Nicole, "Atonement in the Pentateuch," 46; Romerowski, "Old Testament Sacrifices and Reconciliation," 17.

110. Blocher, *La Doctrine du péché et de la redemption*, 132, cited in Romerowski, "Old Testament Sacrifices and Reconciliation," 17.

you, for use at the altar, so that you make atonement for yourselves; yes, it is the blood that makes atonement, by the life which it represents, the life which the animal has been deprived of."[111] This then makes it easier to see how, in cases of extreme poverty, the blood sacrifice for the sin offering could be replaced by a cereal offering: it is purely a matter of divinely instituted convention.[112] Clearly, though, a cereal offering takes us well outside the "evidence of death" explanation and inclines me to gravitate to the gift character of sacrifice to which the killing of an animal need not be the central defining act, but the act of giving up or handing over. Somehow, where an animal rather than cereal was involved, the manipulation of blood was central to that act of giving to God.

Expiation for the Murder of the Animal

In an article in 1971 Jacob Milgrom offered the first point of departure that could be grasped at by scholars who were keen to find a way to undermine distasteful penal substitutionary interpretations of the sacrificial system.[113] It was thought that vicarious and propitiatory meanings were being too readily read *into* the Levitical codes in support of a certain Christian soteriology, with all other possible significances being left behind. Milgrom's view was that to shed the blood of an animal, even for food, was an act of murder, which must be expiated by the offering of sacrificial blood upon the altar. This is not an idea that has found widespread support.

Release of Life

The original significance of blood within the Levitical cult is described in Leviticus 17:11 as centering on the fact that life is in the blood. The blood carries life, and in 17:14, this blood *is* the life of every creature. Finlan interprets both verses as referring to something like what we might describe as an electric current carrying a positive charge. This positive life-charge neutralizes the negative charge that the pollution of sin brings.[114] The life-

111. Romerowski, "Old Testament Sacrifices and Reconciliation," 18.

112. Romerowski, "Old Testament Sacrifices and Reconciliation," 18.

113. Milgrom, "A Prolegomenon to Leviticus 17:11," 149–56. The view was adopted by Joshua Porter, *Leviticus*. Emile Nicole seems to be aware of others who also adopted the idea: Nicole, "Atonement in the Pentateuch," 35 n2.

114. Finlan, *Problems with Atonement*, 13.

SACRIFICE

force undoes the death-force brought about by impurity.[115] Cleansing rituals involving the manipulation of blood lead to people being forgiven (Lev 4:20, 26, 31, 35; 5:10, 13, 18).[116]

This trend towards seeing the blood as a life-force released has been growing in popularity and can be traced at least as far back as B. F. Westcott's commentary on 1 John, the first edition of which was published in 1883.[117] He claimed, on the basis of Leviticus 17, that shed blood signifies life released rather than life taken, and has been followed by scholars of considerable repute.[118] The sacrifices, therefore, had no atoning significance, and the death of Christ therefore was also not about substitutionary sacrifice and his blood was not about propitiating wrath. Rather, his blood was to inaugurate a blood covenant in a sense analogous to blood brothers intermingling their blood.[119] Westcott's main basis for his argument was what he described as a "fundamental Passage":[120] John 6:53–56, where he points out that "participation in Christ's blood is participation in his life."[121] By contrast, Alan Stibbs claimed starkly that "[New Testament] writers who speak of 'the blood of Christ' are interested not in the material substance but in the shed blood, that is, in the death of Christ. For the shedding of blood involves the destruction of the seat of life."[122]

In fact, neither position seems entirely satisfactory: one of which only affirms the life-giving quality of blood, which makes us attribute magic to the worshipers, and the other only affirms its death-evidencing function,

115. Finlan, *Problems with Atonement*, 13.
116. Finlan, *Problems with Atonement*, 17.
117. Westcott, *The Epistles of John*, 34–37, under the heading "The Idea of Christ's Blood in the New Testament."
118. Stibbs listed Nathaniel Micklem, Vincent Taylor, C. H. Dodd, O. C. Quick, Bishop Edward Hicks, P. T. Forsyth, Sanday and Headlam: Stibbs, *The Meaning of the Word "Blood" in Scripture*, 4–7.
119. For an interesting exploration of this possibility from an anthropological perspective but which has been surprisingly influential upon the Word of Faith movement see: Trumbull, *The Blood Covenant*. He cites Westcott with approval (ibid., 212, 214). See also Kenneth Copeland's *Covenant of Blood*.
120. Wescott, *Epistles of John*, 36.
121. Wescott, *Epistles of John*, 36.
122. Stibbs, *Meaning of the Word "Blood" in Scripture*, 8. He bases this not only on the liturgical texts but on a mountain of other texts, such as the blood used as evidence that a wild beast had devoured Joseph. Stibbs' little book literally is a survey of all the uses of the word "blood" in Scripture, including everyday uses. This seems to end up skewing the data towards a bland "evidence of death" interpretation.

which makes the worshipers seem a bit sadistic. It seems to me that by placing gift-giving rather than killing at the center of the sacrifices, the fog begins to clear. What do we think might have been going on in the minds of worshipers as they explained to themselves why they were handing over a perfect animal in the prime of its life to be slaughtered and dismembered by a priest? It was costly. It hurt. But the reasoning would have been that it was worth it, that it pleased God. It was a gesture of putting him first. It was not sacrifice in the sense of killing, as though in the divine scheme of things, some creature somewhere has to die. It is we who have imposed the concept of fixed penalties on the sacrifices. It was sacrifice in the sense that we use the word "sacrifice" in everyday language today: salary sacrifice, making big sacrifices for the kids and so on. It was a necessary but freely offered loss for a greater good.

Conclusion

In conclusion I must admit that, with the writing of this chapter (which I actually wrote quite late, after chapters 1, 3, 4, 6, and 7) I can sense that I will be finishing a different kind of book to the one I started. I started thinking that I would be able to accent the themes of participation in Christ; that I would find that the New Testament is in fact full to the brim of recapitulation and theosis themes of the kind I so enjoyed exploring for *Atonement Theories* and *Old Rugged Cross*. What I actually find is that the New Testament writers mainly understand the death of Christ as a sacrifice for sin. This is heart and center. They would have seen participation as the only way for believers to actually partake of the benefits of atonement but this was not the atonement *itself*. It will never do to take the Anglo-Saxon at-one-ment and say that is it: wherever we see oneness, union, reconciliation, harmony, and peace, that *is* atonement. Biblically, this is a category mistake. However, we have also seen that the death and resurrection of Christ was a victory. It was a victory over the powers, and that victory is experienced by us as liberation via our participation by faith and in the Spirit. This first series of metaphorical explorations responded to the fact that Christ rose from the dead. These pictures were of his death *in the light of his resurrection and glorification*. However, it would soon have been necessary to answer the question: "So why did he die at all?" The sacrifice metaphor is an explanation of the reason for the death of Christ, and it is this explanation that the earliest Christians treasured above all else. This is the second peak

Sacrifice

of interpretation, giving us the second ontological definition of what the atonement actually was. We will see that this sacrifice for sin resulted in the justification of sinners and their reconciliation to God. But ontologically, it was a victory and it was a sacrifice.

It is in the sacrifice metaphor that we are confronted with the most difficult theological problems, and these have already proved impossible to avoid in this chapter. John Stott, in his *The Cross of Christ*, gave us a brilliantly nuanced understanding of penal substitution as though in anticipation of all the controversy the doctrine would be mired in twenty years later. He went out of his way to portray God as being *in Christ* reconciling the world to himself. He gave us a portrait of God so seamlessly identified with the crucified Jesus of Nazareth that, in an extension of patripassionism, it is the whole Godhead undergoing the ordeal. Then, in order to preserve the central role of the justice of God in penal substitution, Stott needed to portray God as absorbing in himself all the punishment due for human sin. There is no escape, even for God, from God's justice. Stott never contemplates making the easy move of Grotius and simply changing the image of Judge, who must uphold the law, to Governor, who is free to make or rescind those laws (or to be "persuaded" as we saw earlier).[123] Rather, the self-substituting God of Stott is a reaction to the punishing God of the cruder interpretations of penal substitution. The God who punishes his own Son because it is the only way he can forgive us is replaced by a self-punishing God who must go through this for the same reason: because it's the only way he can forgive us. To put it crudely, we exchange "cosmic child abuse" for something more like cosmic self-harm: God "sacrificing himself to himself?"[124]

It may be beneficial to reiterate the "is" and "is-not" tension contained in any metaphor. Not every aspect of the source is freighted within the new picture; much is left behind. Even were we to assume the New Testament writers adopted the Levitical system wholesale, unfiltered, as an interpretational grid for the sacrifice of Christ, we would need to bear in mind how doubtful it is that any of the sacrificed animals—even the scapegoat— would have been understood as being punished in place of the offerers. They were bearing away sin. The gift character of the sacrifices meant that they had compensating power, power not to absorb punishment for sin, but to avert it.

123. See Pugh, *Atonement Theories*, 133–36.
124. Bradley, *Power of Sacrifice*, 106.

PICTURES OF ATONEMENT

Yet the sacrificial system is not used without qualification when Christ's death is described as a sacrifice. The New Testament writers tend to access the Levitical system for pictures via the human sin offering depicted in Isaiah 53. Peter tells us that "He himself bore our sins in his body on the cross, so that, free from sins, we might live for righteousness; by his wounds you have been healed," and Paul, that, "For our sake he made him to be sin [that is, a sin offering, a *peri hamartias*] who knew no sin, so that in him we might become the righteousness of God," and Phillip explains to the Ethiopian Eunuch the meaning of the Septuagint of Isaiah 53:7b–8a: "Like a sheep he was led to the slaughter, and like a lamb silent before its shearer, so he does not open his mouth. In his humiliation justice was denied him. Who can describe his generation? For his life is taken away from the earth." He says to the eunuch that this is the good news about Jesus (Acts 8:32–35).

In the Masoretic Text of Isaiah 53, there are cues in verses 5, 6, and 10 for a fully penal reading: God punishes for our peace, lays on him the iniquity of us all, and it was "the will of the LORD to crush him with pain" (NRSV), thus making the Servant's soul an offering for sin. The Septuagint eliminates the penal implications of verse 10, changing it to: "The Lord also is pleased to purge him from his stroke. If ye can give an offering for sin, your soul shall see a long-lived seed" (Brenton). Verse 6 is softened so that the Lord is giving up the Servant for our sins rather than the Lord laying on him the iniquity of us all. Verse 5, the bearing of chastisement leading to peace, seems close to the Masoretic, though this verse is arguably less problematic as it does not explicitly ascribe this action to "the Lord."

What we see in the New Testament when sacrificial imagery is explored is a very similar reluctance to directly ascribe agency to the Father as the one afflicting the scourged and crucified Christ. In *Atonement Theories* I identified Martin Luther's commentary on Galatians of 1535 as the earliest point I could find for an explicitly penal substitutionary interpretation of atonement. Specifically, it is in his exposition of Galatians 3:13. Here, the crucified Christ is told to be Peter the denier, David the adulterer, the sinner who at the fruit in paradise, to be the person who has committed all the sins of everyone. Standing in for God, the law receives full personification: "the law comes and says, 'I find him a sinner . . . let him die on the cross.'"[125] Calvin followed suit in similar fashion in his *Institutes* where Christ becomes Adam in order to present our flesh and pay the due

---

125. Luther, *Galatians*, writing on 3:13.

Sacrifice

penalty.[126] Possibly helped along by changes in the criminal justice system in early modern Europe towards detailed fixed penalties for every crime, the image of inflicting a penalty seems to have acquired a dominant position within evangelical preaching over the centuries that followed.

In fairness to Luther and Calvin, Christ bearing the curse of the law, especially if the judgments threatened in Deuteronomy 28 are what is intended, points to God as cause, even if his causation is not made explicit in Galatians 3:13. More explicit is 2 Corinthians 5:21, where God "made [*epoiēsen*] him to be sin." The Greek points to "causation or appointment."[127] It seems clear that the Father's agency in the suffering of Christ was an angle on the atonement that Paul, at least, was aware of and thought about, especially in the light of the apparently tragic yet ultimately triumphant Suffering Servant figure. What seems to happen in the development of the doctrine of penal substitution between the Reformation and the Princeton theologians of the nineteenth century is that one possible way of reflecting on atonement—one that is approached with extreme caution by the New Testament writers—becomes the all-encompassing way.

By way of contrast, if we allow the gift character of sacrifices greater prominence in our understanding of Levitical theology, we are able to see in a fresh way how important the idea was that Christ freely offered himself. He "*gave* himself for our sins to set us free from the present evil age" (Gal 1:4), he "loved me and *gave* himself for me" (Gal 2:20), he "*gave* himself up for us, a fragrant offering and sacrifice to God" (Eph 5:2), he "*gave* himself up for" the church (Eph 5:25), he "*gave* himself a ransom for all" (1 Tim 2:6), and "*gave* himself for us that he might redeem us from all iniquity" (Titus 2:14).

In short, the New Testament is shy of saying the Father did this to him, loves proclaiming that he did this himself. And this loving self-gift allows us to incorporate the whole of his life of obedience (Rom 5:12–21; Phil 2:5–11) as an offering of fully human humanity, a whole offering that pleases God so much that it averts judgment for all those who claim allegiance to him and bow to his reign.

---

126. Calvin, *Institutes of the Christian Religion* II.12.3.
127. Harris, *The Second Epistle to the Corinthians*, 451.

Reflection

1. The idea of a heroic death for others is as cherished today is it was in ancient times, and the New Testament makes use of this idea but, in one place, twists it into a death for the undeserving, a much less familiar idea (Rom 5:6–8). Might this idea of a heroic death, which turns out to be for the undeserving, be a good way in as you seek to find relevant ways of speaking of Christ's sacrifice to those who do not believe?

2. "For by one offering he has perfected forever those who are being sanctified" (Heb 10:14 NKJV), he "suffered for sins once for all" (1 Pet 3:18). In what ways does the total sufficiency and finality of Christ's self-offering bring you comfort?

3. The worshiping church of today understandably makes a lot of use of the worship songs of Revelation which celebrate the Lamb seated on the throne. Have words like "Lamb" and "blood of Christ" been helpful to you in your worship or do they need some unpacking?

CHAPTER 6

Justification

Introduction

THE BIGGEST QUESTION HERE is: Is justification a metaphor at all?[1] But that is not the only question. The second question is equally drastic: Is justification even related in any direct way to the atonement or is it understood in the New Testament to occur mainly on some other basis? To describe justification as a metaphor is itself to frame it in forensic terms before we have had the chance to decide what it is. A forensic, legal understanding of what it entails goes hand-in-hand with its standing as a law court metaphor. And there are further ramifications: with a judicial act of justification comes the requirement to picture God as judge, humanity in the dock, and the conferring of a new status of harmony with the claims of God's law. This again prejudges many things and commits us too early to a suite of Reformation ideas treasured by some, loathed by others. Such a view would quite readily show itself as related to the atonement but, again, commits us, willingly or otherwise, to a particular view of the atonement as a penal substitutionary sacrifice: Christ bears the legal penalty so that humanity in the dock can be acquitted by God the Judge. Indeed, I made the point in *Atonement Theories* that we could even view penal substitution as a justification-eye-view of the

1. McIntyre does not include it: *Shape of Soteriology*, 26–52. Gunton does but does not engage extensively with the New Testament, preferring to keep his study of atonement metaphors firmly within the discipline of historical theology: *Actuality of Atonement*, 83–113. Stott does famously include justification as a law-court image set alongside the temple, market place, and home images of propitiation, redemption, and reconciliation respectively. This works very well but inevitably prejudges the issue of a penal view of atonement: Stott, *Cross of Christ*, 195–236.

atonement, a doctrine of atonement shaped to fit the Reformation emphasis on justification by faith.

However, developments in the study of Paul over the past half a century and more mean that this forensic option is not by any means the only option on the table. We need neither prematurely accept it nor dismiss it out of hand. Having said that, if it turns out not to be a legal metaphor and not directly related to the atonement, its very status as a chapter in this book stands in jeopardy. But now I'm just sounding over-dramatic.

We will start with a brief review of three options now available to us, which I am hoping are reasonably representative of Pauline studies at the present time. Here, we are naively asking the simple question, What is justification? Which one of the three answers should be chosen, or which combination of them, will hopefully be clarified by attempting after that a study of the likely origins, first of the *concept* and then of the *language* of justification in Paul. Hopefully, we will, along the way, identify whether or not a metaphor is being used, say, from the law courts, and identify how it has been assembled.

What Is It?

A Forensic Declaration: The Old Perspective on Paul (OPP)

This view depends upon a reading of Paul's discussion of God as "just and the justifier" (Rom 3:25) as absolutely reliant upon the atonement as the only solution that squares this circle: God can be both just and justifier because of the propitiatory sacrifice that Paul has just mentioned. This alone then provides the logical underpinning for God being the justifier of the ungodly (Rom 4:5), as well as the reference to Christ being delivered up for our offences and raised for our justification (Rom 4:25) and the reason for the shorthand reference to atonement in Romans 5:9: "justified by his blood." However, within the ranks of those who have adhered to the traditional view, there has been a tendency to abstract justification from atonement, typified by, and perhaps influenced by, John Murray's classic work, *Redemption: Accomplished and Applied*. There has been a tendency within Reformed systematics to locate justification squarely with the *ordo salutis* as part of the *application* of the work of Christ, while atonement tends to be looked at in detail only in what is normally the preceding chapter in a

JUSTIFICATION

systematic theology: the one dealing with the person and work of Christ.[2] Yet, when we read Paul, we find no such division at all.

However, if we do allow a forensic declaration of "not guilty," there is the issue of whether, for the ancients, there was such a thing as a purely legal declaration of innocence. Downing has pointed out that there is no exact equivalent to the modern judicial idea of being acquitted. The Greco-Roman world seems to have known of no division between the formal status conferred in a legal proceeding and the practical effect of it; no distinction between guilt and punishment.[3] To "justify the wicked," therefore, is not to declare someone innocent who is not, but, despite their guilt, to refuse to authorize their punishment.[4] Likewise, in the Old Testament, especially in Job, it is well-being that is sought after as establishing innocence. For as long as Job was suffering he seemed to his friends to be guilty of some unknown sin for which God was punishing him (e.g., Job 9:35; 13:21, 23; 23:27).[5] Downing's conclusion chimes with Douglas Campbell that justification, the decision to leave unpunished, is nothing more or less than a simple "exercise of divine royal prerogative."[6]

Another problem is the idea of retributive justice, which presents an unacceptable picture of God to many people today. Non-forensic categories are often sought for both atonement and justification. There is an understandable desire to frame the good news in concepts of atonement and justification that affirm the benevolence of God, the transformation of communities, and the liberation of individuals. The strength of the two views of justification that we will now look at is that these clearly deliver on all three of these desiderata: in the "new perspective," the loving covenant faithfulness of God replaces immutable retributive justice and corporate inclusion replaces the introspective conscience, while, in the "apocalyptic" view the liberation of believers through participation in Christ replaces a change of legal standing with God, which is slated as scandalously non-transformative.

---

2. Robert Letham devotes a chapter of his *The Work of Christ* to overturning this unhelpful separation between the two doctrines, as well as the equally unhelpful abstraction of justification from sanctification: *The Work of Christ*, 177–94.

3. Downing, "Justification as Acquittal?" 300.

4. Downing, "Justification as Acquittal?" 303.

5. Downing, "Justification as Acquittal?" 309.

6. Downing, "Justification as Acquittal?" 318.

PICTURES OF ATONEMENT

A Means of Inclusion: The New Perspective on Paul (NPP)

Gary Burnett, writing in 2011, pointedly observes:

> [In] New Testament studies over the past twenty-five years . . . more and more emphasis has been given to the relevance of texts to questions of collective identity and social cohesion, and less and less importance attached to how the texts might address issues more to do with the individual, the salvation of the individual and individual behavior.[7]

It is arguable that, even if E. P. Sanders' *Paul and Palestinian Judaism* had never been published, a corporate reading of justification in Paul would have come about some other way. This is simply because of the shift in cultural mood in the West away from rugged individualism and towards an emphasis on the inclusion of the marginalized. There is a new collectivism that goes hand-in-hand with what Réné Girard celebrates as the postmodern concern for victims,[8] a concern for those that once were on the losing side in the onward march of science and progress.

The new perspective stance arrives at its inclusive outcome by way of two prior stages. Firstly, it affirms that Judaism all along was defined by its grateful response to God's electing grace and was never about trying to be saved via religious legalism. The law served as the means of staying in the covenant, not getting in, an arrangement described by Sanders as "covenantal nomism." It was nomistic in that it had reference to an interpretation of the *nomos*, the law that was governing that covenant, but it was not *legalistic* in that it knew little of the approach, common to all religions, of using ethical and ascetic rigors to procure the favor of God. Even the Pharisees of Paul's day, therefore, were not legalists. No, the problem that emerged was more like what we would today call "nationalism." And this is the second stage in the argument. Israel, perhaps in response to its experiences of invasion, exile, and oppression from the nations, had pulled up the drawbridge of its ethnic identity and closed itself off from the gentiles by means of three boundary markers: circumcision, Sabbath-keeping (which was very legalistic but for ethnic, not soteriological reasons), and food laws.[9]

---

7. Burnett, *Paul and the Salvation of the Individual*, 1.

8. "Our society is the most preoccupied with victims of any that ever was. . . . No historical period, no society we know, has ever spoken of victims as we do, . . . a great anthropological first." He goes on: "it is quite obviously Christian. Humanism and humanitarianism develop first on Christian soil." Girard, *I See Satan Fall Like Lightning*, 161, 163.

9. It was James D. G. Dunn who pioneered this threefold concept of what Paul is

JUSTIFICATION

Whatever it was that Paul was arguing against in Galatians, Romans, and Philippians, therefore, cannot have been the soteriology of Second Temple Judaism, since this already held to a form of salvation by grace. And so here is the inclusive outcome of the NPP position. God had already shown his grace to Israel. What Paul was opposing was not some supposed attempt to construe salvation as only possible if you keep lots of rules. Paul was opposing the ethnic exclusionary practices of Jews: not Jews as a whole, but specifically those Jews who had embraced the Messiah, and who therefore ought to have known better. These Jews were in churches where the majority of members were gentiles yet they had not given up their exclusionary ideas. The Judaizers, as we call them, were doing the rounds of Paul's churches actively promoting the idea that the only way for gentile believers to be members of the Jewish covenant is to adopt the three Jewish identity markers, especially circumcision.

On this view, justification, though it may be construed as forensic and declarative in some sense, is primarily an attribute or action of God, or an attribute *in* action, loosely equivalent to the idea of God's covenant faithfulness. This faithfulness of God is not really very much to do with us the beneficiaries in the first instance, and is not a legal metaphor but finds its origins in the story of God's dealings with Israel. It is, however, related to the atonement in that the representative Suffering Servant figure is the climax of God's covenant faithfulness. The Christ event is the means by which God has shown himself faithful to his promises. But justification, on this view, was never the answer to the supposed soteriological legalism that has been assumed to have corrupted Judaism to its very core.

As a result of all this, when it came to the full inclusion of gentiles into God's covenant, Paul argued for the abandonment of the three ethnic boundary markers as the condition of that inclusion. Jews who had embraced their Messiah should throw open their doors to gentiles who had also believed in the Christ, thus making "one new man from the two." There would be "neither Jew nor Greek, neither slave nor free, neither male nor female" (Gal 3:28). And this is how we arrive at a corporate view of justification. God, out of sheer loving faithfulness to Israel, has brought about his own fulfilment of all covenant obligations, thus opening up the covenant to everyone. All Jewish Christ-believers therefore must echo God's acceptance of all by not putting any stumbling blocks in the way of gentiles. Instead, they must receive those others just as God in Christ received them.

---

opposing: Dunn, *The Theology of Paul the Apostle*, 359–66.

Such ideas can be readily embraced today. Many of us might be in churches where some supposedly divinely sanctioned boundary marker is being appealed to as a way of dividing one class of Christians from another. Indeed, has not the emergence of so many confessional groups and denominational splinterings been precisely this: a failure to echo God's justification and pass it on to one another? The NPP forces us to take seriously the relational implications of grace.

The NPP perspective, however, places this relational element front and center, not as an outworking of justification but as its very definition. There are real problems with this. As I will shortly discuss, Psalm 143:2: "Do not enter into judgment with your servant, for no one living is righteous before you," forms the background to two key verses in Paul: Galatians 2:16 and 3:20, both of which are pivotal moments in his argument. The psalm clearly envisages the plight of the individual standing before God. It might well be asked, why would Paul be using such a psalm if the problem he was addressing was a corporate, ethnic one?[10] The tormented conscience highlighted by Stendahl[11] so many years ago, is a human thing, not just a Western thing.[12]

Further, as Hassler has pointed out, even if the problem is not with law-keeping *per se*, even the identity-marking aspects of the law are still law, therefore still legalism of sorts.[13] The differences seem too subtle and evidence of precisely the soteriological legalism that Sanders inveighed against, too great.[14] There is evidence that the rabbinic idea of God weighing up a person's good works and bad works in the balance at the end of life, then deciding on that person's eternal destiny, was more than just a side show. Inevitably, the evidence of legalism increases as one widens the scope to include all forms of first-century Judaism. Sanders narrowed himself to

---

10. Hassler, "Ethnocentric Legalism," 323.

11. Stendahl, "The Apostle Paul and the Introspective Conscience of the West," 199–215.

12. Hassler, "Ethnocentric Legalism," 326.

13. Hassler, 'Ethnocentric Legalism,' 322.

14. 4 Ezra seems to be especially full of the very legalism which supports the OPP, with many passages envisaging eschatological judgment resting on such things as a "treasury of works" (4 Ezra 6:5; 7:76–77; 8:33; 9:7–8; 13:23). However, a recent study has pushed back on this: deSilva, "Grace, the Law and Justification in 4 Ezra and the Pauline Letters: A Dialogue," 25–49, arguing that the author of 4 Ezra is urging a grateful response to God's gracious giving of the Torah, not a legalistic self-righteousness.

JUSTIFICATION

Palestinian Judaism: the rabbis and Qumran, ignoring the Hellenistic and apocalyptic forms, both crucial to an understanding of the New Testament.

At the very least, the claims of NPP were exaggerated and set too starkly over and against the OPP. Even James D. G. Dunn now describes it as merely a "worthwhile hiccup in the ongoing process of receiving what Paul has still to say about the gospel for today."[15] Wright, meanwhile, has developed his position into a both/and scenario in which the early Paul (in Galatians) is speaking only in terms of membership of the covenant, with no legal metaphor in view and only later (in Romans) sees fit to create the courtroom drama and shift to a fully forensic view of justification.[16] John Piper, Wright's chief opponent, remains frustrated that Wright's concept does not seem to have anything to say to "me" the reader in need of a gracious God.

A Liberating Transformation: The Apocalyptic View

The founding father of this view is Douglas Campbell. Most often cited is his landmark book *The Deliverance of God: An Apocalyptic Rereading of Justification in Paul* of 2009, though the same ideas were already articulated in his *The Quest for Paul's Gospel* of 2005, and build on the work of J. Louis Martyn.[17] Followers include Martinus de Boer (a student of Martyn's) and Beverley Roberts Gaventa.[18] The terminology is confusing as "apocalyptic" does not necessarily mean that this group of scholars are basing their views on apocalyptic texts within the Judaism of the period. When Campbell uses the term he seems to mostly have in mind the Greek word *apocalypsis*, an unveiling, a revealing, as it appears in Romans 1:17, though he concedes that the term is misleading.[19] He is making the point that God's saving, liberative, righteousness comes forth from God gratuitously, without any conditions or criteria, as a *fiat*. It is pure revelation.

---

15. Dunn, *The New Perspective on Paul*, 182. See Shaw, "Romans 4 and the Justification of Abraham in Light of Perspectives New and Newer," 50–62 for a helpful overview of the state of play as it looked in 2015.

16. Wright, *Paul and the Faithfulness of God*, 933; 965.

17. Martyn, *Theological Issues in the Letters of Paul*; Martyn, *Galatians: A New Translation with Introduction and Commentary*.

18. Gaventa (ed.), *Apocalyptic Paul: Cosmos and Anthropos in Romans 5–8*.

19. Campbell, *Quest for Paul's Gospel*, 4, 56.

Campbell is influenced by E. P. Sanders and his phrase "participationist eschatology."[20] "Pneumatologically Participatory Martyrological Eschatology" is Campbell's catchy descriptor; PPME for short. The best explanation for it I can find is in *Quest for Paul's Gospel*:

> [A]s the Spirit configures people to the template of Christ—specifically to his descent into death and ascent into glory—they too are thereby delivered from their present oppressed and corrupted condition by means of its termination in Christ's execution and their recreation in a new liberated and transformed condition that is grafted onto his resurrected existence and is now no longer inhabited by the powers of Sin and Death.[21]

In this earlier work, Campbell points out that the heart of Paul's gospel must be in one of the following: Romans 1-4 (the traditional justification by faith model) *or* in Romans 5-8 (the proposed PPME model) *or* in Romans 9-11 (the NPP model), but it cannot be in all three. By the time he writes *Deliverance of God* he is on the war path specifically against the first model, which he calls "justification theory" (JF) and seems determined to eliminate it. "Justification," he claims, "must adapt to a brave new world—or quietly expire."[22] Perhaps the most slated move he makes is to relegate most of Romans 1-4 (specifically 1:18—3:20)—the section which supports JF—to an opponent of Paul's called the Teacher, whom Paul is quoting (echoing similar moves J. Louis Martyn made for Galatians). Campbell's point seems in need of better evidence, especially since his position rests so heavily upon being able to discount the most explicit "retributive" section of Romans.

De Boer and Gaventa have each strengthened the case for PPME by way of a close reading Galatians 2:17-20.[23] The fact that, in this passage, Paul is able to make so frictionless a transition from talk of justification by faith to talk of having been crucified with Christ and apparently living Christ's life, brings the ready conclusion that "The canvas on which

---

20. E.g., Sanders, *Paul and Palestinian Judaism*, 522. This, in turn appears to have been partly inspired Schweitzer's view of Paul as a mystic: Sanders, *Paul and Palestinian Judaism*, 459.

21. Campbell, *Quest for Paul's Gospel*, 59.

22. Campbell, *Deliverance of God*, 936.

23. De Boer, "Paul's Use and Interpretation of a Justification Tradition in Galatians 2:15-21," 189-216. (Campbell also appealed to this passage: Campbell, *Deliverance of God*, 847-49.) Gaventa, "The Singularity of the Gospel Revisited."

JUSTIFICATION

Paul depicts the gospel has enlarged from legal language to existential language."[24] There are clear lines of continuity, it seems, between a living vital union with the crucified and risen Christ and Paul's standing in relation to the law.[25]

Downing has lent further support to this transformational heart to Paul's gospel by redefining the very language itself of justification to mean the actual "righteousing" of those who believe. This righteousing need not involve anything declarative—there is no picture of a law court being painted—but rather this is a state in which a believer is enabled to *actually fulfil* the standards of the Second Table of the Ten Commandments: the ones that have to do with the way we treat other human beings.[26] There are no preliminary atoning and acquitting staging posts on the way to being given the power to live as you should: you get the power straight from the Spirit given as the long promised guarantor of the new covenant arrangement, the one who, in Ezekiel's words, can cause us to walk in God's statutes (Ezek 36: 27). Downing, however, does not take on the issues of context, especially the Romans 1–4 context. Here, justification terminology is deployed by Paul within an argument that seems to have an unmistakably forensic feel, so much so that Campbell has to find a way to discount it from the evidence.

Campbell, however, is aware that he is on firm ground in making the believer's participation in Christ the "key summary motif"[27] of his PPME model, locating himself firmly within the participatory language of Romans 5–8. "Pneumatologically," "martyrologically," and "eschatology" merely qualify the participation as Spirit-forged, cruciform, and triumphant. Indeed, the fundamental idea is so simple and so un-contentious that one wonders why 1,218 pages are needed to explain and defend it.[28] Even in his earlier, slimmer tome, there is so much defense going on that one is

---

24. Gaventa, "The Singularity of the Gospel Revisited," 194.

25. Cowan argues that there has, in fact, been no transition from the legal, courtroom idiom at all, preferring to picture Christ's risen life as a forensic vindication, offering a translation of "Christ lives in me" as something more like: "Christ lives with respect to me": "Christ's resurrection life represents his own status as righteous before God, and Paul can speak of this life and status as his because of his union with Christ." Cowan, "The Legal Significance of Christ's Risen Life," 467.

26. Fredriksen, "Paul's Letter to the Romans, the Ten Commandments, and Pagan 'Justification by Faith,'" 801–8.

27. Campbell, *Quest for Paul's Gospel*, 45.

28. Campbell, *Deliverance of God*.

hard-pressed to find anything more than the briefest of explanations for the PPME concept itself, before the swords are drawn.

A Synthesis?

Together with only a few other voices in this debate,[29] I want to resist the Schweitzerian edict that the only way to make progress is to assert a theory over against another theory and attempt to cancel that other theory out.[30] It seems that the debate has been driven by a desire to get beyond Reformational ways of thinking. There is a widespread distaste for the Reformed tradition, and the desire for a revisionist position seems driven by what it is against: the Reformed faith, now very much resurgent in America and just as sure of itself as ever.

Not only that, but the debate is clouded by a persistent failure to distinguish between that which is fundamentally definitive of the act of justifying someone and the results of that act. The last thing we want to do, of course, is abstract justification from the things to which it is inextricably related. We would strenuously affirm that there is no justification without inward and social transformation, but these are not what justification is. The socially inclusive outcomes and liberative effects of justification, are just that: outcomes and effects. Justification does not *mean* liberation; it does not *mean* social inclusion.[31]

With this in mind we will now see what can be gleaned from a study of the origins of the concept behind what became Paul's doctrine of justification.

What Were the Origins of Paul's Concept?

Second Temple Judaism

Among the Dead Sea Scrolls, a scroll called 1QS11 has long been raided for what seem to be close parallels to Paul. These include the following:

---

29. One is David Shaw, "Romans 4 and the Justification of Abraham," 61.

30. "Progress always consists in taking one or other of two alternatives, in abandoning the attempt to combine them." Schweitzer, *The Mysticism of the Apostle Paul*, 198.

31. Moo, "The Deliverance of God: An Apocalyptic Rereading of Justification in Paul by Douglas A. Campbell," 147.

Justification

    He will wipe out my transgression through His righteousness....
From the source of His righteousness is my justification....
My eyes have gazed on that which is eternal, on wisdom concealed from men,... on a fountain of righteousness and on a storehouse of power....

    As for me, if I stumble, the mercies of God shall be my salvation. If I stagger because of the sin of flesh, my justification shall be by the righteousness of God which endures forever....

    He will draw me near by His grace, and by His mercy will He bring my justification.... He will pardon all my sins. Through His righteousness He will cleanse me of the uncleanness of man.[32]

Despite these Qumran references to a vindicating, pardoning righteousness that comes from God, Wright reckons that justification was not exactly a "hot topic"[33] in Second Temple Judaism. But when the need arose in Paul's ministry for it to become a hot topic, Paul found the language he needed from within his own tradition.[34] After all, the Pharisees, of which he had been one, were "the lawyers of early Judaism."[35] And, of course, as a former member of the Sanhedrin, Paul himself had been a kind of a lawyer.[36] Judicial reasoning was not foreign to him. Wright makes particular use of 4QMMT where those who keep the works of Torah have "'righteousness' reckoned to them."[37] Substitute "works of Torah" for "faith," Wright claims, and you have an exact echo of Paul's theology.[38] One cannot help wondering whether, given the complexity of Paul's arguments for justification by faith, finding genuine parallels could ever be as simple as replacing Torah with faith. Paul weaves his argument together using a careful and creative exposition of passages such as Genesis 15:6, which must surely be the main source for Paul's concept of God "reckoning" on the basis of "believing."

---

32. 1QS XI, in Vermes, *The Complete Dead Sea Scrolls in English*, 115–16.

33. Wright, *Paul and the Faithfulness of God*, 932. Though, many would say that the issue of who is righteous before God was of huge importance. It was certainly more than Schweitzer's "subsidiary crater."

34. Wright, *Paul and the Faithfulness of God*, 933.

35. Peerbolte, "New Perspective on Justification," 148.

36. Peerbolte, "New Perspective on Justification," 151.

37. Wright, *Paul and the Faithfulness of God*, 930.

38. Wright, "4QMMT and Paul: Justification, 'Works,' and Eschatology," 112.

Jesus Himself

A case which, since Jeremias' *The Central Message of the New Testament* of 1965,[39] has not been often enough made is that by far the most likely origin of the *concept* of justification is Christ himself, even though clearly Christ's teachings mostly did not utilize the terminology Paul used.[40] As Jeremias pointed out and is still the case, scholars have been too enamored with 1QS11 and other sources of righteousness terminology. Yet, if one looks closely enough at the way the Qumran community was *using* that terminology, it quickly becomes apparent that we are dealing with two entirely different worlds.[41] Referring to Luke 18:14 (the end of the Parable of the Pharisee and the Tax Collector) Jeremias pointed out that "Jesus was the first to designate the acceptance of the sinner by God as δικαιουσθαι, that is, as an anticipated eschatological acquittal." Jeremias was not alone in seeing the closest possible theological connections between Paul and Jesus in this regard.[42] Further, if Jesus saw himself as the Suffering Servant of Isaiah 53 then there is, in Isaiah 53:10–12, an explicit link between the suffering of the Servant and the justification of the many.[43]

Not only the wider Jesus tradition but smaller creedal formulae may also be significant. Scholars have differed over the extent of traditional material in Romans 3:21–26, yet there is still broad consensus that a significant amount of traditional material is in there. And it may well be that the writer to the Hebrews is also citing that same tradition. Strong verbal similarities between the key atonement terminology of Romans 3:21–26 and Hebrews

---

39. Jeremias, *The Central Message of the New Testament*, based on his Hewett Lectures of 1963.

40. See Stettler, "Did Paul Invent Justification?" 94–196 for an appendix listing a very good range of the literature (as at 2015) discussing continuity and discontinuity between Jesus and Paul, all arranged according to three viewpoints: no continuity, limited continuity, and strong continuity (my terms, not hers).

41. Jeremias, *Central Message*, 66–70. Granted, Jeremias is assuming an OPP view of justification in Paul as anti-legalistic. For the NPP maybe the differences would not be quite so stark.

42. Bruce, *Paul and Jesus*, 2: "Nowhere has Paul more fully entered into the heart of Jesus' teaching about God and man than in his insistence on justification by divine grace;" Farmer, *Jesus and the Gospel*.

43. "The early Christian and Pauline doctrine of justification has taken up the interpretation of Jesus' sacrifice begun by Jesus himself with the help of Isaiah 53, and has further reflected upon it from a post-Easter perspective," Stuhlmacher, *Biblische Theologie des Neuen Testaments* 1, 129. Stettler's translation: Stettler, "Did Paul Invent Justification?" 172.

Justification

9–10 (especially 9:11–15) have been demonstrated.⁴⁴ Interestingly, the one term where there is a verbal difference is in the area of justification, where the writer to the Hebrews uses *teleiō* "I render perfect" (Heb 10:1, 14) instead of *dikaioō* "I justify" (Rom 3:24), but both contexts strongly link justification/perfection with the prior all-sufficient sacrifice of Christ.

So it could be that Paul was tapping into an already very well established common understanding. Christ had modelled a revolutionary gracious approach to human sin and need, and cemented this new age of grace through what he did at Calvary. The church had already sought to preserve this precious new revelation through its creedal statements.

Paul's Conversion

Further, we are on safe ground if we assert that Paul's use of the original grace message of Christ amounted to a lot more than oral (or written) tradition that he "received" and then "passed on as of first importance" (1 Cor 15:3). Paul's understanding of the graciousness of Christ towards the undeserving stemmed from direct encounter on the road to Damascus, which Seyoun Kim's work has so helpfully explored. And not only this, but, in common with so many early Christians, Paul's experience of receiving the Spirit would also have been an illuminating experience: the Spirit was the Spirit of wisdom and revelation in the knowledge of Christ (Eph 1:17). I find common cause here with Campbell:

> And this is not just an idea, or a mental identification. Paul clearly believes that something quite real has happened; it is irreducibly concrete. The process takes place in some relation to the Spirit.⁴⁵

What Gave Paul the Language of Justification?

It is surprising how frequently justification is referred to in the literature as a legal or courtroom "metaphor" yet how infrequently this is explored. What courtroom? Where? If it is a legal metaphor, what specifically might Paul have seen or pictured in his head that sparked the idea? There seems to be little effort to dig any deeper historically into the background of the

---

44. Ribbens, "Forensic-Retributive Justification in Romans 3:21–26," 548–67.
45. Campbell, *Quest for Paul's Gospel*, 40.

image, even on the part of those, such as Stott or Gunton, who seem especially fond of appealing to justification as being essentially an image, a picture.[46]

Wright goes into some detail describing Jewish law courts and how they worked. These descriptions are based mainly on Isaiah 40–55 (43:26LXX actually uses *dikaiōthē*), in which there is a Judge (God), a plaintiff (the prophet bringing the accusation), and a defendant (Israel).[47] The difficulty is that the prophets are themselves using only an *image* of a lawsuit. It is the "prophetic lawsuit," a common trope used by the writing prophets. We are not given much of a window by Isaiah into any real-life proceedings. However, there is one scholar, James Prothro, who has attempted a thorough-going analysis of what might be *behind* the image while still working essentially with biblical, rather than extra-biblical, raw materials. We will explore his findings shortly. First, we take a more simplistic approach and go to the places in the Septuagint that Paul is actually quoting or alluding to when he explains justification by faith.

The Septuagint

There are two places in the Psalms where the verbal similarities are striking. The most significant of these is Psalm 143:2 (142:2LXX): "and do not enter into judgment with your servant, for in your sight no one living will be justified (*enōpion sou pas zōn dikaiōthēsetai*)." There are strong conceptual and verbal echoes in the crucial opening moment, the *propositio*,[48] of Paul's argument in Galatians: "for by the works of the law no flesh will be justified (*hoti ex ergōn nomou ou diakaiōthēsetai pasa sarx*)" (Gal 2:16).[49] Here, appealing to the psalm seems to be a way of giving his argument a "general validity"[50] acknowledged by Peter and the audience of the letter.

---

46. Dunn is similar: Dunn, *Theology of Paul the Apostle*, 328–33, especially 331–32: "These metaphors bring out the reality of the experience of the new beginning for Paul, ... a reality which defied simple or uniform or unifaceted description."

47. Wright, *What St Paul Really Said*, 96–99. Wright rightly takes Seifrid to task for misrepresenting him as assuming a modern courtroom setting: Wright, "4QMMT and Paul," 105 (referring to Mark Seifrid, *Christ, Our Righteousness*, 59, n.66).

48. Betz, *Galatians*, 14–25.

49. Hassler's attention is drawn to these allusions to the psalm because they come at such crucial junctures in both instances: Hassler, "Ethocentric Legalism and the Justification of the Individual," 317.

50. Stettler, "Did Paul Invent Justification by Faith?" 169.

JUSTIFICATION

This audience was likely already accustomed to hearing that psalm alluded to as the rationale for justification by faith. *Eidotes* "knowing" (Gal 2:16) was a tradition-indicator in Paul. He tends to introduce extracts of traditional material with this verb.[51] In Romans 3:20, again a pivotal moment in the argument, the verbal and conceptual similarity is even more striking: "Therefore by the works of the law no one will be justified in his sight . . . (*ou dikaiōthēsetai pasa sarx evōpion autou*)." If this psalm is as crucial as it appears to be for Paul's argument then Paul was unlikely to have ignored the immediate literary context of this phrase within the psalm: "do not enter into judgment with your servant." This is pointedly *not* a plea along the lines of "do not maintain these ethnic boundary markers between Jews and gentiles" but is the cry of a conscience-stricken individual before God.[52]

The other place in the Psalms is Psalm 98:2 (97:2LXX): "The LORD has made known his salvation, in the sight of the nations his righteousness has been revealed." Richard Hays and Douglas Campbell appeal to this as the background for Paul's "righteousness of God" language. The righteousness of God *is* the making known of "his salvation." This supports Campbell's contention that justification is therefore liberative.[53] It also uses the same verb (*apocalyptō*) to refer to the revealing of God's righteousness as is found in Romans 1:17. Further, the psalm specifically refers to the "nations," the gentiles. Indeed, the whole argument of Romans 1:17—3:26 may have been inspired by this one verse of Psalm 98.

A road less travelled in background studies is Ben Sira/Siracides 42:2, which includes the phrase "[Do not be ashamed about] the law of the Most High and the covenant, and about judgment so as to justify the ungodly."[54] Alister McGrath in his famous history of justification by faith pointed out

---

51. *Logizometha* "we maintain" in Romans 3:28 is being used to the same effect: "We maintain that a person is justified by faith without the works of the law."

52. "It would seem that, given the assumptions of the new perspective, in Paul's mind David should have felt fine within the bounds of the covenant. He possessed no tormented conscience or pathological sense of unworthiness." Hassler, "Ethnocentric Legalism and the Justification of the Individual," 326.

53. Of the very long review articles of *Deliverance of God*, Douglas Moo's is probably the easiest to read: Moo, "The Deliverance of God," 143–50. Regarding Psalm 98, Moo makes the point, against Campbell, that the divine king pictured in the psalm is not giving this salvation or deliverance to his people in a criterion-less way. This act of righteousness is not "sheer benevolence" (ibid., 147).

54. An awkward translation recommended with good reasons by James Prothro, "The Strange Case of Δικαιοω in the Septuagint and Paul," 50, n5. See also Downing, "Justification as Acquittal?" 310.

that, in common Greek usage, the verb *dikaioō* almost never referred to a favorable judgment, a justifying of the ungodly or the godly, but almost always to the meting out of a punishment, whilst, in the Septuagint, the reverse is the case: the verb, when referring to a personal object almost always means a positive verdict.[55] James Prothro cites Sirach 42:2 as the only possible *counterexample* to this favorable use of *dikaioō* in the Septuagint: it could translated in such a way that it is about judgment that leads to the punishment of the ungodly. But in the end he decides for a rendering of this passage too as an example of *dikaioō*-as-favorable-verdict. The passage has added significance because it is counseling the reader to not be ashamed of a verdict that ends up justifying the ungodly, an obvious parallel to Paul's shocking designation of God as the one who justifies the ungodly (Rom 4:5).

The Septuagint, it seems, is a *dikaioō*-as-favorable-verdict island in a sea of *dikaioō*-as-punishment usage.[56] Well, not quite. Prothro surveys the possible instances in Greco-Roman usage where *dikaioō* describes a favorable verdict and finds examples in the Greek historians Dio Cassius and Polybius, as well as a passage in Aristotle, and an instance in the writings of the sophist Philostratus. However, these are clearly not the norm. Even Liddell & Scott rightly render the classical use of the noun form (*dikaiōsis*) as "a setting right, doing justice to: punishment."[57] And, more significantly, in specifically judicial contexts, it appears the verb was *never* used in the sense of a judge or a sovereign finding in favor of the accused, whereas, in the Septuagint, the verb carries this meaning *especially* in judicial contexts.[58] This fact provokes a significant question for Prothro:

> If Paul's usage of the term lies outside its range of possible usage in Greco-Roman parlance, it tells against reading justification solely or primarily in Greco-Roman terms. But why, then, would the apostle to the Gentiles use this language in complete disagreement with its common usage?[59]

Despite Paul being the apostle to the gentiles, he seems to have been deploying a use of justification terminology that was widely understood

55. McGrath, *Iustitia Dei*, 18–19.

56. Prothro, "The Strange Case of Δικαιow in the Septuagint and Paul," 48–69.

57. Liddell and Scott, *Greek-English Lexicon*, 173.

58. Prothro, "The Strange Case of Δικαιow in the Septuagint and Paul," 55–56, citing Deut 25:1 as a case in point, and also Exod 23:7.

59. Prothro, "The Strange Case of Δικαιow in the Septuagint and Paul," 51.

only for avid readers of the Septuagint, a use that, incidentally, continued to have a specialized theological sense at variance with its more customary usage well into the patristic era.[60] However, that Paul has in mind a legal setting for the use of justification terminology is clear from the way, in Romans, the argument is constructed around legal phenomena. In other words, he is using the term in precisely the context where it was most likely to be understood to refer to condemnation and punishment rather than justification and favor. Prothro highlights how the argument is built on charges (3:9), accusations (2:15; 8:33-34), witnesses (2:15; 3:21; 8:16), defense (1:20; 2:1), and a sentence of judgment (3:19).[61] Given the way Paul quotes and alludes to key biblical passages when explaining and defending justification, it does seem to be a specifically *biblical* legal setting that Paul has in mind. It is based on "biblical depictions of judgment."[62] He simply expects the gentile component in his audience to keep up!

Prothro provides a comprehensive picture of both bilateral and trilateral contentions from all parts of the Septuagint as well as other places within Hellenistic Judaism. He draws a helpful link to reconciliation, solving, perhaps, the reason why reconciliation language is so closely intertwined with justification language in Romans 5:8-11 as well as curing forensic concepts of justification of the charge that they are too impersonal.[63] He identifies a bilateral contention taking place in Romans: a state of "'enmity' and ruptured relation,"[64] where God is the judge and idolatrous and hypocritical humanity has a case to answer. The works of the law offer no answer and there is no gainsaying God but then, unexpectedly, God justifies those against whom he has a claim: "such justification entailed forgiveness of the offense that set the disputants at odds and effected reconciliation between them."[65] The result is "peace with God" (Rom 5:1), and a shift of allegiance from being allied with sin to being allied to God, a shift of allegiance further cemented by our death with Christ to sin and our new life lived for God.[66] This also helpfully throws back to the kingdom theme

---

60. Prothro, "The Strange Case of Δικαιοω in the Septuagint and Paul," 58
61. Prothro, *Both Judge and Justifier*, 3-4.
62. Prothro, *Judge and Justifier*, 5.
63. Prothro, *Judge and Justifier*, 211.
64. Prothro, *Judge and Justifier*, 211.
65. Prothro, *Judge and Justifier*, 209.
66. Prothro, *Judge and Justifier*, 211-12.

preached within the Synoptics, where allegiance to Christ the King is the central demand.

It seems then that Paul is largely using the prophetic lawsuit image. There is a set of real-life legal practices behind the image but the image itself is what Paul is using, an image in which earthly judges and disputants have already been transposed into a divine-human contention. It is a ready-made image, which he assumes will be equally intelligible to all despite its specialized use of *dikaioō*.

Conclusion

Our concept of justification has been inestimably enriched in recent decades by new perspectives on the backgrounds to Paul's thought. It has undoubtedly been of benefit to see Paul's "anti"-law message as being not necessarily about legalism, at least not legalism as was once commonly understood. The result has been that the socially inclusive implications of God's gracious acceptance of all are given emphasis and made more concrete. It has also been of benefit that the truths of participation in Christ and liberation from the powers of sin and death have been placed back into close relationship with justification, making it a transformative and dynamic thing, not a legal fiction. However, these seem to take us more to the precious results of justification than to a definition of what justification actually is.

Justification itself is indeed a law-court metaphor but the legal setting is far removed from Greco-Roman legal proceedings. The concept is founded upon the Isaianic prophetic lawsuit image and uses language uniquely forged in the translation of the Septuagint. Paul assumes that his gentile hearers will understand the specialized use of justification-as-*favorable*-verdict on the basis of the way he constructs his argument. The whole of Romans 1–3, for example, takes the form of a lawsuit in which Paul speaks for God the judge. Witnesses are called, accusations are made, charges are pronounced, the defense crumbles, and the verdict is given. But then, the truly amazing, epoch-making event takes place: God brings into account his own righteousness as demonstrated by the faithfulness unto death of his Son. On that basis, sinners can be "justified freely by his grace" (Rom 3:24). God "justifies the ungodly" (Rom 4:4). Now, there is a state of "peace with God" (Rom 5:5). No wonder Lloyd-Jones spent an entire week of his Romans series on that one phrase: "But now . . ." (Rom 3:21).

Reflection

1. Think of a time when you experienced serious relationship tensions with someone. How might justification have helped?

2. To be justified is essentially a very simple thing. It means you are unconditionally accepted. CBT counsellors have a remarkably similar concept: "unconditional self-acceptance." Person-centered counsellors use "unconditional positive regard" in the attitude they embody towards the counselee. Feeling accepted is clearly essential to good mental health. In view of the increasing pressures of our meritocratic societies, how might teaching people about justification in Christ arm them against feeling crushed or burnt out by the demands of modern life?

CHAPTER 7

Reconciliation

Introduction

THE THOUGHT OF RECONCILIATION seems to be an uncomplicated concept and an obvious one to use for the atonement. The idea of reconciliation has had increasing currency within discussions of restorative justice over the last few decades, the most obvious example being the Truth and Reconciliation Commission, which was set up to bring healing in the wake of South African apartheid. In more recent times political polarizations make us express a longing, at least for compromise if not reconciliation itself. It might be surprising to the modern reader, then, that the idea of using "reconcile" (*katallassō/apokatallassō*) and "reconciliation" (*katallagē*) as a way of describing the implications of the death of Christ only occurs to Paul of all the New Testament writers, and that, even in his writing, it does not show itself until 2 Corinthians, the second-to-last surviving letter of his ten-year travelling period as a missionary. *Katallassō/katallagē* and their cognates are rare, occurring only in 2 Corinthians 5:18–20, Romans 5:10–11, Colossians 1:20, 22, and Ephesians 2:16. This picture of the atonement, then, presents us with no great puzzles as to why it was chosen; the question is why it was not used more. Hopefully the answer to this question will suggest itself from our discussion of its origins.

For now, it is well to note that there is a significant body of scholars who would claim that the *concept* of reconciliation is so important to New Testament soteriology as to warrant being recognized as central, even though the *term* is rare. Advocates of this position have included James

RECONCILIATION

Denney,[1] Karl Barth,[2] Vincent Taylor,[3] T. H. Hughes,[4] Jacques Dupont,[5] Johannes Weiss,[6] T. W. Manson,[7] Herman Ridderbos,[8] Peter Stuhlmacher,[9] Ralph Martin,[10] and Joseph Fitzmyer,[11] while Ernst Käsemann[12] took entirely the opposite view, arguing mainly from the paucity of the specific terminology and the supposed liturgical setting for what little terminology there is.

Many of these authors were writing before the search for a theological center in Paul fell out of vogue. Of the advocates for the centrality of the concept perhaps none went further than Ralph Martin, whose claim was that reconciliation not only has an implied presence everywhere in Paul but is the supreme interpretive key to Paul's whole theology,[13] with Karl Donfried[14] and others[15] taking exception to such reductionism. Within much of the scholarship on this word, then, there is a built-in discussion between concept and terminology,[16] with the importance of the concept mostly triumphing over the paucity of the term.

---

1. Denney, *The Christian Doctrine of Reconciliation*.
2. Barth, *Church Dogmatics IV,2*.
3. Taylor, *Forgiveness and Reconciliation*.
4. Hughes, *The Atonement*.
5. Dupont, "La Réconciliation dans la théologie de saint Paul," 255-302.
6. Weiss, *Earliest Christianity: A History of the Period AD 30-150, vol. 2*, 497-98.
7. Manson, *On Paul and John*, 50.
8. Ridderbos, *Paul: An Outline of his Theology*.
9. Stuhlmacher, "The Gospel of Reconciliation in Christ," 161-90.
10. Martin, *Reconciliation: A Study of Paul's Theology*.
11. Fitzmyer, "Reconciliation in Pauline Theology," 155-77.
12. Käsemann, "Some Thoughts on the Theme 'The Doctrine of Reconciliation in the New Testament,'" 49-64.
13. Martin, *Reconcilation*, 5.
14. Donfried, "Reconciliation: A Study of Paul's Theology," 83-84 (book review).
15. Constantineanu lists Charles Giblin, Beverly Roberts Gaventa, James Reese, Jeffrey Gillette, John Drane, James Davis, Gregory Allen, and Hulitt Gloer, but gives no specific references to their works: Constantineanu, *Social Significance*, 34 n.31.
16. E.g., Furnish, "The Ministry of Reconciliation," 205.

Pictures of Atonement

A Discussion of the Key Passages

The occurrence of the reconciliation metaphor in 2 Corinthians 5 has been a particular focus of scholarship, with the occurrences in Romans 5, Colossians 1, and Ephesians 2 viewed in the light of it. The 2 Corinthians 5 setting is Paul's conversion. The Damascus Road experience is being related as the occasion when he first encountered God's gracious reconciling initiative, even though he was at that time God's enemy. The setting for Romans 5 is justification. Paul sees "peace with God" as equally the result of justification and reconciliation and deploys both terms in a complementary way to describe God's gracious way of putting former enemies right with himself.[17] In Colossians (where, as with Ephesians, the intensified *apokatallassō* is used) the scene is an underlying "mythology" for want of a better term, in which the rightful ruler of the universe—the firstborn of all creation, God's Wisdom—faces a situation in which beings both embodied and spiritual are hostile to his reign so he pays the price to reconcile the cosmos to himself, though we soon discover that this has not necessarily included the spiritual enemies who seem to end up humiliated in a victory procession.[18] It is towards "an estranged cosmos" that God is "graciously making a diplomatic overture."[19] In Ephesians, the context is the barrier created by the law. The walls are broken down by Christ's reconciling work (Eph 2:14–16), fulfilling as it does, all the claims of the law. Here, Paul echoes Isaiah 57:19a: "Peace, peace, to the far and the near" and the messenger of Isaiah 52:7 who preaches peace: "So he came and proclaimed peace to you who were far off and peace to those who were near" (Eph 2:17). The gentiles who were "once far off have been brought near by the blood of Christ."[20] This passage underlines better than any other the "inseparability of the 'vertical' and the 'horizontal' in God's salvation and peace revealed in Jesus Christ."[21] Seeing

---

17. So Furnish, "The Ministry of Reconciliation," 212–13.

18. Grayston, *Dying, We Live*, 132–41. See especially 133: "It is as if God were a king surrounded by enemies in his own royal court, who wished to draw his people from their support of his enemies and reconcile them to himself. So he set a trap for his enemies, allowing them to kill his Son and thus, by displaying their vicious nature, destroy their own power. When the Son is raised from the dead, he triumphantly mocks the discredited enemies, and their formerly deluded victims are reconciled to God." Also 136 and the literature there cited.

19. Campbell, *Deliverance of God*, 912.

20. See brief but helpful discussion in Snyder-Belousek, *Atonement, Justice, and Peace*, 509–23.

21. Snyder-Belousek, *Atonement, Justice, and Peace*, 511. He goes on to make the

as we are discussing origins it seems right to lean our weight on 2 Corinthians, the earliest and fullest occurrence.

2 Corinthians 2:14—7:4 is the theological heart of 2 Corinthians and seems to exist as a stand-alone unit, prompting numerous source critical speculations about a pre-history of as many as five separate letters which became woven together as a single piece. Within this section, Paul refers to himself using the royal "we" and "our" as part of a sustained defense of his apostleship. In both of the occurrences of the verb *katallassō* within this section, for "we" and "us" we should read "me": 5:18, "God . . . has reconciled us [me] to himself," and 5:20, "God . . . making his appeal through us [me]: be reconciled to God." Likewise, in both occurrences of the noun *katallagē* Paul is using the first person plural to refer to himself: 5:18, "God . . . has given to us [me] the ministry of reconciliation" and 5:19, "he has committed to us [me] the word of reconciliation." This leaves only the participial form *katallassōn* where the reference is to the whole world: 5:19, "God was reconciling the world to himself." The reason for this use of the first person plural seems to be an effort to place the authenticity of his apostleship within the bigger setting of the truth of the gospel he preaches. To call the one into question, as the Corinthians were doing and probably on the basis of his past as an enemy of the church, was to call the other into question.[22] The purpose of chapter 5 in particular appears to be to answer those critics who would write Paul off on the basis of his past life as a persecutor. Paul is emphasizing that God has turned this enemy of God into a friend of God through a dramatic and gratuitous act of reconciliation. He is now a new creation; his old life as an enemy is gone; all things have become new. His defense of his more authentic style of apostleship, in distinction to the super-apostles (11:15; 12:11) and pseudo-apostles (11:13), entails a refusal to even use the term "apostle" anywhere in 2:14—7:4. He underlines his humility by using *diakonos/diakonia/diakonein*, the terminology of serving (3:7, 8, 9; 4:1; 5:18; 6:3).[23]

---

claim, in fact, that human-to-human reconciliation must take place *before* human-to-God reconciliation can become possible, which seems to overstate what the passage itself is saying, though evidence is clearly mustered from elsewhere (e.g., Sermon on the Mount) that human-to-human forgiveness and reconciliation is, at the very least, correlated with divine-human forgiveness and reconciliation. The obvious soteriological problems of apparently needing to be reconciled to others before God can accept us (contra Rom 5:8–11, etc.) are not properly addressed: ibid., 513–21.

22. So Furnish, "The Ministry of Reconciliation," 207.

23. Furnish, "The Ministry of Reconciliation," 208–9: *Diakonos* and related terms

PICTURES OF ATONEMENT

Origins of the Concept and Terminology

The Language of Diplomacy

The background to Paul's use of the term is widely agreed to be diplomatic relations.[24] In modern times we use terms like "talks," "peace talks," "reaching an agreement," "negotiations." In the first-century world, "reconciliation" would have been right at the heart of the collection of technical terms for that context, rather than the more general term that it is for us. It was the language of the peace treaty. 2 Corinthians 5:20 also contains a concentration of other terms commonly used in political diplomacy of the period: "ambassadors" (*prēsbeis*), "appeal" (*parakalein*), and "petition" (*deomai*).[25] In particular, "ambassadors" were officials tasked with "initiating or concluding reconciliation between hostile parties."[26]

The Septuagint

What doubtless helped Paul to think of using the language of diplomacy in a religious context is the fact that 2 Maccabees had already used it in that way.[27] In that setting, the term is used to describe God putting away his

---

occur more frequently in 2 Corinthians (twenty times) than in all of Paul's other letters combined.

24. Based mainly on the work of Cilliers Breytenbach, in his now out of print *Versöhnung: Eine Studie zur paulinischen Soteriology*, though his findings have been at least partially supported more recently by Anthony Bash, *Ambassadors for Christ*, 29–32.

25. Kim, "2 Cor 5:11-21 and the Origins,'" 361. Kim is relying on Breytenbach, *Versöhnung*, 40–83, and especially pp. 64 onwards, which refers to the literature where these words of diplomacy appear. Kim also uses Stanley Porter's Καταλλασσω *in Ancient Greek Literature*, 39–76.

26. Maier, "A Sly Civility," 330 referencing Breytenbach, *Versöhung*, 65–68. Stanley Porter after an exhaustive a survey of the usage of *katallassō* in all the relevant literature, including but not limited to political documents, is able to categorize the usage into six types, but seems unable to draw any strong conclusions about the overall usage of the word, concluding that Paul used it in a unique way: Porter, Καταλλασσω *in Ancient Greek Literature*, 189. What he means is that his "usage E" in which the offended party takes the initiative cannot be traced any further back than Paul and must be an innovation on his part: ibid., 143.

27. So Marshall, "The Meaning of 'Reconciliation,'" 130. Also Breytenbach, *Versöhnung*, 40–83, who points out that, not only the author of 2 Maccabees but also Philo and Josephus used reconciliation terminology in reference to divine-human relations though these are unlikely to be reflected in Paul: ibid., 70–81. Also Kim, "2 Cor 5:11-21 and the Origins," 362. Kim (following Breytenbach) doubts the significance of 2 Maccabees to

hostility and suspending his judgment on Israel's sin in the light of the Jewish martyrs having suffered on behalf of the whole nation (see 2 Macc 5:20; 7:33; and 8:29).[28] It is to be noted, though, that Paul's use of reconciliation terminology might be in deliberate contrast to its usage in the Maccabean martyr tradition,[29] hence my next point.

God the Initiator and Paul's Experience of Grace

A further change in usage comes when Paul describes God's reconciliation as something initiated entirely by God, indeed, something that we merely "receive" (Rom 5:11). Paul is unwavering in this: reconciliation is always about God's gracious initiative even though we are his enemies—in contrast to the martyr tradition in which the martyrs move God to be reconciled. God is the "victim," as it were, and it is humanity that ought to be making reparations. Instead, God assumes total responsibility. Reflecting upon Ephesians 2, Mennonite Thomas Yoder Neufeld says:

> Peace is costly even more because it costs the life of the peacemaker. In contrast to the "peace of this world" (John 14:27) or the Pax Romana, which purchase peace through the death of the enemy, Christ kills enmity with his own blood (v. 13) on the cross (v. 16).[30]

These realities are in some way confirmed by modern concepts of restorative justice in which it is always the victim of a crime who must initiate the process of reconciliation.[31] If the victim is unwilling then no

Paul in order to claim the use of reconciliation terminology as a complete innovation in Paul, which helps bolster (unnecessarily in my view) the Damascus Road argument. See further: Constantineaunu, *Social Significance of Reconciliation*, 26–31 for an overview of the scholarship on origins.

28. Williams, *Maccabean Martyr Traditions*, 104–12.

29. Marshall, "Reconciliation," 129; Kim, "2 Cor 5:11–21 and the Origins," 365. Williams sees more of an exact parallel, even to the point where the martyr tradition informed Paul's whole atonement theology in which a man interposes, at the cost of his life, dying "on behalf of" others and for their sins. There is arguably a Christological synthesis here: it *is* God's gracious initiative that reconciles us (a thought patently absent from 2 Maccabees), yet it is Christ our representative who *effects* it, in a way analogous to the martyrs. Christ in one person is both the divine initiating grace and the human reparation.

30. Nuefeld, "'For He is Our Peace,'" 227.

31. Brink, "From Wrongdoer to New Creation," 302. See also: Myers and Enns, *Ambassadors of Reconciliation vol. 1*.

progress can be made. It is an enormously costly yet necessary first step and inevitably involves moving away from a posture that seeks only the punishment of the wrongdoer. God's reconciling grace must be "discovered" and found "welling up inside" the life of the victim if reconciliation and forgiveness towards the offender is to happen.[32]

The specific trigger that seems to have impelled Paul to use this term was the need to find a suitably exalted way of expressing God's sovereign work of grace in his own life. He is casting his mind back to the Damascus Road as he seeks to describe the about-turn that changed him from an enemy of the gospel to its most ardent proclaimer.[33] Several allusions to Paul's past as a persecutor and his Damascus Road experience can be seen in 2 Corinthians 5:11–21.[34] There are references, for example, to receiving his ministry by the mercy of God (4:1), to having given up underhanded ways (4:2), to having encountered the glory of Christ (4:4, 6), and to a turning point in his perspective on who Christ was (5:16). There was a "paradigm shift" not only in Paul's attitude to Christ and his people but also in what being reconciled to and right with God might look like.[35] Paul is so impacted by God's gracious initiative that he describes himself as having been captured and placed in God's incense-laden cultic procession (2:14).[36] He has gone from "enemy of Christ" to "captive of God,"[37] a turnaround he speaks of especially freely when needing to defend his apostleship.[38]

Isaiah 40–66

There is, in all likelihood a fourth tributary flowing into this river of evolving metaphorical meaning besides diplomacy, 2 Maccabees, and Damascus Road. It seems that the resultant concept is further enriched by Paul's

---

32. Schreiter, *Reconciliation*, 43.

33. Kim, *The Origin of Paul's Gospel*; "2 Cor 5:11–21 and the Origins," 360–84.

34. Kim, *Origin of Paul's Gospel*, 360–66 and 382–84; Brink, "From Wrongdoer to New Creation," 303–7.

35. Constantineaunu, *Social Significance of Reconciliation*, 89–92.

36. Duff, "Metaphor, Motif, and Meaning," 79–92; Brink, "From Wrongdoer to New Creation," 303–5.

37. Brink, "From Wrongdoer to New Creation," 307.

38. Kim, *Origin of Paul's Gospel*, 31. According to Kim, Paul employs the same strategy in 1 Cor 9:1; 15:5–10; Gal 1:13–17 and Phil 3:4–11.

acquaintance with Isaiah 40–66.[39] In particular, his way of defining the result of his reconciliation to God as a "new creation" echoes the language of Isaiah, especially Isaiah 43:18–19, where God urges Israel to not remember the former things because he is about to do a new thing, and 65:17 where God promises to create "new heavens and a new earth." The fact that Isaiah 49:8 is quoted directly at 2 Corinthians 6:2 seems to add weight to the likelihood that Paul had Isaiah in mind while he was forming his thoughts. However, to claim, as Otfried Hofius did,[40] that Paul's entire concept of reconciliation has its origins in Isaiah's great promise in chapters 52–53 of "peace" via the vicarious sufferings of the Servant seems to overstate the Isaianic background.[41] And even Hofius concedes the importance of Paul's encounter with the risen Christ as his closing thought on the subject.[42]

It is sufficient to allow a general Isaianic coloring to Paul's soteriology here as elsewhere but with indebtedness to pagan usage for the actual terminology. So the tenor of the metaphor is Paul's experience enriched a little by Isaiah; the vehicle is diplomatic peace-treaties enlarged by the Jewish martyr tradition.

There is one possible tributary that we have not so far considered and that is the Jesus tradition and other pre-existing Christian sources such as creedal sayings and hymnic fragments. At the height of the source critical study of the letters, Martin could quite confidently rely on material that had formally lain hidden within the dark tunnel that ran between Pentecost and the very first New Testament writings. But now, all was plain to see thanks to the science of source criticism. These days the amount of text in any of the letters that scholars are willing to identify as a quote from something pre-existing is smaller than ever and there is a move towards responding to the text "as it is before us" rather than dissecting it. Nevertheless, as with justification, it can be no coincidence that Jesus himself is portrayed in the Gospels as the friend of sinners, as the advocate of loving one's enemies and as the teller of the Parable of the Prodigal Son. Paul must have been aware of at least some of these parts of the Jesus tradition, though which parts we cannot say.

---

39. See Constantineaunu, *Social Significance of Reconciliation*, 76–87 and the literature there cited.
40. Hofius, "Erwägungen," 11–14.
41. So Kim, "2 Cor 5:11–21 and the Origins," 364.
42. Hofius, "Erwägungen," 14.

Conclusion

The pressure of having to defend his apostleship to people who ought to know better than to question it is what caused Paul to reach for a new word. He wanted to express how God had made an enemy into his friend, how God had done a new thing, made him into a new creation. Then, with only a few occurrences in 2 Maccabees as a precedent for using this word in a religious way, he found his word: *reconciliation*. The very diplomatic coloring of the word sparked more diplomatic language, which seemed very fitting: he is making his appeal as an ambassador for Christ. Once this term had been seized upon, Paul seemed free to use it in widely varied settings: as a synonym for justification in Romans, a cosmic victory in Colossians, and (if it is Paul) a depiction of Jew-gentile unity in Ephesians.

Without doubt the most outstanding and unique quality of reconciliation when the term is applied to God is the fact that God, the victim of our hostility, takes all the initiative, makes all the reparations, and draws near to his enemies to make his offer. Of this Paul was eternally grateful.

Reflection

1. What points of connection are there between this concept and contemporary culture? Is this a picture of atonement that seems relatively easy to explain to someone?

2. God loves his enemies and takes the initiative to engage with them in relationship. What lessons does this teach us in the sphere of political relations, ecumenical relations, families, and friendships?

Conclusion

AT THE END OF *Atonement Theories*, having indulged in what I took to be the richest seam in historical theology, I celebrated the big fat Rachmaninovian chords that can be played once all the different ways theologians have viewed the cross are brought together. We stop playing the usual *Chopsticks* of our tradition and enjoy a much bigger range. We might also find that we discover the foot pedals. These allow us to soft-pedal certain themes, those our culture is less receptive to, and boldly sustain the chords that chime well with the mood music of the contemporary world. This all-embracing approach meant that I had joined the ranks of those who subscribe to a kaleidoscopic view of atonement—yes, it is a thing![1] In fact, in *Atonement Theories* I seemed to reach a point where the situational relevance of an atonement model was of prime importance, while its theological, moral, or biblical authenticity less so, though having dwelt for so long in the biblical passages I did have a certain nose for the biblical rightness or otherwise of a particular view. I soon turned my nose up at theologians who I thought were being too selective in their reading. Theologically too, I intuited that atonement ought to be Christologically centered, not centered on the doctrine of God or anthropology. Nevertheless, my position seemed remarkably close to an easygoing postmodern relativism, and people do not like this. I got quite a backlash of letters from to the editor from angry vicars over a *Church Times* article I wrote that laid out my kaleidoscopic stall. I had thought I would inevitably please everybody by giving every viewpoint some air time. The letters to the editor, as it happens, were particularly annoyed by the way I allowed penal substitution some coverage. But this highlights that theorists, though probably never wholly wrong, are not all equally right: something I tell my students when I'm trying to hone their criticality but don't always remember myself. And some of their models are

1. Beilby and Eddy (eds.), *The Nature of the Atonement*.

woefully lopsided in favor some prior ideological commitment: the theorists that is, not my students (heaven forbid!).

In terms of content, *Atonement Theories* followed Aulen's threefold typology, laid out in chronological order so that the reader could trace developments in thought and how these respond to societal and ecclesiastical shifts. This gave me three big sections: *Christus Victor* Theories, Objective Theories, and Subjective Theories. I then brought Aulen's schema up to date by adding a fourth section, Anthropological Theories, which covered all the non-violent approaches inspired by Girard's scapegoat theory. I was slated by one reviewer of the book for including Karl Barth in the Subjective Theories section. Barth, of course, could not have been less subjective if he'd tried. The category was unfortunate. I put him there because he had in common with all the other thinkers in that section a certain interest in the cross as revelation. Despite everything, the book has been my best seller, probably because it is so even handed. It is, I think, liked best by students, beginning researchers, and informed non-academics, and it has attracted research students to Cliff College.

Then came *Old Rugged Cross*. This was an easygoing meander through the entire history of Christian devotion to the cross beginning with tiny little iconic depictions in Greek manuscripts (staurograms) and finishing with Mel Gibson's *The Passion of the Christ*. This book has been barely read by anyone and it proved impossible to even get anyone to write a few nice words for the back cover. Among those that have read it I know of one who has used it as a daily devotional, which is nice. *Old Rugged Cross* was the volume that did the most to give the Atonement Project its uniqueness. Not only has no single author ever attempted an extensive treatment of the atonement from within the disciplines of historical theology, church history, *and* New Testament, but also, the lay voice as a *source* of theology has almost never been included in academic deliberations about the atonement before. Its contribution, therefore, is potentially very significant. Broadly, it underlined the importance to the faithful of participation in Christ, whether this is through Eucharist, art, poetry, tears, hymn-singing, baptism in the Holy Spirit, or immersion in a film. I concluded with mixed feelings about the excesses and weirdness of some devotion to the cross on the one hand, and some of the most brilliant words ever written and best songs ever sung, on the other. And there were lots of delightfully eccentric people to meet along the way, such as the tearful late-medieval prophet Margery Kempe of Kings Lynn, and all the Italian Catholics for whom devotion to the crucified

CONCLUSION

Christ would result in the bizarre phenomena of wounded hands and feet and oozing foreheads. As for splinters of the cross, let's not even go there. The Turin Shroud, though, I had a lot of time for and felt quite convinced about the evidence. The Participation Imperative emerged so strongly from this work that I reckoned a third volume would need to explore specifically this participation theme from a biblical viewpoint, especially in view of the resurgence of interest in recapitulation and theosis within systematic theology.

After a longer gap than I had planned (there were lots of other books to write), here is the complete final volume and last major output of my Atonement Project. I tackled the participatory theme first and the "Dying and Rising with Christ" chapter was the first to be written—and quite rightly torn to the tiniest of little shreds when I presented an early version of it as a paper. In the end, the itch for a sense of completeness or comprehensiveness drove me to look for a way to write a book that would serve as a complete survey of New Testament atonement theology. This would, of course, need to be within specific parameters. My interest in metaphor generated during the writing of *Old Rugged Cross* and then explored a little further in my *SCM Study Guide to Philosophy and Christian Faith* provided the framework. My introduction to Douglas Farrow's *Ascension and Ecclesia* coalesced with my interest in pneumatology and Pentecostalism to produce a fresh theological vantage point from which to view not only the content of the metaphors but also the process by which they might have been originally created. This vantage point soon became, therefore, not just my own vantage point but an imagined vantage point for the earliest Christians themselves. This idea was slightly (though not greatly) strengthened by my discovery of feminist standpoint theory. Clearly, not all of these formative influences on this work have ended up playing a decisive role in the outcomes. They are more like an only-just-tamed tendency toward eclecticism on my part.

I am pleased, however, with what has resulted from all these years of work. Once again, here is a volume that will serve as a general survey, a textbook, an introduction, but which also I hope gently moves the scholarly conversation forward. So, what atonement theology does this book give us? Strong themes have included victory over powers—both those outside of us and those within our own selves—and somehow dying and rising with him as the only way of tapping into that victory and living truly free. It claims that the New Testament writers do not tire of celebrating and proclaiming

Christ's death as the final sacrifice for the sins of the whole world, a loving self-donation on behalf of all of us, more than compensating for our miserable catalogue failures to give to our glorious Creator what is owed. Christ's offering was a representative making up for, a measuring up on our behalf, a doing-enough, a satisfaction. This all-sufficient sacrifice means that God has practiced what Christ preached: he has loved his enemies and taken all the initiative in reconciling them to himself. Once we receive the reconciliation we find ourselves the object of a surprise outcome to the prophetic lawsuit; there is a "but now" moment in which all accusations are dropped and a status of acceptance is given. You will notice I have just rearranged the pictures. It seems they are now: victory, participation, redemption, and sacrifice, reconciliation, justification. I have rearranged these chapters so many times now I think I will just pretend that did not just happen.

What is clear is that Christ's atonement is very, very good news today, just as it was in the first century. The truths I have just so glibly trotted out are dynamite. They remain absolutely on point as remedies for a whole host of personal and social ills. The task of contextualizing this, however, is something I was hoping you would take care of. For my part I will do my best to do something within my own context that offers these pictures of atonement to a badly broken world.

Bibliography

Abraham, William. *The Logic of Evangelism*. London: Hodder & Stoughton, 1989.
Allison, Greg. "Theological Interpretation of Scripture: An Introduction and Evaluation." *The Southern Baptist Journal of Theology* 14.2 (2010) 28–36.
Angus, Samuel. *The Mystery Religions and Christianity*. London: John Murray, 1925.
———. *The Mystery Religions: A Study in the Religious Background of Early Christianity*. London: John Murray, 1925.
Arnold, Clinton. *Powers of Darkness: A Thoughtful, Biblical Look at an Urgent Challenge Facing the Church*. Leicester, UK: IVP, 1992.
Aulén, Gustav. *Christus Victor*. Translated by A. G. Herbert. London: SPCK, 1931.
Bailey, Daniel. "Jesus as the Mercy Seat: The Semantics and Theology of Paul's Use of *Hilasterion* in Romans 3:25." PhD diss., University of Cambridge, 1999.
———. "Jesus as the Mercy Seat: The Semantics and Theology of Paul's Use of *Hilasterion* in Romans 3:25." *Tyndale Bulletin* 51.1 (2000) 155–58.
Barth, Karl. *Church Dogmatics*. Edited and translated by Geoffrey Bromiley and T. F. Torrance. Edinburgh: T. & T. Clark, 1945–58.
Bash, Anthony. *Ambassadors for Christ: An Exploration of Ambassadorial Language in the New Testament*. Tübingen: Mohr-Siebeck, 1997.
Bauckham, Richard. *Bible and Mission: Christian Witness in a Postmodern World*. Milton Keynes, UK: Paternoster, 2003.
———. "Markan Christology according to Richard Hays: Some Addenda." *Journal of Theological Interpretation* 11.1 (2017) 21–30.
Baum, Gregory. "Baptism." In *Sacramentum Mundi: An Encyclopedia of Theology* I, edited by Adolf Darlap, 136–46. London: Burns and Oates, 1968.
Beasley-Murray, G. R. *Baptism in the New Testament*. London: MacMillan, 1962.
Beker, J. Christiaan. *Paul the Apostle: The Triumph of God in Life and Thought*. Philadelphia: Fortress, 1980.
Bell, Richard. *Deliver us from Evil: Interpreting the Redemption from the Power of Satan in New Testament Theology*. Tübingen: Mohr Siebeck, 2007.
Benoit, Pierre. "Pauline Angelology and Demonology: Reflexions on the Designations of the Heavenly Powers and the Origin of Angelic Evil according to Paul." *Religious Studies Bulletin* 3.1 (1983) 1–18.
Best, Ernest. *Following Jesus: Discipleship in the Gospel of Mark*. Sheffield, UK: Sheffield University Press, 1981.
Betz, Hans Dieter, ed. *The Greek Magical Papyri*. Chicago: University of Chicago Press, 1986.

Bibliography

———. *Galatians: A Commentary on Paul's Letter to the Churches in Galatia*. Hermeneia. Philadelphia: Fortress, 1979.
Black, Max. *Models and Metaphors: Studies in Language and Philosophy*. Ithaca, NY: Cornell University Press, 1962.
Blocher, Henri. *La Doctrine du péché et de la redemption*. Vaux-sur-Siene: Édifac, 2000.
Block, Daniel. "The Burden of Leadership: The Mosaic Paradigm of Kingship (Deut. 17:14–20)." *Bibliotheca Sacra* 162 (2005) 259–78.
Boer, Martinus de. "Paul's Use and Interpretation of a Justification Tradition in Galatians 2:15–21." *Journal for the Study of the New Testament* 28.2 (2005) 189–216.
Bolt, Peter. *The Cross from a Distance: Atonement in Mark's Gospel*. Downers Grove, IL: IVP, 2004.
———. "Feeling the Cross: Mark's Message of Atonement." *Reformed Theological Review* 60 (2001) 10–32.
Bond, Helen. "E. P. Sanders and the 'Trial' of Jesus." *Journal for the Study of the Historical Jesus* 13 (2015) 93–115.
Boyd, Gregory. "Christus Victor View." In *The Nature of the Atonement: Four Views*, edited by James Beilby and Paul Eddy, 23–49. Downers Grove, IL: IVP, 2006.
———. *God at War: The Bible and Spiritual Conflict*. Downers Grove, IL: IVP, 1997.
Bradley, Ian. *The Power of Sacrifice*. London: Darton, Longman & Todd, 1995.
Braund, Susanna Morton. "The Anger of Tyrants and the Forgiveness of Kings." In *Ancient Forgiveness: Classical, Judaic, and Christian*, edited by C. L. Griswold and D. Konstan, 79–96. Cambridge: Cambridge University Press, 2010.
Bremmer, Jan. "Greek Normative Animal Sacrifice." In *A Companion to Greek Religion*, edited by D. Ogden, 132–44. Oxford: Wiley-Blackwell, 2007.
Breytenbach, Cilliers. *Versöhnung: Eine Studie zur paulinischen Soteriology*. Neukirchen-Vluyn: Neukirchener, 1989.
Brink, Laurie. "From Wrongdoer to New Creation: Reconciliation in 2 Corinthians." *Interpretation* 71.3 (2017) 298–309.
Brondos, David. "The Cross and the Curse: Galatians 3:13 and Paul's Doctrine of Redemption." *Journal for the Study of the New Testament* 81 (2001) 3–32.
Brown, David. *God and Mystery in Words: Experience through Metaphor and Drama*. Oxford: Oxford University Press, 2008.
Bruce, F. F. *The Epistle to the Hebrews*. NICNT. Grand Rapids: Eerdmans, 1990.
———. *Paul and Jesus*. London: SPCK, 1977.
———. *Paul: Apostle of the Heart Set Free*. Exeter, UK: Paternoster, 1977.
Brueggemann, Walter. "Ancient Israel on Political Leadership: Between the Book Ends." *Political Theology* 8.4 (2007) 455–69.
Buker, Bill. "Spiritual Development and the Epistemology of Systems Theory." *Journal of Psychology and Theology* 31.2 (2003) 143–53.
Bultmann, Rudolf. *Theology of the New Testament, Vol. 1*. London: SCM, 1951.
Burkert, Walter. *Ancient Mystery Cults*. Oxford: Blackwell, 1987.
Burnett, Gary. *Paul and the Salvation of the Individual*. Leiden: Brill, 2001.
Burnhope, Stephen. *Atonement and the New Perspective: The God of Israel, Covenant, and the Cross*. Eugene, OR: Pickwick, 2018.
Caird, George. *Principalities and Powers: A Study in Pauline Theology*. Oxford: Oxford University Press, 1956.
Calvin, John. *Institutes of the Christian Religion*. 2 vols. Translated by Henry Beveridge. London: James Clarke, 1962.

Bibliography

Campbell, Douglas. *The Deliverance of God: An Apocalyptic Rereading of Justification in Paul.* Grand Rapids: Eerdmans, 2013.
———. *The Quest for Paul's Gospel: A Suggested Strategy.* London: T. & T. Clark, 2005.
Caragounis, C. C. "Kingdom of God/Heaven." In *Dictionary of Jesus and the Gospels*, edited by Joel B. Green, Scot McKnight, and I. Howard Marshall, 417–30. Leicester, UK: IVP, 1992.
Carey, George. "Lamb of God and Atonement Theories." *Tyndale Bulletin* 32 (1981) 97–121.
Carpinelli, Francis. "'Do This as *My* Memorial': (Luke 22:19): Lucan Soteriology of Atonement." *Catholic Biblical Quarterly* 61 (1999) 74–91.
Carr, Wesley. *Angels and Principalities: The Background, Meaning, and Development of the Pauline Phrase 'hai Archai kai hai Exousiai'.* Cambridge: Cambridge University Press, 1981.
Carson, Don. "What Is the Gospel?—Revisited." In *For the Fame of God's Name: Essays in Honor of John Piper*, edited by Sam Storms and Justin Taylor, 147–70. Wheaton. IL: Crossway, 2010.
Clauss, Manfred. *The Roman Cult of Mithras.* Edinburgh: Edinburgh University Press, 2000.
Cockburn, Cynthia. "Standpoint Theory." In *Marxism and Feminism*, edited by Shahrzad Mojab, 331–46. London: Zed, 2015.
Collins, Adela Yarbro. "Mark's Interpretation of the Death of Jesus." *Journal of Biblical Literature* 128.3 (2009) 545–54.
———. "The Signification of Mark 10:45 among Gentile Christians." *Harvard Theological Review* 90.4 (1997) 371–82.
Constantineanu, Corneliu. *The Social Significance of Reconciliation in Paul's Theology.* London: T. & T. Clark, 2010.
Copeland, Kenneth. *Covenant of Blood.* Fort Worth, TX: KCM, 1987.
Cortez, Felix. "From the Holy to the Most Holy Place: The Period of Hebrews 9:6–10 and the Day of Atonement as a Metaphor of Transition." *Journal of Biblical Literature* 125.3 (2006) 527–47.
Cowan, J. Andrew. "The Legal Significance of Christ's Risen Life: Union with Christ and Justification in Galatians 2:17–20." *Journal for the Study of the New Testament* 40.4 (2018) 453–72.
Cross, Anthony. "Spirit- and Water-Baptism in 1 Corinthians 12:13." In *Dimensions of Baptism*, edited by Stanley Porter and Athony Cross, 120–48. Sheffield, UK: Sheffield Academic Press, 2002.
Daly, Robert. *Sacrifice Unveiled: The True Meaning of Christian Sacrifice.* London: T. & T. Clark, 2009.
Deissmann, Adolf. *Light from the Ancient Near East.* London: Hodder & Stoughton, 1927.
———. *St Paul: A Study in Social and Religious History*, translated by Lionel Strachan. London: Hodder & Stoughton, 1912.
Denny, James. *The Christian Doctrine of Reconciliation.* London: James Clarke, 1959.
deSilva, David. "Grace, the Law and Justification in 4 Ezra and the Pauline Letters: A Dialogue." *Journal for the Study of the New Testament* 37.1 (2014) 25–49.
Dodd, C. H. *The Apostolic Preaching and Its Developments.* London: Hodder and Stoughton, 1936.
———. *The Bible and the Greeks.* London: Hodder and Stoughton, 1935.

Bibliography

Dowd, Sharyn, and Elizabeth Struthers Malbon. "The Significance of Jesus' Death in Mark: Narrative Context and Authorial Audience." *Journal of Biblical Literature* 125.2 (2006) 271–97.

Downing, F. Gerald. "Justification as Acquittal? A Critical Examination of Judicial Verdicts in Paul's Literary and Actual Contexts." *The Catholic Biblical Quarterly* 74 (2012) 298–318.

Duff, Paul. "Metaphor, Motif, and Meaning: The Rhetorical Strategy behind the Image 'Led in Triumph' in 2 Corinthians 2:14." *Catholic Biblical Quarterly* 53 (1991) 79–92.

Dunn, James D. G. *Jesus and the Spirit*. London: SCM, 1973.

———. *The New Perspective on Paul*. Grand Rapids: Eerdmans, 2007.

———. *The Theology of Paul the Apostle*. Edinburgh: T. & T. Clark, 1998.

Dupont, Jacques. "La Réconciliation dans la théologie de saint Paul." *Estudios Biblicos* XI (1952) 255–302.

Ellingworth, Paul. *The Epistle to the Hebrews: A Commentary on the Greek Text*. NIGTC. Carlisle, UK: Paternoster, 1993.

Esler, Philip. *Community and Gospel in Luke-Acts: The Social and Political Motivations of Lucan Theology*. Cambridge: Cambridge University Press, 1987.

———. *Conflict and Community in Romans*. Minneapolis: Fortress, 2003.

———. *The First Christians in Their Social Worlds: Social-Scientific Approaches to New Testament Interpretation*. London: Routledge, 1994.

Ezra, Daniel Stökl ben. *The Impact of Yom Kippur on Early Christianity: The Day of Atonement from Second Temple Judaism to the Fifth Century*. Tübingen: Mohr Siebeck, 2003.

Faraone, C. A., and F. S. Naiden, eds. *Greek and Roman Animal Sacrifice: Ancient Victims, Modern Observers*. Cambridge: Cambridge University Press, 2012.

Farmer, William. *Jesus and the Gospel: Tradition, Scripture, and Canon*. Philadelphia: Fortress, 1982.

Finlan, Stephen. *Problems with Atonement: The Origins of, and Controversy about, the Atonement Doctrine*. Collegeville, MN: Liturgical, 2005.

Fitzmyer, Joseph. "Reconciliation in Pauline Theology." In *No Famine in the Land: Studies in Honor of John L. McKenzie*, edited by J. Flanagan and A. Robinson, 155–77. Missoula: Scholars, 1975.

———. "Reconciliation: A Study of Paul's Theology." *Interpretation* 37.1 (1983) 83–84.

Ford, J. Massingberd. "'Mingled Blood' from the Side of Christ (John XIX.34)." *New Testament Studies* 15.3 (1969) 337–38.

Fowl, Stephen, ed. *The Theological Interpretation of Scripture: Classic and Contemporary Readings*. Oxford: Blackwell, 1997.

Fredriksen, Paula. "Paul's Letter to the Romans, the Ten Commandments, and Pagan 'Justification by Faith.'" *Journal of Biblical Literature* 133.4 (2014) 801–8.

Furnish, Victor Paul. "The Ministry of Reconciliation." *Currents in Theology and Mission* 4 (1977) 204–18.

Gadamer, Hans Georg. *Truth and Method*. Translated by Joel Weinsheimer and Donald G. Marshall. New York: Seabury, 1989.

Galvin, John. "The Death of Jesus in Contemporary Theology: Systematic Perspectives and Historical Issues." *Horizons* 13.2 (1986) 239–52.

———. "The Resurrection of Jesus in Contemporary Catholic Systematics." *Heythrop Journal* 20 (1979) 123–45.

Bibliography

Gathercole, Simon. *Defending Substitution: An Essay on Atonement in Paul.* Grand Rapids: Baker, 2015.
Gaventa, Beverley Roberts, ed. *Apocalyptic Paul: Cosmos and Anthropos in Romans 5–8.* Waco, TX: Baylor University Press, 2013.
———. *From Darkness to Light: Aspects of Conversion in the New Testament.* Philadelphia: Fortress, 1986.
———. "The Singularity of the Gospel Revisited." In *Galatians and Christian Theology: Justification, the Gospel, and Ethics in Paul's Letter,* edited by Mark Elliott et al., 187–99. Grand Rapids: Baker, 2014.
Girard, Réné. *I See Satan Fall Like Lightning.* Maryknoll, NY: Orbis, 2001.
Goheen, Michael. "A History and Introduction to a Missional Reading of the Bible." In *Reading the Bible Missionally,* edited by Michael Goheen, 3–27. Grand Rapids: Eerdmans, 2016.
Goldingay, John. "Old Testament Sacrifice and the Death of Christ." In *Atonement Today,* edited by John Goldingay, 3–20. London: SPCK, 1995.
Goodman, Nelson. *Languages of Art: An Approach to a Theory of Symbols.* Oxford: Oxford University Press, 1969.
Gorman, Michael. *Apostle of the Crucified Lord: A Theological Introduction to Paul and His Letters.* Grand Rapids: Eerdmans, 2017.
———. *Becoming the Gospel: Paul, Participation, and Mission.* Grand Rapids: Eerdmans, 2015.
———. "Cruciformity according to Jesus and Paul." In *Unity and Diversity in the Gospels and Paul: Essays in Honor of Frank J. Matera,* edited by Christopher Skinner and Kelly Iveson, 173–201. Atlanta: SBL, 2012.
———. *Cruciformity: Paul's Narrative Spirituality of the Cross.* Grand Rapids: Eerdmans, 2001.
———. *The Death of the Messiah and the Birth of the New Covenant: A (Not So) New Model of the Atonement.* Eugene, OR: Cascade, 2014.
———. *Inhabiting the Cruciform God: Kenosis, Justification, and Theosis in Paul's Narrative Soteriology.* Grand Rapids: Eerdmans, 2009.
———. *Participating in Christ: Explorations in Paul's Theology and Spirituality.* Grand Rapids: Baker, 2019.
———. "Paul's Corporate, Cruciform, Missional Theosis in Second Corinthians." In *"In Christ" in Paul: Explorations in Paul's Theology of Union and Participation,* edited by Kevin Vanhoozer, Constantine Campbell, and Michael Thate, 181–208. Tübingen: Mohr/Siebeck, 2014.
Grayston, Kenneth. *Dying, We Live: A New Enquiry into the Death of Christ in the New Testament.* London: Darton, Longman & Todd, 1990.
Green, Joel. "Kaleidoscopic Response." In *The Nature of the Atonement: Four Views,* edited by James Beilby and Paul Eddy, 61–5. Downers Grove, IL: IVP, 2006.
Gundry, Robert. *Mark: A Commentary on His Apology for the Cross.* Grand Rapids: Eerdmans, 2000.
Gunton, Colin. *The Actuality of Atonement: A Study of Metaphor, Rationality and the Christian Tradition.* Edinburgh: T. & T. Clark, 1988.
Guy, Laurie. "Back to the Future: The Millennium and the Exodus in Revelation 20." *Evangelical Quarterly* 86.3 (2014) 227–38.
Hahn, Scott. "A Broken Covenant and the Curse of Death: A Study of Hebrews 9:15–22." *Catholic Biblical Quarterly* 66.3 (2004) 416–36.

Bibliography

Harding, Sandra, ed. *The Feminist Standpoint Theory Reader: Intellectual and Political Controversies*. London: Routledge, 2004.
Hare, Douglas. *Mark*. Louisville, KY: Westminster John Knox, 1996.
Harris, Murray J. "Prepositions and Theology in the Greek New Testament." In *The New International Dictionary of New Testament Theology*, Vol. 3, edited by Colin Brown, 1171–1215. Exeter, UK: Paternoster, 1978.
———. *The Second Epistle to the Corinthians: A Commentary on the Greek Text*. NIGTC. Grand Rapids: Eerdmans, 2005.
Hartsock, Nancy. "Comment on Hekman's 'Truth and Method: Feminist Standpoint Theory Revisited.' Where's the Power?" *Signs* 22.2 (1997) 367–74.
Hartsock, Nancy. *The Feminist Standpoint Revisited and Other Essays*. Boulder, CO: Westview, 1998.
Hassler, Andrew. "Ethnocentric Legalism and the Justification of the Individual: Rethinking Some New Perspective Assumptions." *Journal of the Evangelical Theological Society* 54.2 (2011) 311–27.
Hayes, John. "Atonement in the Book of Leviticus." *Interpretation* 52.1 (1998) 5–15.
Hays, Richard. *The Faith of Jesus Christ: The Narrative Substructure of Galatians 3:1—4:11*. Grand Rapids: Eerdmans, 2002.
Hengel, Martin. *The Atonement: The Origins of the Doctrine in the New Testament*. Translated by John Bowden. London: SCM, 1981.
———. *Crucifixion*. Philadelphia: Fortress, 1977.
Henten, Jan Willem van. *The Maccabean Martyrs as Saviours of the Jewish People: A Study of 2 & 4 Maccabees*. Leiden: Brill, 1997.
———. "The Tradition-Historical Background of Rom 3:25: A Search for Pagan and Jewish Parallels." In *From Jesus to John: Essays on Jesus and New Testament Christology in Honour of Martinus de Jonge*, edited by Martinus C. De Boer, 101–28. Sheffield, UK: Sheffield Academic Press, 1993.
Hicks, Frederick. *The Fullness of Sacrifice: A Essay on Reconciliation*. London: SPCK, 1953.
Hiebert, Paul. "The Flaw of the Excluded Middle." *Missiology: An International Review* 10.1 (1982) 35–47.
Hock, Andreas. "Christ the Parade: A Comparative Study of Triumphal Procession in 2 Cor 2,14 and Col 2,15." *Biblica* 88 (2007) 110–19.
Hofius, Otfried. "Erwägungen zur Gestalt und Herkunft des paulinischen Versöhnungsgedankens," *Wissenschaftliche Untersuchungen zum Neuen Testament* 77 (1980) 11–14.
Hood, Jason. "Evangelicals and the Imitation of the Cross: Peter Bolt on Mark 13 as a Test Case." *Evangelical Quarterly* 81.2 (2009) 116–25.
Hooker, Morna. *Jesus and the Servant*. London: SPCK, 1959.
Hoskyns, E. C. *The Fourth Gospel*. London: Faber & Faber, 1961.
Hughes, John. "Hebrews IX 15ff. and Galatians III 15ff.: A Study in Covenant Practice and Procedure." *Novum Testamentum* XXI, fasc.I (1979) 27–96.
Hughes, T. H. *The Atonement*. London: Allen and Unwin, 1949.
James, E. O. *Sacrifice and Sacrament*. London: Thames and Hudson, 1962.
James, William. *Varieties of Religious Experience*. London: Penguin, 1985.
Janowski, Bernd. "He Bore Our Sins: Isaiah 53 and the Drama of Taking Another's Place." In *The Suffering Servant: Isaiah 53 in Jewish and Christian Sources*, edited by Bernd Janowski and Peter Stuhlmacher, translated by D. P. Bailey, 48–74. Grand Rapids: Eerdmans, 2004.

Bibliography

Jeremias, Joachim. *The Central Message of the New Testament*. London: SCM, 1965.
Käsemann, Ernst. *Commentary on Romans*. London: SCM, 1980.
———. "Some Thoughts on the Theme 'The Doctrine of Reconciliation in the New Testament.'" In *The Future of Our Religious Past: Essays in Honour of Rudolf Bultmann*, edited by J. M. Robinson, 49–64. London: SCM, 1964.
———. *Perspectives on Paul*. London: SCM, 1971.
Keil, Friedrich, and Franz Delitzsch. *Biblical Commentary on the Old Testament, Vol. II: The Pentateuch*. Grand Rapids: Eerdmans, 1978.
Kennedy, H. A. A. *St Paul and the Mystery Religions*. London: Hodder and Stoughton, 1913.
Kidner, Derek. "Sacrifice: Metaphors and Meaning." *Tyndale Bulletin* 33 (1982) 119–36.
Kim, Jintae. "The Concept of Atonement in Early Rabbinic Thought and the New Testament Writings." *Journal of Greco-Roman Christianity and Judaism* 2 (2001) 117–45.
Kim, Seyoon. "2 Cor. 5:11–21 and the Origins of Paul's Concept of 'Reconciliation.'" *Novum Testamentum* 39.4 (1997) 360–84.
———. *The Origin of Paul's Gospel*. Grand Rapids: Eerdmans, 1981.
Klauck, Hans-Josef. *The Religious Context of Early Christianity: A Guide to Graeco-Roman Religions*. Minneapolis: Fortress, 2003.
Klein, Ralph. "Liberated Leadership: Masters and 'Lords' in Biblical Perspective." *Currents in Theology and Mission* 9.5 (1982) 282–90.
Lakoff, George, and Mark Johnson. *Metaphors We Live By*. Chicago: Chicago University Press, 1980.
Lane, William. *Hebrews 9–13*. WBC. Waco, TX: Word, 1991.
Larsson, Göran. *Bound for Freedom*. Peabody, MA: Hendrickson, 1999.
Letham, Robert. *The Work of Christ*. Leicester, UK: IVP, 1993.
Levison, John. *Filled with the Spirit*. Grand Rapids: Eerdmans, 2009.
———. "*Filled with the Spirit*: A Conversation with Pentecostal and Charismatic Scholars." *Journal of Pentecostal Theology* 20 (2011) 213–31.
Lévi-Strauss, Claude. *The Savage Mind*. Translated by George Weidenfield. London: Weidenfeld and Nicolson, 1972.
Liddell, H. G., and R. Scott. *Greek-English Lexicon*. Abridged. Oxford: Oxford University Press, 1994.
Lloyd Jones, Martyn. *Romans: Exposition of Chapter 6: The New Man*. Edinburgh: Banner of Truth, 1972.
Lohse, Eduard. *Märtyrer und Gottesknecht: Untersuchungen zur urchristlichen Verkündigung vom Sühne Jesus Christi*. Göttingen: Vandenhoeck & Ruprecht, 1963.
Louth, Andrew, ed. *Ancient Christian Commentary on Scripture, Old Testament I*. Downers Grove, IL: IVP, 2001.
Luc, Alex. "The Kingdom of God and His Mission." In *Discovering the Mission of God*, edited by Mike Barnet and Robin Martin, 85–98. Downers Grove, IL: IVP, 2012.
Luther, Martin. *Galatians*. Wheaton, IL: Crossway, 1998.
Macaskill. Grant. *Union with Christ in the New Testament*. Oxford: Oxford University Press, 2013.
Maccoby, Hyam. *The Sacred Executioner*. London: Thames and Hudson, 1982.
Mackenzie, Ed. "The Quest for the Political Paul: Assessing the Apostle's Approach to Empire." *European Journal of Theology* 20.1 (2011) 40–50.

BIBLIOGRAPHY

Maier, Harry. "A Sly Civility: Colossians and Empire." *Journal for the Study of the New Testament* 27.3 (2005) 323–49.
Malbon, Elizabeth. "Fallible Followers: Women and Men in the Gospel of Mark." *Semeia* 28 (1983) 29–48.
Manson, T. W. *On Paul and John*. London: SCM, 1963.
Marcus, Joel. "Crucifixion as Parodic Exaltation." *Journal of Biblical Literature* 125 (2006) 73–87.
Marshall, I. Howard. "The Meaning of 'Reconciliation.'" In *Unity and Diversity in New Testament Theology*, edited by Robert Guelich, 117–32. Grand Rapids: Eerdmans, 1978.
Martin, R. A. "The Earliest Messianic Interpretation of Genesis 3:15." *Journal of Biblical Literature* 84.4 (1965) 425–27.
Martin, Ralph. *Carmen Christi*. Cambridge: Cambridge University Press, 1967.
———. *Reconciliation: A Study of Paul's Theology*. London: Marshall, Morgan & Scott, 1981.
Martyn, J. Louis. *Galatians: A New Translation with Introduction and Commentary*. New York: Doubleday, 1997.
———. *Theological Issues in the Letters of Paul*. Edinburgh: T. & T. Clark, 1997.
Marx, Alfred. *Les Sacrifices de l'Ancien Testament*. Cahiers Évangile III. Paris: Cerf, 2000.
McCarthy, Dennis. "The Symbolism of Blood and Sacrifice." *Journal of Biblical Literature* 88.2 (1969) 166–76.
McGilchrist, Iain. *The Master and His Emissary: The Divided Brain and the Making of the Western World*. New Haven, CT: Yale University Press, 2009.
McGrath, Alister. *Iustitia Dei: A History of the Doctrine of Justification*. Cambridge: Cambridge University Press, 2005.
McIntyre, John. *The Shape of Soteriology: Studies in the Doctrine of the Death of Christ*. Edinburgh: T. & T. Clark, 1992.
Meeks, Wayne. "Inventing the Christ: Multicultural Process and Poetry among the First Christians." *Studia Theologica* 58 (2004) 77–96.
Meyer, Marvin. *The Ancient Mysteries: A Sourcebook of Sacred Texts*. London: HarperCollins, 1987.
Milgrom, Jacob. *Cult and Conscience: The ASHAM and the Priestly Doctrine of Repentance*. Leiden: Brill, 1976.
———. *Leviticus 1–16*. Anchor Bible. New York: Doubleday, 1991.
———. "A Prolegomenon to Leviticus 17:11." *Journal of Biblical Literature* 90 (1971) 149–56.
Moffitt, David. "It is Not Finished: Jesus's Perpetual Atoning Work as the Heavenly High Priest in Hebrews." In *So Great a Salvation: A Dialogue on the Atonement in Hebrews*, edited by Jon Laansma, et al., 157–75. London: T. & T. Clark, 2019.
Moo, Douglas. Review of *The Deliverance of God: An Apocalyptic Rereading of Justification in Paul* by Douglas A. Campbell. *Journal of the European Theological Society* 53.1 (2010) 143–50.
Morales, Michael. "Atonement in Ancient Israel: The Whole Burnt Offering as Central to Israel's Cult." In *So Great a Salvation: A Dialogue on the Atonement in Hebrews*, edited by Jon Laansma, et al., 27–39. London: T. & T. Clark, 2019.
Morris, Leon. *The Apostolic Preaching of the Cross*. London: Tyndale, 1965.
Munro, Winsome. "Women in Mark's Gospel: An Early Christian View of Woman's Role." *The Bible Today* 19 (1981) 228–33.

Bibliography

Murray, Andrew. *The Blood of the Cross.* Springdale, PA: Whitaker House, 1981.
———. *The Holiest of All: An Exposition of the Epistle to the Hebrews.* Grand Rapids: Revell, 1993.
Myers, Ched, and Elaine Enns. *Ambassadors of Reconciliation, Vol. 1: New Testament Reflections on Restorative Justice and Peacemaking.* Maryknoll, NY: Orbis, 2009.
Nabarz, Payam. *The Mysteries of Mithras.* Rochester, NY: Princeton University Press, 2005.
Nicole, Emile. "Atonement in the Pentateuch." In *The Glory of the Atonement: Biblical, Theological and Practical Perspectives*, edited by Charles Hill & Frank James III, 35–50. Downers Grove, IL: IVP, 2004.
Nuefeld, Thomas Yoder. "'For He is Our Peace': Ephesians 2:11–22." In *Beautiful Upon the Mountains: Biblical Essays on Mission, Peace, and the Reign of God*, edited by Mary Schertz and Ivan Friesn, 215–33. Elkhart, IN: Institute of Mennonite Studies, 2003.
Ott, Craig. "The Power of Biblical Metaphors for the Contextualized Communication of the Gospel." *Missiology* 42.4 (2014) 357–74.
Pao, David. *Acts and the Isaianic New Exodus.* Tübingen: Mohr/Siebeck, 2000.
Peerbolte, Bert Jan Lietaert. "A New Perspective on Justification: Recent Developments in the Study of Paul." *Zeitschrift für Dialektische Theologie* 6 (2014) 128–52.
Pelser, Gert. "Could the 'Formulas' Dying and rising with Christ be Expressions of Pauline Mysticism?" *Neotestamentica* 32.1 (1998) 115–34.
Penn-Lewis, Jessie. *The Battle for the Mind.* Poole, UK: Overcomer, nd.
———. *The Centrality of the Cross.* Poole, UK: Overcomer, nd.
———. *The Glorious Secret.* Poole, UK: Overcomer, 1898.
———. *The Leading of the Lord.* Poole, UK: Overcomer, 1903.
———. *More than Conquerors.* Poole, UK: Overcomer, nd.
Pfleiderer, Otto. *Christian Origins.* New York: Huebsch, 1906.
Plummer, Robert. *40 Questions about Interpreting the Bible.* Grand Rapids: Kregel, 2010.
Poe, Harry. *The Gospel and Its Meaning.* Grand Rapids: Zondervan, 1996.
Porter, Joshua. *Leviticus.* Cambridge: Cambridge University Press, 1976.
Porter, Stanley. Καταλλασσω *in Ancient Greek Literature, with Reference to the Pauline Writings.* Cordoba, Spain: Ediciones El Almendra, 1994.
Prothro, James. "The Strange Case of Δικαιοω in the Septuagint and Paul: The Oddity and Origins of Paul's Talk of 'Justification.'" *ZNW* 107.1 (2016) 48–69.
Pugh, Ben. *Atonement Theories: A Way through the Maze.* Eugene, OR: Cascade, 2014.
———. *Bold Faith: A Closer Look at the Five Key Ideas of Charismatic Christianity.* Eugene, OR: Wipf & Stock, 2017.
———. *Old Rugged Cross: A History of the Atonement in Popular Christian Devotion.* Eugene, OR: Cascade, 2016.
Rainey, A. F. "The Order of Sacrifices in Old Testament Ritual Texts." *Biblia* 51 (1970) 485–98.
Reichenbach, Bruce. "Healing Response." In *The Nature of the Atonement: Four Views*, edited by James Beilby and Paul Eddy, 54–60. Downers Grove, IL: IVP, 2006.
Rempel, Morgan. "Nietzsche, Mithras, and 'Complete Heathendom.'" *Comparative and Continental Philosophy* 2.1 (2010) 27–43.
Ribbens, Benjamin. "Forensic-Retributive Justification in Romans 3:21–26: Paul's Doctrine of Justification in Dialogue with Hebrews." *Catholic Biblical Quarterly* 74 (2012) 548–67.
Ricoeur, Paul, and Harry Prosch. *Meaning.* Chicaho: University of Chicago Press, 1975.
Ricoeur, Paul. "The Metaphorical Process." *Semeia* 4 (1975) 78–79.

Bibliography

———. *The Rule of Metaphor: Multi-Disciplinary Studies in the Creation of Meaning in Language*. Translated by Robert Czerny with Kathleen McLaughlin and John Costello, S.J. London: Routledge and Kegan Paul, 1978.

Ridderbos, Herman. *Paul: An Outline of his Theology*. Grand Rapids: Eerdmans, 1975.

Romerowski, Sylvain. "Old Testament Sacrifices and Reconciliation." *European Journal of Theology* 16.1 (2006) 13–24.

Rosenberg, R. A. "Jesus, Isaac, and the 'Suffering Servant.'" *Journal of Biblical Literature* 84 (1965) 381–88.

Routledge, Robin. *Old Testament Theology*. Leicester, UK: Apollos, 2008.

Salter, Martin. "Does Baptism Replace Circumcision? An Examination of the Relationship between Circumcision and Baptism in Colossians 2:11–12." *Themelios* 35.1 (2010) 15–29.

Sanders, E. P. *Paul and Palestinian Judaism: A Comparison of Patterns of Religion*. London: SCM, 1977.

Sandnes, Karl Olav. "The Death of Jesus for Human Sins: The Historical Basis for a Theological Concept." *Themelios* 20.1 (1994) 20–23.

Schnabel, Eckhard. "Jesus's Atoning Sacrifice in Hebrews and Atonement for Sin in the Greco-Roman World." In *So Great a Salvation: A Dialogue on the Atonement in Hebrews*, edited by Laansma, et al., 65–86. London: T. & T. Clark, 2019.

Schreiner, Thomas. *Romans*. Grand Rapids: Baker, 1998.

Schreiter, Robert. *Reconciliation: Mission and Ministry in a Changing Social Order*. Maryknoll, NY: Orbis, 1992.

Schwartz, Daniel. "Two Pauline Allusions to the Redemptive Mechanism of the Crucifixion." *Journal of Biblical Literature* 102.2 (1983) 259–68.

Schweitzer, Albert. *The Mysticism of Paul the Apostle*. London: A. & C. Black, 1931.

Scott, E. F. *The Epistles of Paul to the Colossians, to Philemon, and to the Ephesians*. London: Hodder & Stoughton, 1930.

Seely, David. *The Noble Death: Graeco-Roman Martyrology and Paul's Concept of Salvation*. Sheffield, UK: Sheffield Academic Press, 1990.

Seifrid, Mark. *Christ, Our Righteousness*. Leicester, UK: IVP, 2000.

Shaw, David. "Apocalyptic and Covenant: Perspectives on Paul or Antinomies at War?" *Journal for the Study of the New Testament* 36.2 (2013) 155–71.

———. "Romans 4 and the Justification of Abraham in Light of Perspectives New and Newer." *Themelios* 40.1 (2015) 50–62.

Shelton, Larry. *Cross and Covenant: Interpreting the Atonement for 21st Century Mission*. Waynesboro, GA: Paternoster, 2006.

Silvoso, Ed. *That None Should Perish*. Ventura, CA: Regal, 1994.

Snyder-Belousek, Darrin W. *Atonement, Justice, and Peace: The Message of the Cross and the Mission of the Church*. Grand Rapids: Eerdmans, 2012.

Soskice, Janet Martin. *Metaphor and Religious Language*. Oxford: Clarendon, 1985.

Stein, Robert. *The Law and Its Fulfilment: A Pauline Theology of Law*. Grand Rapids: Baker, 1993.

Stendahl, Krister. "The Apostle Paul and the Introspective Conscience of the West." *Harvard Theological Review* 56 (1963) 199–215.

Stettler, Hanna. "Did Paul Invent Justification by Faith?" *Tyndale Bulletin* 66.2 (2015) 161–96.

Stibbs, Alan. *The Meaning of the Word "Blood" in Scripture*. London: Tyndale, 1947.

Stott, John. *The Cross of Christ*. Leicester, UK: IVP, 1986.

Bibliography

Stuhlmacher, Peter. *Biblische Theologie des Neuen Testaments 1: Grundlegung: Von Jesus zu Paulus.* Göttingen: Vandenhoeck & Ruprecht, 2005.

———. "The Gospel of Reconciliation in Christ—Basic Features of a Biblical Theology of the New Testament." *Horizons in Biblical Theology* 1 (1979) 161–90.

Swora, Maria. "The Rhetoric of Transformation in the Healing of Alcoholism: The Twelve Steps of Alcoholics Anonymous." *Mental Health, Religion and Culture* 7.3 (2004) 187–209.

Talbert, Charles. *Romans.* Macon, GA: Smyth & Helwys, 2002.

Tannehill, Robert. "The Disciples in Mark: The Function of a Narrative Role." *Journal of Religion* 57 (1977) 386–405.

———. *Dying and Rising with Christ: A Study of Pauline Theology.* Reprint, Eugene, OR: Wipf & Stock, 2006.

Taylor, Vincent. *Forgiveness and Reconciliation.* London: Macmillan, 1946.

———. *Jesus and His Sacrifice: A Study of the Passion Sayings in the Gospels.* London: Macmillan, 1959.

Tiede, David. "Proclaiming the Hidden Kingdom: Preaching on Gospel Lessons on Mark." *Currents in Theology and Mission* 11.6 (1984) 325–32.

Torrance, T. F. *Atonement: The Person and Work of Christ.* Milton Keynes, UK: Paternoster, 2009.

Tozer, A. W. *I Talk Back to the Devil: The Fighting Fervor of the Victorious Christian.* Chicago: Moody, 1972.

Trumbull, H. Clay. *The Blood Covenant: A Primitive Rite and its Bearing on Scripture* Kirkwood, MO: Impact, 1975.

Vanhoozer, Kevin. "The Atonement in Postmodernity: Guilt, Goats, and Gifts." In *The Glory of the Atonement: Biblical, Theological and Practical Perspectives*, edited by Charles Hill & Frank James III, 367–404. Downers Grove, IL: IVP, 2004.

———. *The Drama of Doctrine: A Canonical Linguistic Approach to Christian Doctrine.* Louisville, KY: Westminster John Knox, 2005.

Várhalyi, Zsuzsanna. "'To Forgive is Divine': Gods as Models of Forgiveness in Late Republican and Early Imperial Rome." In *Ancient Forgiveness: Classical, Judaic, and Christian*, edited by C. L. Griswold and D. Konstan, 115–33. Cambridge: Cambridge University Press, 2010.

Vassiliadis, Petros. "Beyond *Theologia Crucis*: Jesus of Nazareth from Q to John *via* Paul (or John as a Radical Reinterpretation of Jesus of Nazareth)." *Greek Orthodox Theological Review* 47.1–4 (2002) 139–63.

Vermes, Geza. *The Complete Dead Sea Scrolls in English.* London: Allen Lane, 1962.

Versnel, Henk. "Making Sense of Jesus' Death: The Pagan Contribution." In *Deutungen des Todes Jesu im Neuen Testament*, edited by J. Frey and J. Schröter, 215–94. Tübingen: Mohr 2005.

———. *Triumphus: An Inquiry into the Origin, Development, and Meaning of the Roman Triumph.* Leiden: Brill, 1970.

Vickers, Brian. "The Kingdom of God in Paul's Gospel." *Southern Baptist Journal of Theology* 12.1 (2008) 52–67.

Waddell, Robby. "The Holy Spirit of Life, Work, and Inspired Speech: Responding to John (Jack) R. Levison, *Filled with the Spirit*." *Journal of Pentecostal Theology* 20 (2011) 207–12.

Walsh, Julie. "Jael's Story as Initial Fulfillment of Genesis 3:15." *Priscilla Papers* 33.4 (2019) 22–37.

Bibliography

Wasserman, Emma. "Paul among the Philosophers: The Case of Sin in Romans 6–8." *Journal for the Study of the New Testament* 30.4 (2008) 387–415.

Watts, Rikki. "Exodus." In *New Dictionary of Biblical Theology*, edited by T. D. Alexander and Brian Rosner, 478–87. Downers Grove, IL: IVP, 2000.

———. *Isaiah's New Exodus and Mark*. Tübingen: Mohr/Siebeck, 1997.

Wedderburn, A. J. M. *Baptism and Resurrection: Studies in Pauline Theology against its Graeco-Roman Background*. Tübingen: Mohr, 1987.

———. "The Soteriology of the Mysteries and Pauline Baptismal Theology." *Novum Testamentum* XIX.1 (1987) 53–72.

Weiss, Johannes. *Earliest Christianity: A History of the Period AD 30–150, Vol. 2*. New York: Harper and Row, 1959.

Wenham, Gordon. *Genesis 1–15*. WBC. Waco, TX: Word, 1987.

Wescott, B. F. *The Epistles of John*. London: Macmillan, 1886.

White, Robert. *The Interpretation of Dreams, Oneirocritica by Artemodorus: Translation and Commentary*. Park Ridge, NJ: Noyes, 1975.

Wiliams, Joel. "Discipleship and Minor Characters in Mark's Gospel." *Bibliotheca Sacra* 153 (1996) 332–43.

Williams, Jarvis. *Maccabean Martyr Traditions in Paul's Theology of Atonement: Did Martyr Theology Shape Paul's Conception of Jesus's Death?* Eugene, OR: Wipf & Stock, 2010.

Williams, Sam. *Jesus' Death as Saving Event: The Background and Origin of a Concept*. Missoula, MO: Scholars, 1975.

Wink, Walter. *Naming the Powers: The Language of Power in the New Testament*. Philadelphia: Fortress, 1984.

Wittgenstein, Ludwig. "Lecture on Religious Belief." In *Wittgenstein: Lectures and Conversations on Aesthetics, Psychology and Religious Belief*, edited by Cyril Barrett, 53–72. Berkeley: University of California Press, 1966.

Wrede, William. *Paul*. Translated by Edward Lummis. London: Philip Green, 1907.

Wright, N. T. "4QMMT and Paul: Justification, 'Works,' and Eschatology." In *History and Exegesis: New Testament Essays in Honor of Dr E. Earle Ellis for his 80th Birthday*, edited by Aang-Won Son, 104–32. London: T. & T. Clark, 2006.

———. *The Climax of the Covenant: Christ and the Law in Pauline Theology*. Edinburgh: T. & T. Clark, 1991.

———. *The Day the Revolution Began: Reconsidering the Meaning of Jesus's Crucifixion*. San Francisco: Harper One, 2016.

———. *How God Became King*. London: SPCK, 2012.

———. *Jesus and the Victory of God*. London: SPCK, 1997.

———. *Paul and the Faithfulness of God*. London: SPCK, 2013.

———. *What St Paul Really Said*. Oxford: Lion, 1997.

Ziesler, John. *Pauline Christianity*. Oxford: Oxford University Press, 1990.

Zoccali, Christopher. "'And so all Israel will be saved': Competing Interpretations of Romans 11.26 in Pauline Scholarship." *Journal for the Study of the New Testament* 30.3 (2008) 289–318.

Ancient Literature Index

Epistle of Barnabas,	87–88	Leviticus Rabba	
7:4–11	88n77	32:43	70n3

2 Baruch,	20	1 Maccabees	
		2:52	74n15
Ben Sira (Ecclesiasticus)		5:20	73
42:2	119–20		
50:14–15	87n74	2 Maccabees	
50:20–21	87n74		75, 128, 128n27, 129n29, 130
		5:20	75, 128
Dead Sea Scrolls		7:30–38	75
1QS11	114, 115n32, 116	7:33	128
4QMMT	115	8:29	75, 128

1 Enoch		4 Maccabees	
1–36	20		75–76, 76n20, 77
51:1–3	34n11	6:22	73
69:27	34n11	6:27–29	75
89:58	33n7	17	76
		17:21–22	75
		17:22	76n19

4 Ezra			
	20, 110n14	Mithras Liturgy	
3:32	33n6	Lines 719–25	51
6:5	110n14		
7:76–77	110n14		
7:113	33n10	Palestinian Targum	
8:33	110n14	Poem of the Four Nights	74–75
9:7–8	110n14		
13:23	110n14		

Scripture Index

OLD TESTAMENT

Genesis

3	20, 23
3:15	22–24
6	20
15	74, 74n15
15:6	115
22	74, 74n15, 75

Exodus

14:13	30
14:30	30
15:2	30
21:29	39
23:7	120n58
24	70, 97
24:8	39
24:29–35	90
30:11–16	39

Leviticus

1:5	81
1:11	81
1:15	81
3:2	81
3:8	81
3:13	81
4:13	83
4:20	99
4:22	83
4:26	99
4:27	83
4:30	81
4:31	99
4:32–35	96
4:35	99
5:1	81
5:4	81
5:9	81
5:10	99
5:13	99
5:18	99
8:14–15	82
10:17	82
14:22	70
16	86–88
16:2	76
16:13–15	76
16:21	41, 81, 87
16:22	41–42
16:31	87
17	99
17:11	81, 97–98
17:14	97–98
25	37

Numbers

7:15–16	86
15:30–31	83

Deuteronomy

17	32

Scripture Index

21:23	69	27:1	28, 40–55
21:23	41		33, 118
25:1	120n58	40–55	130–31
28	42, 103	40–66	30
29:64	42	43:3	130
		43:18–19	118
		43:26	30
Judges		45:22	30, 131
4–5	23	49:8	10
5:24	23	51	28
8:23	32	51:9	10
		52	131
		52–53	10
1 Samuel		52:1	30, 95, 126
8	32	52:7	10
8:11–17	32n4	52:7–8	38n22
10:9–11	32	52:13	39
		52:13—53:12	38, 40, 67, 71–73,
1 Kings		53	76n19, 77, 83, 95,
20	70n3		102, 116
		53:1	72
Job		53:5	102
9:35	106	53:6	102
13:21	106	53:6b	72
13:23	106	53:7b–8a	102
23:27	106	53:10	72, 83, 102
		53:10–12	116
Psalms		53:12	38n23–24, 41, 72
22:1	21–22	57:19a	126
22:21–23	21–22	65:17	131
27:4	56		
40:6	77n24	**Jeremiah**	89
50:12–13	77n24	11:19	96
74:13–15	28	31:31	89n83
90:1	56		
91	56	**Ezekiel**	89
91:1–2	56	36:27	113
91:9–10	56		
98	119n53		
98:2	119	**Daniel**	
110:1	21, 67	7:13–14	21, 38
141:2	78		
143:2	110, 118	**Hosea**	
		6:6	77n24
Isaiah		13:14	29
1–39	10		

Scripture Index

Amos

5:21	77n24

Micah

6:6–7	77n24

∽

NEW TESTAMENT

Matthew

9:13	77n24
12:6	70
12:7	77n24
12:44	21
13:10–11	34
16:28	89
23:23	77n24
26:26–29	70
26:28	40
26:36–46	85
26:54	40n33

Mark

3:21	72
4:40	62
5:22–24a	62
5:35–43	62
6:52	62
7:24–30	62
8:17–18	62
8:27	63
8:27–30	62
8:27—10:52	63
8:31	38
8:34	63
9:30–31	38
9:33	63
10:17–31	63
10:32	63
10:33–34	38
10:45	35, 36n15, 16, 38–40, 38n24, 40, 69
10:46–52	62–63
11:18	77
12:28–34	62
12:36	21
13:1–2	70
14:3–9	62
14:22–25	70
14:24	89
14:57–58	70
14:62	21–22
14:24	39
15:29	70
15:39	62
15:40–41	62
15:42–46	62
16:1–9	62

Luke

1:42	23
1:68	35, 43
2:38	35, 43
4:18–19	37
7:18–23	34
9:51	78
10:19	23
18:14	116
20:43	21
22:14–20	70
22:20b	89
22:42	78
24:21	43
24:26	78
24:26–27	40n33
24:50–53	87

John

1:1	96n107
2:18–22	70
3:3, 5	8
3:16	75
6:53–56	99
7:1–15	72
10:11	71

Scripture Index

10:17–18	71	4	74n15
11:48	69	4:4	122
12:31	15	4:5	106, 120
12:31–33	13	4:25	72, 106
14:27	129	5	126
15:13	71, 77	5–6	54
18:36	8	5–8	111, 113
19:14	95	5:1	121
19:29	95	5:5	122
19:31	95	5:6–8	73n13, 104
19:33–36	95	5:8–11	121
19:34	95–96n104	5:9	106
19:42	95	5:10–11	124
		5:11	128
Acts		5:12–21	57, 103
1:14	72	5:14	55
2:32–36	21	5:17	55
2:33	3, 12	5:18	17
3:18	40n33	5:21	55
5:31	21	6	57–59, 64
6:14	70	6–8	56
8:32	95	6:1	57n51
8:32–35	102	6:1–11	48n11
17:2–3	40n33	6:2–11	56
17:23	93	6:3	46, 48
26:17–18	30n73	6:3–4	58
		6:4	45, 58
		6:6	29
Romans		6:9	55
1–3	122	6:10	55
1–4	112–13	6:11	55
1:17	111, 119	6:12	55
1:17—3:26	119	6:12–13	16
1:18—3:20	111	6:13	55, 66
1:20	121	6:14	55
2:1	121	6:15	57n51
2:15	121	6:16	55, 66
3	76n20	6:16–23	57
3:8	57n51	6:17	55
3:9	121	6:18	16
3:19	121	6:19	55, 66
3:20	119	6:20	16
3:21	76, 122	6:22	55
3:21–26	116–17	6:23	55
3:24	35, 117, 122	7	27
3:25	75, 88, 93, 106	7:4	17
3:28	119n51	7:7	57n51

Scripture Index

Romans (continued)

7:9	17
7:10–11	16
7:13–14	16
7:23	16
8	57
8:10–13	65
8:17	45, 65
8:32	72, 74n15, 75
8:33–34	28, 121
9–11	111
10:3	65
10:4	17
12:1	78
16:20	23–24

1 Corinthians

1:18	2, 11
1:18–25	29
1:22–24	2
2:1–8	29
2:6	27
2:8	27
5:7	95
6:17	48
6:20	37
7:23	36–37
9:1	130
10:1–4	56
11:23–25	70
11:25a	89
12:13	58, 58n54
15:3	72, 77, 118
15:3–4	40n33
15:4	27
15:5–10	130
15:7	72
15:22–25	21
15:24	15
15:26	17
15:55	29
15:56	17, 29

2 Corinthians

1:3–9	65
2:14	26, 130
2:14—7:4	127
3	90
3:7–9	127
4:1	127, 130
4:2	130
4:4	130
4:6	130
4:7–14	65
5	126
5:8	31
5:11–21	130
5:15	71
5:16	130
5:18	127
5:18–20	124
5:19	127
5:20	128
5:21	83, 103
6:2	131
6:3	127
7:3	65
9:7	93
11:13	127
11:15	127
12:9	65
12:11	127
13:4	65

Galatians

1:4	30, 30n73, 103
1:13–17	130
2:16	110, 118–19
2:17–20	112
2:19–20	57
2:19–21	47
2:20	45, 59, 103
3:10	17
3:13	17, 37–38, 40–43, 69, 92, 102–3, 102n125
3:20	110
3:28	109
4:4–5	41–42
4:5	37
4:6	41
5:1	36

Scripture Index

5:11	2		3:4	45
5:24	57			
6:14	29		**1 Thessalonians**	
			1:5–8	65
Ephesians			2:13–16	65
1:7	35		4:14	47
1:17	118		5:10	47, 71
1:21	16			
1:21–22	27		**1 Timothy**	
2	126		2:6	35, 103
2:6	45			
2:8	47n6			
2:13	129		**Titus**	
2:14–16	126		2:14	35, 103
2:16	124, 129		3:1	16
2:17	126			
3:10	16			
5:2	84, 103		**Hebrews**	90
5:25	103		1:3	21
6:12	16		2:14–15	13, 28–29
			6:19–20	88
Philippians			7:14	85
1:23	31		8:1—10:18	87
2:5–11	103		8:4	85
3:2–11	65		8:8	88
3:4–11	130		8:8–13	89
3:9	65		9–10	117
			9:6–8	88
			9:11–15	117
Colossians			9:12	35, 43, 88
1	126		9:12–13	86
1:13	24		9:13	83, 86
1:13–14	30n73		9:15	35, 43, 92
1:14	35		9:16–17	91–92, 92n94
1:15	17–18, 24		9:24—10:4	88
1:15–20	17–18		9:25—10:3	86
1:16	14–15, 17, 26		10:1	117
1:20	14, 24, 26–27, 124		10:1–10	85
1:22	124		10:11	86
2	58		10:12	88
2:10	15		10:12–13	13, 21
2:12	58		10:14	104, 117
2:14	17		10:16–18	89
2:14–15	13, 24–27		10:18	93
2:15	15–16		10:19–21	88
2:20	57		11:17–20	75
3:1–3	57		12:2	2

Scripture Index

James

2:14–26	74
2:21–23	74n15

1 Peter

1:2	90
1:18–19	35, 95
2:20–23	61
2:24	83
3:9	61
3:13–18	61
3:18	104
3:21–22	21
4:1–2	61
4:12–19	61

1 John

2:2	93
3:8	13, 24
3:16	71
4:9–10	75
4:10	93

Revelation

	104
1:5	35
1:6	37
5:9	38
12	28
12:4	28
12:6	28
12:9	28
12:10	27
12:11	13, 27–28
12:12–17	28
12:14	28
13:1	28
14:3–4	37–38
20	28
20:1	28
20:2	28
20:4	28
20:7–10	28
20:14	29

Subject Index

Apocalyptic, apocalypticism, 8, 14–15, 19–20, 19n33–34, 53, 107, 111
Ascension, ascended, ix, 2–3, 13, 30, 44, 50, 84–85, 84n54, 87, 135
Blood, xii, 27–28, 31, 35, 37, 39–40, 52, 75n19, 78n29, 80, 82–85, 84n52, 85n63, 86–87, 87n74, 89, 90–92, 95, 95n104, 97–99, 99n117, 99n118–22, 104, 106, 126, 129,
Burnt Offering, 81, 84–86, 96–97
Church, xi–xiv, xvii, 3, 7, 16–17, 21–22, 49–50, 78, 90, 103–4, 109–10, 117, 127
Crucifixion, 1–2, 10–11, 21–22, 47, 63, 68–70, 84, 95
Christus Victor, 16–17, 24, 134
Diplomacy, 128, 128n25, 130
Discipleship, 44, 61–63, 63n73
Eucharist, xi–xii, 134
Feminist Standpoint Theory, 2–3, 135
Flesh, 16–18, 20, 28, 31, 54, 57, 60, 75, 102, 115, 118
Heroic death/deaths, xiv, 75–76, 76n52–53, 94, 104
Incarnation Criterion, xi, xiv
Lamb, lambs, 27–28, 31, 34, 84, 84n59, 95–96, 95n103–4, 96n105–7, 104
Last Supper, 89, 92
Law court, 105–6, 105n1, 113, 118, 122
Maccabean martyrs, 73, 75–76, 75n18

Market place, 37, 105n1
Metaphor, metaphorical, xiv–xvii, 1–5, 13, 24, 26, 29–31, 36, 44–50, 53–54, 57, 67, 70, 76n20, 78–80, 83, 88, 91, 94–95, 100–101, 105–6, 109, 111, 117, 118n46, 122, 126, 130–31, 135
Moral Influence Theory, xi
Mystery Religions, 47n7, 48–54, 58, 66
New Perspective (on Paul), 19, 89n82, 90, 107–11, 111n15, 115n35–36, 119n52
Participation Imperative, xi, xiv, 63, 135
Penal Substitution, penal substitutionary, 12, 41–43, 101, 103, 105–6, 133
Pentecost, 3–4, 7–8, 12–13, 22, 47, 53, 70, 72, 131
Plato, Platonists, platonic, 16, 78
Political, 1, 1n2, 15, 15n11, 17n22, 19, 24, 32, 33n5, 39, 124, 128, 128n26, 132,
Powers, 5, 13–20, 16n16, 24–27, 25n54, 29–31, 33, 39–40, 40n34, 45, 54, 60, 67, 100, 112, 122, 135
PPME, 112–14
Protoevangelium, 22–23
Propitiation, propitiating, propitiatory, 36–37, 36n16, 43, 75, 80, 84n53, 92–94, 98–99, 105–6, 105n1

157

Subject Index

Ransom, ransoming, 35, 37–38, 38n24, 39, 39n29, 61, 103
Resurrection, resurrected, risen, xiv, 3–4, 6–9, 6n13, 11, 13, 13n2, 17, 21, 24, 25n54, 30, 40, 44–45, 47–48, 48n11, 51, 56–57, 59, 60, 62, 64–66, 69–70, 72–73, 75, 79, 100, 112–13, 113n25, 131,
Salvation, 7–9, 27, 30, 30n73, 51–52, 73n12, 74, 96n105, 108, 108n7, 109, 115, 119, 119n53, 126
Scapegoat, scapegoats, 41–43, 87–88, 101, 134
Second Temple Judaism, 19, 32, 76, 82, 109, 114–15
Sin, sins, 25n54, 27, 29, 31, 34, 42–44, 54–55, 57, 57n51, 60–61, 64, 66–67, 72, 77, 79–83, 86, 88, 93, 95–96, 96n105, 98, 116, 100–103, 107, 112, 115, 117, 121–22, 129

Sin offering, 79, 81–83, 86, 96, 98, 102
Slave, slaves, slavery, enslaved, 3n8, 13n2, 16, 18–20, 28–29, 31–32, 36–37, 43, 56–57, 68–69, 109
Spirit, Holy Spirit, 3–4, 7–8, 11–12, 16–17, 41, 45, 47–48, 50n17, 53, 56–60, 64–65, 100, 112–13, 117, 134
Spiritualization, 78, 78n29–30
Suffering Servant, 10, 38, 41, 67, 74n17, 103, 109, 116,
Temple, 35–36, 46, 52, 69–70, 75, 77–78, 80, 84, 86, 96n105, 105n1,
Theological Interpretation of Scripture, xii–xiv
Theosis, 56, 100, 135
Yom Kippur, 83, 86–88, 87n76, 90

www.ingramcontent.com/pod-product-compliance
Lightning Source LLC
Chambersburg PA
CBHW030114170426
43198CB00009B/619